A real-life fairy tale
MICHAEL JACKSON
AND ME

TALITHA LINEHAN

Copyright © 2021 Talitha Linehan

ISBN 978-1-7360246-6-9 *Hardback*
978-1-7360246-0-7 *Paperback*
978-1-7360246-8-3 *eBook*

Library of Congress Control Number: 2020921077

Design and layout by Arus Tashchyan
Illustrations by Ariel Aguire, @arielaguire on Instagram,
@ariel_aguire on Twitter,
and @arielsartwork777 on Facebook
Proofread by Talin MacArthur

Photographs taken by paparazzi in Los Angeles and Las Vegas used with permission from Bauer-Griffin and National Photo Group. Newspaper articles from 1997 and photograph taken outside UCLA in 2009 used with permission from relevant copyright owner. All other photographs used courtesy of author and friends.

Front cover photo: Michael Jackson and Talitha Linehan,
inside a hotel suite at the Hotel Bel-Air, Los Angeles, November 2008.
Back cover photo: Michael and Talitha inside a studio at CenterStaging,
Burbank, April 2009.

Talitha Linehan, Los Angeles, California, USA
www.michaeljacksonandme.com

For Michael, who is there, and Jill, who is here.
Between you both, I remain tethered.

Contents

PROLOGUE

Written in the stars

ike all great fairy tales, mine begins once upon a time in a land far away. The time is before I am born and the place is the realm where we all exist before and after life on earth. It is here, as the destiny for my life is being decided upon, that an angel plants a seed in my heart. The seed contains the purest form of love for the purest soul to walk the earth in my time, a soul made of light and magic, whose presence raises the planet's vibrational field to a higher level, who reaches millions through his creative endeavours, inspires through his humanity and compassion, and illuminates through his vision of a brighter tomorrow.

The seed is planted and I come into the world as any other and live unaware of it for some years. Then, when I am seven years old, the seed sprouts, provoked by the formation of my first memory of the soul to whom my destiny is linked. I do not know his name, I do not truly know his face or his character, for he appears in this instance in the guise of a Scarecrow in a 1978 film called *The Wiz*. All I know is that I find him captivating, though I can hardly articulate that in such a manner at the time, and when my mother comes to collect me from my nana's house before the film ends, I cry because, "I have to find out what happens to the Scarecrow!" So desperate are my pleas that when we arrive home a few minutes later, my mother insists my brothers change the channel so I can watch the film's conclusion.

The seed has become a bud, initiating my intrigue with the soul whose name I soon learn to be Michael Jackson, though it will be several years before I realise that the Scarecrow and he are one and the same. I become a fan of his music and decorate my bedroom with more posters of him than any other pop star. But it is when I am thirteen and watch his film *Moonwalker* for the first time that the bud, with the promise of all that love still locked inside, finally blossoms. In that instance, I see Michael, more clearly than ever before, and I know on some deep level that my destiny is linked to his and that he will always be a huge part of my life.

*   *   *

Most of what I have just written is pure fantasy, the exception being my first memory and experience of Michael, and the sudden revelation at the age of thirteen, but it is as good an explanation as any of my love for him and the compulsion I felt to go to him ever since I watched *Moonwalker* for the first time. I didn't decide to love Michael, any more than we decide to love anyone; the love was simply a part of me that once released into my heart could never be subdued or dismissed.

It was as inescapable as destiny, and years later, when I embraced this aspect of myself more than ever before, when I gave myself permission to go to Michael without fear or reservation, I felt certain that I was in perfect alignment with some prescribed fate – something that Michael affirmed to me during a late-night phone conversation in 2008, when he told me that what we shared was written in the stars. "I love you, I really do," he said in his soft, melodious voice. "It's all cosmic, you know. We are connected to each other. We are drawn to one another. Even tonight, this phone call, it's cosmic. You wanted to talk to me. And I wanted to hear your voice. And that's why we're talking now. The universe made it happen."

While I have no memory or knowledge of another dimension, my fantasy of a higher realm offers one possible answer to one of the biggest questions of my life, a question that prompts a series of other questions... Why do I love Michael so much? Why did I feel compelled to go to him? Why, of all of the fans who felt similarly, was I given a quantity and quality of encounters that was far beyond the norm, often alone, in private, with his children? And perhaps the answer to this latter question lies in my natural propensity to write, because perhaps if I truly was destined to go to Michael, then I was also destined to write this book.

This book could and would not exist had I not been given the gift of countless experiences of and encounters with Michael over a thirteen-year period, and had I not recorded so many of them in writing, because without such a record, much of their content would have been lost to me in the darkness that followed his sudden passing in June 2009. And it could not exist without my ability to write it now, more than a decade later, to convey as fully and honestly as I can not only the facts of my life as they pertain to Michael Jackson, the why, the what, the when, and so on, but also the truth of my experience, emotionally and intuitively.

I will try to convey fully, through the limitation of words and my ability as a writer, my experience of Michael and why I know with absolute conviction that he was a man who embodied all that we consider to be good and pure and true.

ONE

First contact

As a young girl living in the countryside in Ireland, I would often stand in a field at night gazing up at the stars, marvelling at the thought that somewhere out there, Michael stood beneath the same sky as I did. That he existed, that he lived and breathed, seemed impossible, for he was so much more than a man, he was an elevated being, as magical as any fairy-tale character could be. I would search for the brightest star in the sky and wish upon it, pleading with the universe to carry me to him one day, that I might deliver to him all the love for him that my heart contained.

From the day I awoke to my destiny, at the age of thirteen, I began to experience and express my love for Michael in ways that were tangible and intangible, external and internal, material and ethereal. I collected and absorbed everything related to him that I could and turned my bedroom into a veritable shrine, its walls and ceiling covered with posters of him, every surface stacked high with his albums and other merchandise: books, magazines, t-shirts, bags, badges, and so on. Even my bed was covered with a bedspread bearing his image, and on it lay a doll created in his likeness, wearing a miniature version of his trademark sequinned glove.

When the bud in my young heart blossomed, it not only allowed me to experience and express my love for Michael but also to receive him, through his music, his dance, and his words, sung, spoken, and written. He told me that we are all equal, and I believed him, that we are all connected to each other and to Mother Earth, that we can achieve a brighter tomorrow if we work together in a spirit of love and compassion. His message to the world, which I believe he was sent here to deliver, sank deep into my heart and shaped who I am. "Inspire" literally means "to breathe," and as I grew through my formative years, from a young girl into a young woman, I inhaled everything that Michael channelled into the world, and through him became a better version of myself than I otherwise would be.

It was always Michael's essence, his heart and soul, that I connected with, but it was through his public persona that I discovered him, and it was as an artist, an entertainer, a performer, that I experienced him in person for the first time, at his *Dangerous* concert in Lansdowne Road Stadium (which has since been demolished and where Aviva Stadium now stands) in Dublin on 25 July 1992. I was fifteen years old at the time and I spent the concert in the stands with my aunt, utterly transfixed. I couldn't take my eyes off the figure on stage, but I also couldn't make it be him, not really. He was too perfect, robotically perfect, inhumanly perfect, as impossible as I'd always feared him to be. And he was so far away, so out of reach, further removed from me than I'd ever allowed myself to consider.

In the bubble of my early youth, it was just him and me, but here I was confronted by the fact that I wasn't alone, that I wasn't unique in my love of him, and so it seemed to follow, my desire to go to him, to know him, to be known by him. In that concert, I was one of tens of thousands of people, and now I realised that in order to reach him, I would have to navigate through or around this mass of strangers, to stand out from the crowd in order to connect with him, and that seemed to me, an ordinary girl from a village in Ireland, an impossible task.

While seeing Michael in concert was the single best experience of the first eighteen years of my life (I would be nineteen before I saw him again.), I cried myself to sleep that night, both with the longing to reach him, which I now feared would go unmet, and the certainty that I would have to wait an eternity of four years to see him again. That was the period since his previous world tour, and I felt certain that I wouldn't see him again until his next tour, by which time I at least would have entered adulthood and could finally take control of my own destiny.

*   *   *

My life outside of Michael's world was full and colourful, but from the first moment of discovery, part of me was always waiting to go to him. The four years after the *Dangerous* concert, during which I finished school and began a degree programme in journalism at Dublin City University, passed, and in September 1996, the debut of Michael's *HIStory* tour in Prague in the Czech Republic presented my second opportunity to see him in real life.

Although at nineteen, I was technically an adult, I was still financially dependent on my parents, and so had to secure their permission to travel to Prague for the tour's opening concert. A couple of days beforehand, I boarded a plane for the first time in my life, and left Ireland for the first time in my life, to fly to Prague, and the day after I arrived, on 6 September, I saw Michael off-stage for the first time, outside the Intercontinental Hotel, where he was occupying a top-floor suite.

I joined the throngs of people standing behind barriers, many of them holding banners they'd made bearing his image and declaring their love for him. We chanted his name, "Mi-chael, Mi-chael, Mi-chael," sang his songs, and shouted out the names of the countries we'd travelled from: "Ireland loves you, Michael," in the case of me and my travel companion, a guy coincidentally named Michael who I'd met at a fan event in Dublin and convinced to come to Prague with me because I was too nervous to travel alone.

I barely remember Michael (Jackson) leaving the hotel that day but I know he did so in a black minivan with heavily tinted windows. The van was no doubt swarmed by those waiting to see him, the savviest of whom would have hopped in cars or taxis to follow him, something that never even occurred to me that day but that I would do many times in later years. But I clearly remember when Michael returned because I was standing against his car when he emerged through its sunroof wearing a black fedora, a black surgical mask, and a red and gold jacket.

I had never before seen him so close-up and my eyes drank him in, the reality of him, the humanity of him, because I could finally see that, while he shone brighter than any soul on the planet, he was made of flesh and blood like me. He turned slowly, his eyes, his beautiful, brown eyes, scanning the crowd, who were pressed against the car, reaching towards him and calling his name. I waited for his gaze to meet mine, feeling certain that if he saw me, he would know me, he would know how much I loved him, and some kind of connection would instantaneously be made. But his gaze fell around me but never on me, and then he was gone, back in the car, back in the hotel, and the wait to see him began again.

*　　*　　*

That evening, as darkness fell, I found myself with a group of young people from Prague. They pointed out the window to Michael's room, which was directly above us, and told me they'd seen him there several times over the previous days. We kept our eyes fixed on that window as we chatted, a few of them translating what I said to the others, who expressed amazement that I'd travelled all the way from Ireland to see Michael. Suddenly, there was movement at the window and then Michael was there, leaning out with a big cuddly toy in his hand, which he threw down to the jubilant crowd. We waved at him, we called to him, we pleaded with him to throw one of the toys our way, and finally, we got his attention.

Michael pointed at us excitedly, disappeared for a moment, and reappeared with a giant green toy in his hands. It might have been a frog or a dragon, I'm not sure, because as it flew down towards us, everyone reached for it, snatched it out of the air, and pulled it apart. Someone got its head, another an arm, a leg. One of the guys I'd been speaking with grabbed one of its limbs, bright green with white stuffing bursting through the opening where he had ripped it from its torso.

We all congratulated him on his prize, part of a toy that Michael, this ethereal being, had touched, that he had gifted to us. I asked him tentatively if I could hold it for a moment, and he told me that he had caught it for me and that it was mine to keep. I refused to take it at first because, as much as my heart desired it, I didn't feel I could accept anything so precious from this kind stranger, but he insisted, and to this day, that plush green partial toy takes pride of place among my collection of treasures from Michael's world.

In retrospect, it seems to me that right from the beginning, a wave of good fortune carried me to Michael. Of course, I had to take the tangible steps towards him: to come up with the money, which I borrowed in this instance from my parents, and later earned by working; to get the approval I needed from my parents or the time off from my boss; to book the flights and hotels and tickets; and to wait, often for hours on end, day after day, in the cold and rain, to see him.

But there were forces at play that were beyond my control, that dictated my fortune one way or another, and they always seemed to smile on me, to grant me an unnatural level of good luck. This phenomenon began in Prague, with the acquisition of that treasured keepsake, and would continue that night, when Michael left the hotel for a second time.

As Michael's car pulled away from the hotel, my newfound friends grabbed my hands and told me, "We know where he's going, come with us." We ran through the streets of Prague, holding hands and singing, filling the cold night air with the chorus of Michael's song "Heal the World." We came to a barrier with a guard standing behind it and, now a few dozen strong, we broke through it, the guard seemingly too stunned to try to stop us. We were inside Letná Park, where Michael was to perform the first ever *HIStory* concert to a crowd of 125,000 the following evening, and now we were at the front of the stage, which was guarded by men that were not as easily intimidated as their counterpart outside.

One of the guards let their dog free and it knocked me down and pinned me to the ground. My friends admonished him in their language and pulled me to my feet: I was fine, I assured them, as we backed away from the stage, behind a large, black tarp erected to hide it from view. A few minutes later, Michael, who we could see projected onto the jumbotron screens, which stood on each side of the stage, and occasionally around the sides of the tarp or through rips people had made in it, appeared, and he performed the *HIStory* concert in its entirety, from the spectacular opening, in which he emerged from a space rocket, to the grand finale, in which he performed the tour's titular song.

I could hardly believe my luck, because here I was, an ordinary girl from a village in Ireland, more than a thousand miles from home, seeing not only the man who was my everything, but also arguably the most famous person on the planet, performing his long-awaited *HIStory* concert before it was even unveiled to the world.

*   *   *

The concert the next day was, in fact, attended by far more than 125,000 people, which was the park's capacity and the number of tickets sold, as thousands of non-ticket-holders broke through the stadium's barriers, as we had done, climbed over walls, and entered in other ways illicitly. It was chaotic from the beginning and brutal at times, but it also held a moment of magic that I would carry in my heart forever.

My friend Michael and I arrived at Letná Park early in the morning, by which time several hundred people had arrived and were waiting in a chain link tunnel, behind a locked gate. We joined them and, a few minutes later, they began to surge forward: one, two, three, surge, and again and again, until the gate collapsed and they flooded across it, into the park. We ran with them, of course, all the way to the stage, and I made it to the second row behind the front barrier, where I clung on to the guy in front of me, who invited me to do so as the crowd thickened behind us.

What followed was the worst crowd experience of my life, one that would leave me black and blue from head to toe, my long, dark hair a clump of matted tangles. Throughout the day and into the evening, a stream of people were passed over the crowd to the front, where the security staff stationed between the front barrier and the stage would pull them to safety. Some of them had passed out, while others, including my friend Michael, simply couldn't take the force of the crush anymore.

Several times, I got hit in the head by the limb of an unconscious body, and one of the guards repeatedly offered to pull me out, no doubt fearful for the safety of this one slight girl among a sea of hefty guys, but every time I refused. I had waited what had felt like an eternity to watch a concert from the front, as opposed to from the stands, halfway across the stadium, and when Michael finally blasted onto the stage in a space rocket, it was worth every ounce of pain and discomfort to see him perform from just a few feet away.

As each song began to play, people would call out its title: "Stranger in Moscow," "Smooth Criminal," "You Are Not Alone," and so on, and I joined them. But when Michael emerged in a black pants and white t-shirt, carrying a suitcase, no music played, and I was the only one to shout, "Billie Jean!"

"How do you know it's 'Billie Jean?'" a guy beside me asked.

"Because I saw him rehearse the entire concert last night," I said.

"Yeah right," he replied.

Of course, he didn't believe me, but I didn't care. I shouted it again: "'Billie Jean,' 'Billie Jean,' 'Billie Jean,'" my voice rising in excitement. This was my favourite in-concert song, the performance that had captivated me the most, ever since I'd seen a video of the 1983 *Motown 25* television special, during which Michael had performed the song while wearing his now trademark silver sequinned glove for the first time, and debuted his illusive moonwalk, which had become his signature dance move.

On the dark and silent stage, the spotlight followed Michael as he walked to the centre, put his suitcase on a stool, and clicked it open. He took out a black sequinned jacket and put it on, then a silver sequinned glove, then a black fedora, and all the while I continued to shout, "Billie Jean!" And then, remarkably, incredibly, unbelievably, just before he entered the opening stance of the performance, he looked at me, he looked right at me, and he winked, a wink that seemed to say, "That's it, you got it, it's 'Billie Jean.'"

Somehow, I had achieved the impossible: in a sea of people, I had won Michael's attention, expressed to me through a gesture that was right out of a scene in *Moonwalker*, in which he winks at a young girl watching through the window of a 1930s'-style club as he performs "Smooth Criminal." I had dreamt of being that girl ever since I'd watched the film for the first time, at the age of thirteen, and that night, for one magical moment, I got to be her.

TWO

On tour

y journey through Michael's world began, in my mind, with my trip to Prague, and ended, tragically and unexpectedly, on 25 June 2009, with Michael's sudden passing. Within those thirteen years, there are many experiences that stand out, and among them are all of the "firsts": the first time I saw him, the first time he saw me, the first time I met him, the first time he hugged me…

The next "first" that I achieved, the next dream to become a reality, was at the next *HIStory* concert that I attended, on the second leg of the tour, at the Don Valley Stadium in Sheffield, England, on 9 July 1997. This time, I travelled alone, and the evening before the concert, I went to the stadium to spend the night there. As was typical in Europe, the stadium had several gated entrances, each with a set of turnstiles. The entrances were equidistant from the stage and would open at the same time, to give those who were at the top of each queue an equal chance of reaching the front.

When I arrived at my entrance, as indicated on my ticket, there were only a handful of people there. We were joined by a few dozen more by dawn, after which our numbers quickly swelled, from dozens to hundreds to thousands. As the time neared for the gates to open, in the early afternoon, the crowd tightened and the tension grew. I had had butterflies in my tummy for weeks at the prospect of seeing Michael again, a goal I'd been working towards since returning from Prague.

I had got my first ever job at the start of the university year, working weekends at a restaurant, to save up the money; bought tickets to the four concerts in England and one in Ireland as soon as they'd gone on sale; and waited at the stadium for eighteen hours already, huddled with the other fans through the night to keep warm, and forgoing water all morning to avoid needing the bathroom all evening, when I'd be pinned in place inside the stadium – and it all came down to this.

What if our turnstiles didn't open? What if I tripped and fell? What if everyone outran me and I ended up at the back of the crowd? Finally, the moment arrived. The staff at the gate told us to get ready. The turnstiles opened. I stepped through and handed over my ticket. And then I took off, sprinting through a concrete tunnel, down a set of steps through the stands, and across an open field. But this time, instead of one barrier in front of the stage, there were two, the second a few dozen feet behind the first. I noticed an opening on each end of the second barrier, and I veered towards the one on the left, and now I was through it, flying across the final stretch of grass.

Unlike the second barrier, which ran straight across the field, the front barrier was t-shaped to accommodate the catwalk that jutted out from the centre of the stage. The most coveted spots were where the barrier curved away from the stage, and as I approached, only these corners were lined with people. I ran towards the catwalk end of the curve and slammed into the barrier, and I immediately burst into tears. For the first time in my life, I had made it to the front row of a Michael Jackson concert, something I had dreamt about for years but thought virtually impossible.

The barrier quickly filled and a crowd began to form behind us. The security guards positioned in the gap between the barrier and the stage told us all to sit down on the ground, a safety procedure that, along with the double-barrier system, was employed on the second leg of the tour to minimise the risk of people getting crushed and passing out. When the crowd was about twenty rows thick, the staff closed the entrances on each side of this front section, known as the front pit, and directed the stream of new arrivals to the second barrier behind us.

I sat on the black metal platform of the barrier but I never relaxed, and neither did the people around me, all of us too fearful of losing our hard-earned spots. We sat on our haunches, facing the stage, ready to leap up at any moment. Every so often, perhaps in a moment of paranoia, someone would spring up and everyone in the front pit would follow in a wave, and the security guards would have to tell us all to sit down again. Eventually, however, the guards gave up the battle and we, the lucky occupiers of the front row, stood shoulder to shoulder against the wall of black metal, occasionally linking arms to stop those behind us from pushing through and dislodging us.

As the hours passed, the stadium filled, the excitement built, and my body began to ache. The discomfort was nothing compared to what I'd endured in Prague, but the sleepless night and the crush of the crowd inevitably took their toll, and I had to keep shifting position and leaning over the barrier to alleviate the pain in the small of my back. At around 6.30 p.m., the support act, an Australian band called Human Nature, took to the stage, providing a welcome distraction, and then a medley of hits that ended with Michael's song "Ben" played, and my tears of love and excitement began to flow again.

To a deafening chorus of cheers and chants of Michael's name, the jumbotron screens lit up with the concert's opening film, which depicted a rocket ship zooming along a track, past international landmarks and video clips of historical events. As it ended, there was a loud rumble and, with the crowd now in a state of hysteria, the rocket exploded onto the stage.

The door slid open, revealing a figure wearing a helmet with a dark visor, a shiny gold jacket, and matching pants. He stepped out and slowly, teasingly, removed his helmet. It was Michael. It was really him, not a poster, not a picture, not a projection on a television screen, but the real, live human being. I screamed his name and reached towards him, and one of the photographers at the front of the stage snapped a photo of me, which appeared in a British newspaper the next day.

The concert was more or less the same as the one I'd seen in Prague, but my experience of it was entirely different. I was much closer to the central area of the stage for one thing (in Prague, I'd been along the top of the T, on the right side of the stage), and this time, I wasn't distracted by the constant pushing and shoving of tens of thousands of people, all fighting for my place. In the front pit, I was in a crowd of perhaps no more than a thousand, and my body was against the barrier, which provided a much more solid anchor than the man I'd clung to in Prague.

Me, with a gloved hand in the air, watching Michael perform live from the front row of his HIStory concert in Copenhagen, Denmark, on 14 August 1997. (Photo: Tommy Mardell)

Besides all of that, being at the front barrier, so close to the stage, offered the ultimate concert experience; I could feel the rhythm of the music pulsating through my body, the base pounding against my chest, and the heat of the pyrotechnics that blasted from the front of the stage. Best of all, however, was the view of Michael, closer, clearer, more intimate. I savoured every moment, every note, every move, every expression, and when he emerged to perform "Billie Jean," I again shouted out the name of the song and won his attention, this time with a look and a point directed at me. This was my song, my in-concert song, and this was my way to do what I'd thought impossible at the age of fifteen: to stand out to Michael, if only for a moment, in a stadium full of adoring fans.

*   *   *

From Sheffield, I travelled to London for the three concerts at Wembley Stadium, where I again spent the night at a set of turnstiles, located at the top of a set of concrete steps, and, miraculously in my mind, considering the stadium's size and iconic status, reached the front barrier the next day. It was while waiting outside the stadium overnight that I met a girl from England who I will refer to by her nickname, Tick. Tick and I immediately struck up a friendship and seemed to share the same motivation to win Michael's attention. She joined me at the front barrier, where we chanted "Billie Jean" together, and she came up with an idea for a banner for the final Wembley concert that would certainly stand out.

In February 1996, while Michael was performing his song "Earth Song" at the Brit Awards, a singer called Jarvis Cocker had run on stage and shook his bum at him in protest. To express our disgust at this, we bought a poster of Cocker, had it laminated, and wrote across it in large black lettering, "You can't wiggle your bum at this. It's 70,000 to one." The 70,000 was a reference to the capacity of Wembley Stadium, which was sold out for all three concerts. At the front barrier, we stood side by side at the same spot I'd occupied in Sheffield, in the hope that Michael would begin to recognise me and look for me there, and we unrolled our banner. At first, some of the people around us were taken aback by it, but then they read the message and laughed.

Before every concert, Michael's cameraman, Hamid, would go along the front barrier filming the crowd, and the footage would be projected onto the jumbotron screens and, as I later found out, a small screen that Michael was watching backstage. The camera panned across us, we were on the big screens for a moment, and… the entire stadium booed! They booed because all they saw was a poster of Jarvis Cocker, a known enemy of Michael, hated by his fans.

After some discussion and despite some reservations, we kept the banner in place. The concert began and, as usual, we erupted in tears of excitement, screaming Michael's name and dancing along with him, copying his arm movements during the opening medley. He threw us a few nervous glances, no doubt misinterpreting our banner, as the crowd had done, but our response must have made it clear to him that we were, in fact, mega-fans.

After the first succession of songs, Michael took a short break on stage to drink some juice and wipe his face with a towel. We held out the banner and pointed at it excitedly. He took a few steps towards us, bent forward, shaded his eyes from the glare of the stage lights, and read the words across the image of Jarvis Cocker: "You can't wiggle your bum at this. It's 70,000 to one." And he burst out laughing! We made Michael Jackson laugh!!! This was more than a wink or a point, glorious as they were, this was a far more solid interaction, an action from us and a reaction from Michael, and it seemed to establish us in his observational field. Throughout the concert, he kept looking at us, pointing at us, and gesturing to us, interacting with us in ways I would later discover he did with every regular along the front barrier.

He had acknowledged me for a moment at previous concerts, but this was when he began to recognise me, to recognise us, something that would be evident to my friends who accompanied us to the concert in Dublin and stood beside us at the front barrier there. "He keeps looking at you guys," my friend Noreen told me during the concert. "I know," I told her. I knew it but I could hardly believe it. That I fell under his gaze, that I existed to him, as someone who so obviously loved him, was already more than I'd been told was possible by adults around me, who'd promised me throughout my teenage years that I'd grow out of my love of him, that I'd never get anywhere near him, and that I was one of millions and would never be anything more to him than that. I was already beginning to prove them wrong.

*   *   *

I had convinced Tick to travel to Dublin for the concert at the RDS Arena on 19 July 1997, which was to be my last, and it was at a restaurant on the north side of the city that we had a conversation that would alter the course of our summer, and in my case at least, my entire life. By this time, we had heard that there was a special group of fans, called followers, who travelled the world to see Michael and had been to dozens of his concerts. He recognised them and acknowledged them whenever he saw them, and most, if not all, of them had met him, in many cases several times.

That fateful conversation between Tick and me went something like this:

Me: "I don't want this to end already."

Tick: "Me neither."

Me: "I want to do what those other fans do and follow the tour."

"Me too."

"I'll do it if you do it."

"I'll do it if you do it."

And we did it! After getting permission from our parents (Tick was only seventeen so required their permission, and I had used up all of my savings and had to borrow from mine again, necessitating their approval and support.), we got the supplies we needed: a rucksack, a bumbag, a sleeping bag, and a roll mat; booked our transport; and bought whatever concert tickets we could get our hands on; and rejoined the tour on 1 August in Berlin, Germany.

We began by spending our days travelling and seeing concerts, and our nights sleeping outside stadiums, at train stations and, on occasion, outside Michael's hotel, though most of the time he flew back to Paris, where he was staying in a castle and enjoying being a father for the first time, to his infant son, Prince.

Things didn't always go smoothly for us, like at the stadium in Leipzig, Germany, where a sudden surge at the gate caused us to lose our spot at the top of the queue. Then, when we reached the front pit, only the entrance on one end was open, the other half of the pit was cordoned off by security tape, and the barrier was already full on our side. We ended up bursting through the tape as the second entrance opened and fans spilled in, and planting ourselves at the front barrier at the end of the catwalk; it wasn't our usual spot but at least we were at the front, and Michael still found us there.

Things didn't always go smoothly for Michael either. At one concert, one of the dancers fell off the catwalk section of the stage during "Black or White" and had to fight off security guards who mistook him for a fan, and at another concert, Michael couldn't do his gravity-defying lean during "Smooth Criminal" because the crew member underneath the stage failed to properly insert the bolts that slotted into the bottom of his shoes, enabling this seemingly impossible feat.

Tick and I experienced another near-disaster at the stadium in Hockenheim, Germany, when, after sleeping at the entrance all night, we couldn't find anywhere to store our rucksacks. On previous occasions, we had left early in the morning to go to a local train station and deposit them in a locker, while the fans we'd befriended overnight saved our spots. But this time, there was no such facility and we were at a loss as to what to do. Fortunately, perhaps due to that wave of good fortune that seemed to carry me through Michael's world, we ran into a crew member who we'd befriended, a guy from England called Mick, and he offered to store our rucksacks in his truck.

After the concert, when Tick and I went to retrieve our rucksacks, Mick offered to drive us to the next venue, which was over five hundred miles away, in Copenhagen, Denmark. And that's how we travelled from then on, in the cabin of Mick's truck, which transported part of the stage rigging from venue to venue. We'd take turns sitting in the passenger seat and lying in the sleeper cab, and often wake up to find ourselves parked in front of the stage as it was being erected for the following night's concert.

"Why me?" I questioned, perhaps for the first time but by no means for the last in the context of Michael's world. Why, of all the fans, of all the followers, was I, along with Tick in this case, singled out in such a way? We were two of only four girls, all but me from England, who were adopted by the crew in such a manner, perhaps in our case because we seemed rather helpless. Tick was only seventeen but at least was an experienced traveller, having regularly visited Germany, where her father was from. And I was twenty but appeared much younger to people, who often mistook me for being in my early teens.

Whatever the reason, we felt extremely spoilt to be given such a privilege, not only because it eliminated the stress of navigating the transport system and finding our own way from one venue to the next, but also because it gave us access to the backstage area and a glimpse into a world that had been such a huge part of Michael's, ever since he'd begun touring with The Jackson 5 as a little boy.

* * *

It was a conversation between Tick and me in Ireland that had led to us following the tour through Europe, where we attended eleven more *HIStory* concerts, bringing my total to seventeen. And it was a conversation outside the stadium in Copenhagen on 14 August, when we faced yet another potential disaster, that I believe led to us being granted the greatest privilege of all by the crew. The disaster in this case was that we didn't have any tickets to that evening's concert, having been unable to buy them in advance or on arrival in the city.

We had left our place at the front of the queue and were sitting at a picnic table by the stadium, shortly before the gates were due to open, bemoaning our fate. We knew by then that some of the other fans who were following the tour were being given early access to the stadiums, something we'd discovered in Dublin, after we'd seen one of them arriving on the morning of the concert. When we'd asked him why he hadn't queued out overnight, he'd given us a friendly but evasive answer, but when we'd reached the front barrier, we'd found him standing there, along the curve, with the other regulars. It was then that we'd realised that these fans were being allowed into the stadiums before the gates opened to the public.

Tick and I often complained to each other about the unfairness of this arrangement, not only because they didn't have to endure the stress of queuing that we did, but more so because it meant that we could never secure a place on the coveted curve of the barrier. "It's not fair that some fans get in early," I said to Tick now, as we faced the prospect of spending the evening outside the stadium. She agreed with me, and then she asked, "Would you do it if you got the chance?" I could have lied, but after a moment's reflection, I admitted that yes, I would, and she echoed my response.

Me standing in front of the stage where Michael was to perform his next HIStory concert, inside a stadium in Europe, in the summer of 1997. The bumbag I was wearing remains in my possession to this day, filled with ticket stubs from the HIStory tour, notes and coins in various European currencies, and some of the shiny, metallic, gold confetti that would rain down on the front of the crowd at the end of every concert.

Almost as soon as these words were out of our mouths, one of the crew members approached us to ask why we weren't in the queue. We told him that we didn't have any tickets to the concert, and he said, "Come on, I'll take you inside right now." We gaped at each other, then scrambled to our feet and accompanied him through a staff entrance and across the stadium's open field to the front barrier, where the other regulars were already waiting in single file along the curve, and where we took up our usual spot beside them, still in a state of disbelief. We were inside a near-empty stadium, standing at the front barrier, a position that we'd had to fight so hard for on all previous occasions. We absolutely could not believe our luck, even less so when it repeated itself at the next concert, and then every concert after that.

Tick (right) and me (middle) sitting at the front barrier inside a stadium in Europe, on the afternoon of a HIStory concert in August 1997, before the gates opened to the public and the tens of thousands of other fans streamed inside.

I know many people would dismiss the link between our conversation that afternoon and the events that followed as purely coincidental, but I believe in my heart that if we'd lied to each other, if we'd failed to admit our hypocrisy, we would have rejected on some level this possible fate, and it never would have occurred. I say this based not only on my feeling at the time but also on my thirteen years inside Michael's world, where energy seemed to be intensified and intuition heightened; karmic forces, such as those that I believe were in operation that day, were often apparent, and time and again, I visualised my dreams into existence, seemingly manifesting them through willpower alone.

For the rest of the tour, Tick and I continued to sleep outside the stadiums but would leave the queue in the morning and be escorted to the front barrier in the early afternoon. While waiting outside stadiums, we got a lot of attention from the media, and were featured in newspapers and on television stations across Europe, mainly because we were following the tour but also because of our matching Michael Jackson masks and sequinned gloves, and because of the tattoo of Michael I had got on my left shoulder blade the previous summer, in an era before tattoos on teenage girls were considered the norm.

We also got a lot of attention from Michael, who continued to acknowledge us with stares and points and gestures at every concert, every moment of contact thrilling our souls. I lost myself in his performance and wept every time, especially during "Earth Song," a humanitarian anthem that perfectly encompasses his message of peace and compassion, but I was always waiting for his gaze to return to us again.

*   *   *

I never met Michael on the *HIStory* tour but I had two interactions

En megastjärna för alla åldrar. Både Johanna ██████ och mamma Anki ██████ ska på kvällens konsert. Fast mamma Anki har inte sovit utanför Ullevi i natt.

Michael är den eviga drömmen

AV LOTTA ENGELBREKTSON / GÖTEBORG
031-689051

Att få stå på scenen tillsammans med Michael Jackson - det är den största drömmen av dem alla.

- Under varje framträdande tar han upp en tjej och dansar med henne, säger Marie-Louise ██████ ikonsert.

Sedan i tisdags har de väntat utanför Ullevi i Göteborg. De har övernattat i svenskalet på asfalten, och de har levt på kakor och vatten från bensinstationen intill.

- Men jag har varit så nervös att jag knappast har ätit något alls, berättar Caroline ██████.

Alla umbäranden, bara för att komma så nära som möjligt under megastjärnans scenframträdande ikväll. Den lilla samlingen av ungdomar kommer att vara den första som släpps in. Och det är de som kommer att inta de eftertraktade platserna längst fram på fotbollsplanen.

- Man ska stå så nära att man kan känna lukten av honom, säger Caroline.

Michael Jackson är den bäste, den vackraste, och den underbaraste människan i hela världen, enligt henne.

- Han är helt perfekt.

De svenska tjejerna och killarna utanför insläppet, har också fått sällskap av två riktiga proffsfans från Storbritannien. Jill ██████ och Talitha Linehan har följt sin idol under ett tiotal konserter i Europa på slutalfärtfart och konstant övernattat

Jill ██████ och Talitha Linehan har redan följt Michael Jackson under ett tiotal konserter.

utanför arenorna. Ändå har de väldigt stora förväntningar inför kvällen.

- I Köpenhamn var han fantastisk. Han har aldrig varit så bra som nu, berättar de.

Michael Jackson hade spexat med publiken och pratat med fansen som de aldrig hade sett honom göra tidigare. Annizzig!

Men vad säger alla föräldrar egentligen, om att deras ungdomar sover utomhus mitt i stan?

- Mammorna ska också på konserten i kväll, menar Anki ██████ som tittar förbi på lunchen för att se hur dottern Johanna ██████ har det.

- Fast åtminstone jag, nöjer mig med en plats längre bak, skrattar hon.

Michael Jackson för evigt inristad i skinnet. Talitha Linehan från Irland är en övertygad fan.
FOTO: STEFAN EDETOFT

Här är ungdomarna som kommer vara först på plan i kväll. Då har de tillbringat två dygn på asfalten utanför Ullevis entré.

One of several European newspaper articles featuring Tick and me from the summer of 1997, this one depicting us waiting with other fans at the stadium in Gothenburg, Sweden, where Michael was to perform his next HIStory concert the following evening, and a photo of my tattoo. (Photos: Stefan Edetoft)

with him that stand out above all others. The first occurred because of a chance encounter backstage in Hockenheim with his guitarist, Jennifer Batten, who performed on stage with him at every concert, wearing black leathers and a giant neon wig. She told us that while preparing for that night's concert, Michael had pointed us out to her on a screen backstage, as his cameraman, Hamid, had filmed us at the front barrier, and said he'd thought we were kids who'd run away from home to follow the tour.

Touched that Michael had perceived us in such a way, we told Jennifer who we were and where we were from, and gave her a gift for Michael: a pair of small teddy bears attached with a love heart. Pinned on the front was a photo of us, taken outside the stadium in Leipzig, and written across it in silver lettering were the words, "With you 'til Ostend," which was the location in Belgium of our last concert (which ended up being postponed by three days because of the untimely passing of Michael's beloved friend Princess Diana). On the back was another photo of us, with the message, "Wish it were forever."

At the next concert, in Copenhagen, on 14 August, Michael kept looking and pointing at us, more than ever before, and during "Heal the World," he pointed at us mid-song, bowed, and then looked at us again, no doubt to see our reaction, which was one of joyful incredulity. The next time we met Jennifer, which was at a meet and greet in Scandinavia, she told us that she'd given our gift to Michael just before that concert, and we told her, "We know, oh we know!" and thanked her from the bottom of our hearts.

After Copenhagen, we went to concerts in Sweden, Norway, Finland, and Estonia, before returning to Copenhagen for a concert on Michael's thirty-ninth birthday, on 29 August. Our dream above all others, long before we'd begun travelling together, was to meet Michael, and to achieve this, we knew that we'd have to separate ourselves from the crowd. So, shortly after rejoining the tour in Berlin, we'd made the decision to leave every concert towards the end of the second last song, which was "Heal the World." We would then head to the backstage exit and try to figure out which route Michael was taking to the airport, based on maps we'd studied earlier and/or the direction his police escorts were facing. We would hurry along this route until we heard the fireworks that exploded above the stage at the end of every concert, at which point we'd stand under a streetlight at the nearest intersection, and wait.

When Michael left the stadium, police on motorcycles would accompany him until he was a safe distance away. But by the time he reached us, the police would have departed, and it would just be the car he was travelling in, with his personal bodyguard, Wayne Nagin, followed by a security vehicle. We guessed the route correctly more often than not, and would stand on the pavement, jumping up and down, waving and blowing kisses as his car drove past or, on those lucky occasions when the traffic light was red, approach his car and profess our love to him through its tinted back window.

In Copenhagen, on the night of 29 August, we not only guessed the route correctly, an easy task since it was the same one he'd taken after his previous concert there, on 14 August, but also chose the best possible intersection, because as Michael approached it, the traffic light turned red, and it stayed red for what seemed like an inordinately long time. We took a few steps towards the back window and projected all of our love through it, telling Michael how much we loved him and how much we'd miss him after his next concert, which was to be our last. And then, just before the light turned green, we heard banging on the window and Michael's voice shouting, "I love you! I love you! I love you!"

Me (right) with guitarist Jennifer Batten, backstage following the HIStory concert in Hockenheim, Germany, in August 1997. Jennifer is holding a gift from Tick and me that she would give to Michael just before he took to the stage to perform the following concert, in Copenhagen, Denmark.

Thanks to Jennifer Batten, we knew that Michael had spoken about us, but this was the first time he'd spoken *to* us, and, standing on that road under a starlit sky, I captured those precious first words with my heart, where they remain forever lodged.

THREE
Meeting Michael

ust as a wave of good fortune carried me through Michael's world, a wave of happiness carried me through the intervening years, from the day I exited his world, after my final *HIStory* concert in Ostend, Belgium, in September 1997, until I re-entered it almost two years later, in Munich, Germany, in June 1999, when Michael went there to perform as the final act at a star-studded concert called MJ & Friends.

While waiting to return to Michael, I became absorbed in my life, which included a short stint in Paris and the completion of my journalism degree, all the while glowing with the radiance of the shiny new treasures that I carried inside. I often basked in my memories of the tour, extracting each treasure and re-experiencing the feelings it evoked, and in the knowledge that after carrying my love for Michael for seven years unrequited, I now knew that he loved me too. I knew because he'd told me so, projecting the sentiment through a darkened car window under a starry night sky.

In Munich, Tick and I headed straight to the Hotel Bayerischer Hof, where Michael was to arrive the following day, and camped overnight to secure our spot at the barricade, directly across from the hotel's main entrance. While waiting there, we saw many of the regulars from the *HIStory* tour, as well as fans we'd met at various countries along the way. Most of the latter group had been to only one or two concerts, but since we'd last seen them, several of them had taken a giant leap forward, by achieving the dream that still eluded us, and meeting Michael for the first time. For some, their opportunity had come during a previous visit Michael had made to Munich, in March 1998, while for others, it had been when he'd emerged from a building in London in April 1999 and spoken to awaiting fans for more than an hour. We were as happy for them as we could be while reassuring each other that our long-awaited opportunity would soon come.

The next day, fans flocked to the hotel, many of them draping banners over the barricade, the crowd thickened behind us, and the air became electrified with the prospect of seeing Michael. "He's coming soon," his German tour promoter, Teddy Lakis, promised repeatedly as the hours ticked by. Among the crowd was an English fan called Peter, aka Pete the Clown, who was a fixture outside Michael's hotels in Europe. Sporting a clown wig and shouting into a megaphone, he led the crowd in cheers and chants of Michael's name, and throughout the afternoon, the level of excitement continued to intensify. Finally, with the crowd in a state of frenzy, Michael's convoy of cars pulled into the courtyard, and Michael emerged, wearing a black jacket with gold embellishments.

A member of Michael's entourage handed him a blue and white striped umbrella, and he stood under its canopy surveying the crowd. His gaze swept across the barricade and landed on us, standing side by side, as we had at every concert, holding our Michael Jackson masks and wearing our sequinned gloves. His face lit up in recognition and he pointed directly at us. He recognised us, he remembered us, and now he was moving towards the barricade to our right, and we wondered if he might walk along it greeting his fans. We couldn't help hoping that this was our chance to meet him at last, if only for a moment, and with our hearts pounding, we waited for him to return our way.

As he walked along the cordoned-off road between the hotel and the barricade, he pointed to several banners and paintings, which his entourage collected for him. Suddenly, a woman broke through a line of police officers to his left and flew towards him, but his entourage caught her before she could reach him and held her back. A few minutes later, another followed suit and, perhaps fearing that the situation was becoming too chaotic, his entourage ushered Michael inside the safety of the hotel, and any prospect of achieving our long-held dream slipped out of grasp.

We didn't come close to meeting Michael again in Munich, and our next venture into his world was almost a year later, in Monte Carlo, Monaco, in May 2000, when he went there to receive the Best-selling Male Pop Artist of the Millennium Award at the World Music Awards. The day after the awards show, Michael emerged from a side door of the Hotel de Paris, where he was staying, wearing a black shirt and a red surgical mask, and got into a tiny, two-seater Smart car, where he sat on the passenger seat, looking larger than life. The crowd swarmed the car and I found myself pressed against the window on the driver's side, as close to Michael as I had ever been. He looked my way and our eyes met, and while his gaze was open and curious, it held no glint of recognition. It was in that moment that I realised that Michael didn't know me nearly as well as I had thought he did.

Michael knew me only as he'd first come to recognise me, standing at the front barrier on the *HIStory* tour with Tick, both of us holding our masks and wearing our gloves. Remarkably, he'd recognised us instantaneously almost two years later, in Munich, but alone, without my other half, he had no idea who I was; he did not know my face. It was a huge blow. I felt stripped of my greatest treasure, which was the knowledge that he knew me, something I now knew held true only under rigid conditions, in a specific configuration. It felt like a giant step backwards because I'd have to climb a hill I thought I'd already conquered and establish myself again within his field of recognition, alone and without the necessity of props, and so would Tick, as we suspected that what was true for me was true for her as well.

Despite this setback and the disappointment in Munich, I still felt like the luckiest girl in the world. In Munich, I had arrived late to the concert, having foregone queuing at the stadium to stay at the hotel in the hope of meeting Michael, but still got to watch his performance from the back of the front pit – as opposed to the back of the stadium – having acquired wristbands to enter this area. And in Monte Carlo, I had used my press credentials to gain access to the red carpet and the backstage area at the World Music Awards, and then talked someone into allowing Tick and me into the heart of the venue, where we'd watched Michael accept his award and give a speech, live and in person. Even when I was waiting in the rain for hours with little prospect of seeing, let alone meeting, Michael, I was exactly where I wanted to be, bar in his actual presence. I was within his world, and that is where I belonged.

*   *   *

In the end, Tick and I met Michael not because of the impression we'd made on him during the *HIStory* tour but because of the impression we'd made on his bodyguard, Wayne Nagin. Wayne had worked for Michael for many years and was seen as something of a father figure to him, as well as the gateway between him and his fans.

One day during the tour, while Tick and I were hanging out backstage in Scandinavia, we saw Wayne in the distance, looking our way. We froze, fearing that he would have us removed, since we weren't really supposed to be there, but instead he smiled at us and gave us a solid thumbs up. We knew he could have recognised us only from the roadside, as he always travelled in the car with Michael after every concert, and interpreted his gesture as an approval of our behaviour, which was in stark contrast to that of fans we'd seen outside the stadium in Berlin, running at Michael's car and pounding their fists against its windows.

A couple of weeks after our trip to Monaco, Tick and I went to see Michael again, this time in London, where he was to accompany the legendary Hollywood actress and his dear friend Elizabeth Taylor to a tribute concert to her at the Royal Albert Hall. On 25 May 2000, Michael arrived at the Dorchester Hotel to all the usual chaos, and greeted his fans from his hotel window, as was the norm. A short time later, he emerged from the hotel with his entourage and got into the back of a black minivan, and Wayne got into the front passenger seat.

Tick and I were standing a few feet in front of the van and, as it eased forward, Wayne began pointing at us. We thought he was indicating to us to move aside, so we did so, but then the van stopped and he jumped out. Some of the other fans gathered around him, pleading for a meeting with Michael, but he pushed past them and made a beeline for us, saying, "These two, these two." He put one hand on Tick's shoulder and one on mine, and he steered us towards the van, and our friend, who goes by the name Moonstreet, got swept along with us.

Wayne planted us by the van's back door and slid it open, and there, sitting inside, all alone, wearing a black jacket and a red surgical mask, his eyes blissfully un-hidden by shades, was Michael. While our friend stood stunned into silence, Tick and I babbled, telling him how much we loved him and how long we'd dreamed of this moment. We gave him our masks and he thanked us and told all three of us that he loved us, and he squeezed our outstretched hands in his, but mostly he just stared at us in turn, as if reading our faces, committing them to memory. The door slid shut and we erupted in joy at finally achieving what had begun to feel like an impossible dream.

After that, everything changed. The number of trips I went on a year multiplied, from two in 2000, to five in 2001, to seven in 2002. I began making friends with other rookie followers, and planning trips and staying in hotels with them. And I began meeting Michael every time I travelled to see him, often numerous times.

My first trip after London in May 2000 was my first trip to the US and my first trip without Tick since we'd met. In February 2001, I flew to New York to watch Michael give a speech at a seminar at Carnegie Hall for a new charity he was launching called Heal the Kids. When he arrived backstage, he spotted me at the red carpet, and he smiled and flashed me a peace sign. It was confirmation that he now knew me, at least within the context of the fan world and not just in the context of a *HIStory* tour duo.

*   *   *

The early 2000s were a whirlwind of adventures and blissful moments within Michael's world, which I often equated to Narnia. My friends and I all lived relatively ordinary lives, in which we worked and studied and socialised. But every so often, we would disappear through a metaphorical wardrobe door into a magical land of wonder, where all of our dreams had the potential to come true, and where many of them already had.

The followers I met in those years were all young adults, mostly female, and, with the exception of one American, all from Europe, with the largest contingents hailing from England, Germany, France, and Spain. Tick and I were part of a new wave of followers who had begun following during or after the *HIStory* tour, and we were all learning the tricks of the trade from the older, more seasoned followers: where to go and what to do for the best possible chance of seeing and meeting Michael.

We could only go to Michael when we knew where he was, and we only knew where he was when it was announced by the media or an online fan forum. Most of the trips we went on involved a public appearance of some kind by Michael, whether at a concert, an awards show, or another event. Typically, we would hear about such appearances months, weeks, or days in advance, and have to scramble in such latter cases to make all of the necessary arrangements.

Whenever possible, I would use my press credentials to acquire media passes for Tick and me to any events that Michael was to attend. On other occasions, my friends and I would go to the venue a day or two before the event, take photos with the crew members, and then go to a printing shop, such as Kinkos in the US, to duplicate the passes dangling from the lanyards around their necks. Normally, all we needed to do was copy the logo from the event's website, type something like "VIP" or "All Access" across it, and laminate it, and even if it wasn't an exact duplicate, it worked.

The goal on these trips was to always be where Michael was, or as close to him as possible. In 2002, Tick and I began staying at his hotels in Europe, where room rates were a lot more affordable than in the US. In June of that year, Michael spent a week in London, where he attended a protest against Sony for mistreating him and other artists, and a fan event called the Killer Thriller Party, and where he took a train from London to Exeter, on which all of us fans joined him, to give a speech at a local football club.

After a frustrating day outside London's Renaissance Chancery Court hotel (now the Rosewood London hotel), where he was staying and where a crowd surge had deprived us of seeing him, Tick and I heard from other followers that unlike in some hotels, where Michael took the elevator directly from his room to the garage, he was using the lobby here, passing through it every time he came or went, and stopping to greet any waiting fans. Immediately, we booked a room, and clever Tick figured out that the stairway from the lobby led directly to Michael's floor. So, whenever he returned and disappeared into the elevator, we would fly up the stairway to meet him again. He laughed the first time we did this, popping out of the stairwell as he stepped out of the elevator, and stopped to greet us every time.

It was also at the Renaissance Chancery Court hotel that Tick and I got our first photograph with Michael, something we'd never felt comfortable asking for but long desired, mainly as a tangible treasure for us to savour but also to show our family and friends, who didn't think we were lying exactly but also couldn't quite believe our stories of meeting Michael, so impossible were they to conceive.

Following the Sony protest, during which Michael had ridden on the top deck of an open-air bus through London, we raced back to the hotel, where we found him in a small room greeting fans. He spotted us at the window holding a banner he'd pointed at repeatedly from the bus. It had a photo of the head of Sony, Tommy Mottola, who Michael had told us a few weeks earlier, in New York, was trying to destroy his career, and a quote from Michael's 1996 short film *Ghosts*: "Are you scared yet? You should be."

Michael beckoned us inside the room, and when we went to the door, his bodyguard, Mike LaPerruque, who had replaced a retired Wayne Nagin the previous year, came to get us. Inside, Michael asked us to pose with him for a photo, which he said was to appear in *Time* magazine, though as far as I know, it never did. He held up the banner and we stood on each side of him, as a photographer snapped a series of photos of us, capturing our togetherness in a permanent, physical form.

*   *   *

Our next stay at Michael's hotel, the Adlon in Berlin, where he went in November 2002 to accept a Bambi Award for Pop Star of the Millennium, was almost as stressful as it was amazing. Based on a rumour that Michael was flying into a private airport, we went there to greet him, only to discover that the rumour was unfounded, and so we missed him arriving at the hotel. This turned out to be a blessing in disguise, as when he'd stepped into the lobby, chaos had ensued, with fans knocking over furnishings to reach him, and the hotel manager had promptly cancelled the reservation of every guest he could identify as a fan.

When Tick and I arrived at the hotel, we checked in under a veil of anonymity, and hurried to our room to plan our next move. We knew we couldn't hang out in the lobby for hours, as we had in London, without arousing suspicion, and at any rate, it soon became apparent that Michael was no longer using the lobby, but instead taking the elevator directly to the underground garage.

By this time, Tick and I were both living in Munich, and we had arrived in Berlin in a rental car, which was parked in the same underground garage as Michael's convoy of SUVs. So, with two of our friends in tow, we descended to the garage, parked a few rows from Michael's convoy, and sat waiting in our car. Hours passed before the crowd outside erupted, a sure sign that Michael was at the window, and a few minutes later, a team of security guards emerged from the elevator and began milling around.

We shifted further down on our seats so they wouldn't see us, but kept our eyes trained on the elevator doors. If we got out of our car too early, we would alert the security guards, who would no doubt send us away. If we got out too late, Michael would already be inside his car and might not see us. We had to time it just right. Finally, Michael stepped out of the elevator and, while everyone was focused on him, we sprung out of our car and approached. The security guards, startled by our sudden appearance, blocked our path, so we gently called out Michael's name, and he turned to us and told them to let us through.

We chatted and giggled with Michael, and when he returned that evening, we handed him a water pistol to match the two that Tick and I had, and engaged him in a water-fight. We continued to use the same tactic, much to the amusement of his entourage, who, after seeing his reaction to us the first time, told us, "You can go to him if he calls you over," and he always did. Towards the end of his visit, other fans began sneaking into the garage, at which point Tick and I began meeting him on his floor, where a few of our friends were staying and invited us to wait in their room with them.

Eventually, though, we attracted the ire of the hotel manager, who, after seeing us with Michael one evening, marched us to the front desk to check us out. As he turned away to speak with the clerk, we ran off and hid, delighting at our mischief, because so often in Michael's world, we felt like mischievous children hiding from the big bad wolf, be that a security guard or a hotel manager or anyone else who was threatening to quash our dreams. That wave of good fortune must have still been in force because we managed to stay at the hotel until Michael left for the airport, even chatting to him one last time in the garage before waving him goodbye.

*　　*　　*

Whether in Europe or the US, whenever Michael left his hotel or any other location, we followed if possible, either by car, taxi, or the local subway system. In London, we often heard through the grapevine when he was planning to visit the toy store Hamleys or the department store Harrods, or attend a musical at the West End. We would wait for him to leave the hotel where he was staying, then hop on the Tube to beat him to his destination, so we could greet him on his arrival.

In early 2002, Tick and I each bought a Razor scooter, a two-wheeled compact scooter that you propel along by foot, and began taking it with us on trips to New York. So clogged were the streets of Manhattan that whenever Michael left his hotel, which was always either the Palace or the Four Seasons, we were able to use our scooters to keep up with his car, which at that time was a white truck limousine with the licence plate 4WMM398, a sequence that my brain has retained even after all these years, no doubt because of the promise it once held. Tick and I would whiz along on the sidewalk, and whenever the limousine, which was wonderfully slow-moving and awkward to manoeuvre, got stuck in traffic or stopped at a red light, we would approach the back window and Michael would roll it down to talk to us, often laughing at our antics and urging us to be careful.

In Los Angeles, a rental car was a necessity and although, like many of my friends from Europe, – where a car was an unnecessary burden and driving lessons were prohibitively expensive – I couldn't drive at that time, fortunately Tick could. We made our first trip to Los Angeles in February 2002, and were the only fans to greet Michael backstage at an AIDS benefit and tribute to Rock Hudson at Laguna Beach in Orange County, to which he accompanied his dear friend Elizabeth Taylor.

On our next trip to LA, in April 2002, we were among three

or four car-fulls of fans from Europe who went to see Michael perform at the American Bandstand 50th Anniversary Celebration in Pasadena, and at the hotel where he was staying in Bel Air. At one point, we pulled up next to him at a red light, Tick and I leaned out to hand him a gift, and Michael climbed halfway out of his car window to get it. He was always an equal participant in our game of cat and mouse, egging us on and rewarding us whenever we navigated around all of the obstacles to place ourselves within his reach.

*   *   *

Throughout those glorious years, I lived in a state of permanent anticipation, ever waiting for that next phone call or email about an upcoming appearance, never knowing when or where my next adventure would be, or what new treasures it might contain. At the centre of this Narnia-type world was Michael, but my journey to him brought an abundance of friendship and travel that enriched my life.

Because of Michael, I met people with whom I share a special bond, a deeper knowing, an unspoken understanding. One of these people turned out to be my soul mate, my twin flame, and several others have become my closest friends and confidants. Because of Michael, I got to travel the world, and while admittedly most of my time abroad was spent focused on him, I often found time to explore the local culture, and on that first trip to Los Angeles in 2002, I discovered what I felt certain would become my future home, so strong was my connection to it.

In many ways, my friends and I, who made up this new wave of followers, were especially lucky, to be part of this golden era in the fan world. Meeting Michael came a lot easier to us than it had to followers in the past, not because of them or us but because of Michael. While he remained painfully shy, I think he was forcing himself to overcome his shyness in those years, and while I can't say for sure why, I suspect it was because of his children, whose love gave him the courage to climb out of his shell.

Also, when we went to the US to see Michael, we were often alone or among very few fans there, in part because some of the followers were taking a step back to pay off loans that they had taken out to follow the *HIStory* tour, but also because most fans from Europe travelled to the US to see Michael only if it was for a major event, like the two concerts he performed in New York in 2001, or the birthday celebration he attended in Los Angeles two years later.

In March 2002, my friends and I, who between us represented a contingent from Ireland, England, Germany, Sweden, and Spain, went to New York because we heard that Michael was going to be the best man at the wedding of Hollywood star Liza Minnelli to David Gest there. We met Michael several times a day, either inside the garage of his hotel or out and about in the city, and he introduced us to his infant son, Prince Michael Jackson II, who became known as Blanket, and whose existence was not yet known to the world, and to Elizabeth Taylor, who was accompanying him to the wedding.

A month later, while on another trip to New York, I relayed these experiences to a follower from England called Justin, who Michael had nicknamed Waldo and who he was crazy about. Justin had first seen Michael during the *Bad* era in the late 1980s, and he told me that we were very spoilt, because back in those early days and indeed well into the 90s, it had been incredibly difficult to meet Michael, and even catching a glimpse of his hand as he waved out of a car window had been considered a rare treat.

It was up to us to close the distance between Michael and us, but it was up to Michael to bridge that final gap, whether by calling us to him or rolling down his car window to talk to us. We couldn't force ourselves into his presence and we wouldn't have dreamt of doing so; it would have felt so wrong, so unnatural.

There was one girl who followed for a few years in the early 2000s. She was perfectly nice but whenever she saw Michael, she would run at him and try to hug him, at which point he would be whisked away. Afterwards, she would apologise to us, for cutting our time with him short, to his bodyguard, for posing a security threat, and to Michael, for being so forceful. In the end, Michael became visibly wary of her and would back away whenever he saw her, a response that no other follower I knew ever evoked.

The rest of us enjoyed an exchange of love with Michael that was gentle and sweet. The first couple of times that Tick and I met him, we did babble quite a bit, but after that, we forced ourselves to remain calm and would plan with our friends questions to ask him so we could hear him speak. We listened intently as he told us what projects he was working on or what trips he was planning; during one conversation, he said he was working on a movie based on a book called *They Cage the Animals At Night*, by Jennings Michael Burch, and he told us about his trip to Berlin to receive the Bambi Awards months before it was announced to the world.

Whenever we talked to him through his open car window, we would each reach a hand in, which he would squeeze while telling us how much he loved us and how happy we made him. Then, as he drove away, he would wave and blow us kisses, and we would respond in kind until he was out of sight and we were left to relive the encounter while holding up our hands to breathe in the scent of his cologne and making empty promises to never wash them again, because doing so would mean washing away his touch.

*   *   *

Michael often told us we were his family, and he always treated us as such. In April 2002, after seeing him at the American Bandstand 50th Anniversary Celebration in Los Angeles, we flew directly to New York, where he was to perform at a Democratic celebration called A Night at the Apollo at the Apollo Theater in Harlem. However, because it was a political event, we were unable to buy tickets, for which proof of US citizenship was required. Some of the followers relayed this to Michael, and on the day of the event, his bodyguard, Mike, told us that Michael was refusing to perform unless the organisers granted us access; he was not going on stage without us there.

We felt bad for putting Michael in this position, unintentional though it had been, but also touched that he was insisting on our presence. That evening, Mike told us to go to the Apollo Theater, where we greeted Michael on his arrival. Then, minutes before he took to the stage, the venue's security team came out to get us and escorted us inside, where we cheered and applauded and shouted out our love for Michael, as we watched him perform three of his hit songs.

Perhaps at no other time did Michael make more apparent his love and concern for us as a whole, however, than in the aftermath of the terrorist attacks on the US on 11 September 2001. Tick and I, along with hundreds of other fans from Europe, woke up in New York that morning, having attended a duo of concerts there that were in honour of Michael and at which he'd performed, at Madison Square Garden, on 7 and 10 September.

After hearing about the terrorist attacks from a stranger on the streets of Manhattan and watching the infamous footage of an aeroplane flying into the Twin Towers on a TV screen in Time Square, Tick and I headed to the Palace hotel, where Michael was staying and where other fans were gathered, many of them relaying rumours of further attacks on the city, which thankfully proved to be unfounded.

Shortly after we arrived, Michael left the hotel, but that evening, he sent his entourage back to the city to check on us, to make sure we had accommodation and enough money to get by. Gradually, our numbers dwindled, as people secured flights home, many of which, including ours, had been rescheduled, and a few days after the attacks, members of Michael's entourage arrived on his tour bus and invited the remaining 15 or so of us on board.

Under Michael's instruction and on his dime, they took us to see a movie and to eat at McDonald's, and then drove us to the hotel in New Jersey where he was staying. We spent the night there on the bus, which was fitted with rows of bunk beds, each with its own DVD screen, and although we didn't get to see Michael, he kept calling to check on us. In a time of fear and uncertainty, he made us feel safe and loved and cherished. He made us feel like family.

FOUR
Inside Neverland

f Michael were a magical being, an impression that never wavered in my mind, then Neverland Valley was his fairytale kingdom. Developed by him beginning in the late 1980s, and located in Santa Barbara County, about 130 miles northwest of Los Angeles, the 2,700-acre estate was his private haven, his retreat from the world, accessible only to invited guests, which included family members, close friends, and the busloads of sick children who would visit often, to frolic and play in this sweet wonderland.

During my early youth, I got to peer inside Neverland through the photographs and footage captured during two interviews with Michael there, the first of which was carried out by the owner and editor of the fanzine *Off The Wall*, Adrian Grant, in 1990. The second interview was conducted by American talk show host Oprah Winfrey three years later, in Michael's softly furnished living room and private movie theatre, and on the grounds of his amusement park, and was televised live to an audience of about ninety million people. How I absorbed those precious few images, channelling them into my imagination, which was the only place I ever expected to step through the golden gates that opened into the heart of the estate.

While most fans I knew had met Michael at least once, some even hugging him, a dream that by the end of 2002 I had yet to fulfil, no fan I knew had set foot beyond the exterior gates of Neverland, which

Tick and I had stopped by during our first visit to California earlier that year. That all changed, suddenly and unexpectedly, in August 2002. Tick and I were among about a dozen European fans in New York, where Michael was to attend the MTV Video Music Awards on his forty-fourth birthday, when we heard a rumour that he had invited members of an American fan club to visit Neverland in his absence a few days later.

When we met Michael at the Palace hotel, he confirmed to us that the rumour was true, and invited us to join those other fans in visiting his home. Tick and I found ourselves in quite the dilemma, having to choose between staying in New York, where Michael was, and flying thousands of miles across the country, to visit his home. In the end, we decided to stay, hoping and praying that another opportunity to fulfil this heretofore impossible dream would one day come our way. Neverland was at the heart of Michael's world, but Michael was the heart of the heart, and not even an invitation to his kingdom could draw us away from him.

The next time I went to Neverland Valley was sadly without Tick but was with four other good friends, all female, one from Germany, one from Sweden, and two from Spain. It was in February 2003, following the release of a documentary called *Living with Michael Jackson*, in which the host, British journalist Martin Bashir, had corrupted the content through a commentary track in which he'd suggested, based on nothing but his own distorted viewpoint, that Michael's relationship with children was in some way inappropriate. The documentary, which without Bashir's sinister overtone would have merely substantiated what a beautiful and loving human being Michael was, no doubt had had the effect that the journalist had intended. It had proven extremely controversial, evoking harsh criticism of Michael from people who took every opportunity to condemn all that he said and did.

My friends and I decided to make the trip to Neverland, where Michael was rumoured to be at the time – though we could never be sure that such rumours were well founded – in order to show our love and support during what must have been a difficult time for him. We spent several days outside the estate's entrance, which was marked by a pair of brown wooden gates that gave no indication of the wonders that lay within. We gave letters for Michael to the guards stationed in the security hut just inside the entrance, and we chatted with staff members and guests, who included Marlon Brando's son Miko, as they came and went. Many of them wanted to know who we were and why we were there, and marvelled at our past adventures and our devotion to Michael.

On 19 February, I was due to catch a flight back to Germany, where I was still living at the time, but had time to spend a final few hours outside Neverland before leaving for the airport. Shortly after 10 a.m., one of the girls said, in a calm, clear voice, "limo," and, knowing exactly what she was referring to, the rest of us scrambled out of our rental car to see. There, meandering towards us, along the road that cut through the estate, was Michael's white truck limousine. It pulled up at the security hut, where the driver, Jesus, chatted to the guard for a few minutes, then eased through the gateway and came to a stop.

"It's just some guests leaving," shouted the guard, but we weren't sure whether or not to believe him, as people in such positions often felt obligated to lie to keep secret Michael's whereabouts. The back door of the limousine opened and a deep male voice (which we later discovered belonged to TV host Maury Povich) said, "Come in and say hi!" We all assumed at that point that it really was a group of Michael's guests inside the limousine, but when we leaned in to see, we let out a collective gasp, because sitting on the leather seating along the interior cabin was Michael with his three children, and a man we would come to recognise as American TV presenter Maury Povich. On return to Europe, we would discover that Maury was the host of a rebuttal video called *Take Two: The Footage You Were Never Meant To See*, which revealed how Bashir had manipulated Michael into trusting him, before betraying him in a deliberate and heartless way.

We told Michael we had come to show our support, on our own behalf and on behalf of our friends in Europe, and he said, "Tell the fans I love them all." He told us he was on his way to Miami, Florida, and one of the girls asked him if it would be okay if we followed him, to which he replied in a pained voice, "I could never say no to you girls." We all laughed and said, "No, you have to tell us no Michael, so we can control ourselves," then reassured him that we wouldn't follow, as it was clearly a private trip.

We asked him how he was feeling, and he said he still had a lot of pain from the spider bite he'd endured a few months earlier. Funnily enough, at that very moment, a spider appeared on the TV screen at the back of the limousine, which was showing that year's *Spider-Man* film. "Spider," I shouted, pointing at it, and everyone laughed. Then Michael said, "Do you want to see it?" meaning the spider bite, and of course, we all said we did. "When you see it, you're going to go, 'Uuugh!'" he said. We promised we wouldn't, but as soon as he started to pull up his pant leg, we all said, "Uuugh!" and he laughed again. He lowered his sock to reveal a large yellowed wound on his shin, with strips of tape across it, and we all ooh-ed and aah-ed in sympathy.

One of the girls then asked Michael if we could take a photo with him, and he agreed, and we all piled into the limousine and handed a camera to Maury Povich, who snapped a picture that later ended up on a message board, where fans fawned over the image of a beaming

Michael surrounded by five adoring girls. While I sat perched on Michael's lap, he asked me where I was from and told me how much he loved Ireland and dreamed of living in a castle there. "Find me one," he said, with boyish enthusiasm, and I promised him, "I will, and if I can't find you one, I'll build you one instead!"

Just before we left, one of the girls, the one among us brave enough to request all of the things that our hearts desired, asked Michael if it would be possible for us to go inside Neverland, and he said, "Of course, just ask the guards," as if it were the most casual thing in the world. We told him that he'd have to tell the guards it was okay, because there was no way they would believe us, and his driver, Jesus, promised he would take us inside as soon as he returned from the airport.

As Michael's limousine disappeared down Figueroa Mountain Road, we all fell into each other's arms, savouring the aftermath of the encounter and the anticipation of entering Neverland. A few minutes later, the guard came out of the security hut to tell us, "They called," presumably meaning Michael and Jesus, and, "You can come inside now." Our car carried the five of us past the outer bounds of Neverland, three of us for the first time, two for the second, as the Spanish girls had taken up the invitation that Michael had extended to us in New York and joined the other fans on a tour of the grounds the previous August.

We drove along the road behind a security car, past a sign that depicted an iconic image of the Peter Pan characters flying through the air, with the words "Children at play" underneath. We pulled into a parking lot, where the estate manager, Joe Marcus, came to greet us. He told us that he would be our tour guide for the day, later remarking that Michael had instructed him to treat us "like royalty," which he and the other staff members went out of their way to do, greeting us everywhere we went with big smiles and kind words.

We followed Joe across the parking area and there, before us, gleaming in the sun, were the golden gates of my dreams. They glided open, and as we passed through them, under an arched sign that said "Neverland" in gold lettering, tears slid down my face. They were tears of overwhelming happiness tinged with sadness that Tick, my closest friend within this magical world, wasn't there to share this moment with me.

Joe led us into a quaint building that he explained was the train station, where guests waited to begin their tour. In the lobby stood a waxwork of a butler holding a silver tray scattered with hard candies, and under our feet was a carpet with the Neverland logo, a boy in a blue jumpsuit sitting in the crest of a moon.

A red train that looked like a storybook version of an old-fashioned steam locomotive pulled up outside, and we climbed into the front carriage, then gazed around as it carried us deeper into the estate, past perfectly manicured gardens and bronze statues of children frozen in a moment of playfulness: performing a summersault, engaged in a game of chase, joining hands in a circle that brought to mind the nursery rhyme "Ring a Ring o' Roses." We disembarked from the train and crossed the bridge, only to find ourselves gazing up at the Giving Tree, which Michael had explained in Bashir's documentary was the tree he most liked to climb and where he had composed several of his songs, including "Heal the World," "Will You Be There," "Black or White," and "Childhood."

When about forty fans, including my two friends from Spain, had broken new ground the previous August by becoming the first that we knew of to visit Neverland, Michael's house had, understandably, remained off limits. So when Joe led us towards the Tudor-style mansion, my heart skipped a beat. This couldn't possibly be happening, and yet it was: we were going inside Michael's house! Standing on each side of the stone steps leading up to the doorway was a row of staff members dressed in neat uniforms, and as we passed between them, they said, with huge smiles, "Welcome to Neverland." We were touched and flattered but also wanted to tell them that we were just five ordinary girls, and in no way warranted such formality.

We stepped inside, into a home that was warm and cosy, with a glowing fireplace, a large, intricate model of a castle, and Christmas decorations that Michael kept up all year round, partly in compensation for the holiday celebrations he had missed out on as the son of Katherine, a devout Jehovah's Witness, and partly because he simply enjoyed them. What captured our attention the most, however, were all of the paintings and photographs that hung on the walls and, in the latter case, also stood in frames on the mantelpiece, the piano top, and other surfaces, and lay inside photo albums that Joe invited us to browse through.

We stood gazing at the paintings, several of which we recognised from Michael's 1992 book of poems and reflections, *Dancing the Dream*, and pored over the photos of him and his children at various ages, of him with celebrity friends like Elizabeth Taylor, Bill Clinton, and Princess Diana, and performing with his brothers as part of The Jackson 5. Like every other visitor to the estate, we had signed contracts before entering, promising not to take any photographs, so we would have to rely on memory alone to hold on to the details of the day, at least until we had a chance to capture them in writing.

We wandered from room to room, recognising the one in which Oprah Winfrey (another person who had won Michael's trust and then, tragically, gone on to betray him) had interviewed Michael a decade earlier. In the library, among the shelves full of leather-bound books, one of the Spanish girls found, to her amazement, a book she and her brother had made and given to Michael years earlier, an indication that what he always told us was true: that he kept everything we gave him, every letter, every gift, cherishing each one for the sweet sentiment it contained.

Joe invited us to have breakfast, and we sat at a round table in the dining area, separated from the kitchen, where the staff were preparing food, by a counter lined with bar stools. On the wall hung a cuckoo clock, and I stared at it, wishing I could freeze time and remain here forever, captured in a state of perpetual happiness, like the bronze statues outside. One of the staff members, called Maria, presented each of us with a Neverland breakfast menu, and I ordered a cheese omelette, hoping that I could eat despite the fluttering in my tummy. One of the girls glanced out the window and exclaimed; strolling by outside, being led by a carer, was an elephant, a real live elephant! We ran to the window to gaze out, and had just returned to our seats when we spotted a camel, whose carer had perform a series of tricks for us, much to our delight.

After breakfast, Joe escorted us to the back door of the house. Just inside, above a pile of children's shoes, hung a dry-erase board scribbled with messages of love from Michael's children to him, providing a glimpse into their daily life and the closeness that they shared. Outside, Disney music played softly in the background, piped through speakers that were hidden throughout the grounds. Joe led us into another building, which housed a games arcade, and we played on the machines and posed for photos in the photo booth, which printed them in the style of hand-drawn portraits, providing us with treasured mementos of the day.

Back on the train, we passed by an Indian village that Joe told us Michael and his friend Macaulay Culkin, a Hollywood actor and former child star, had built together. The train meandered further into the estate and then pulled up at the zoo, which housed everything from farm animals to crocodiles to monkeys and tigers. We fed the llamas from cone-shaped paper cups, held a snake and a tarantula in the reptile house, and watched a chimpanzee perform tricks as her carer, Stacy, fed her bubblegum, which she chewed and chewed and chewed, making us all laugh hysterically.

It was a day of laughter and of almost uncontainable bliss, to be inside Michael's haven, which he'd dreamt up and created. It wasn't just a place, it was an extension of his soul, a reflection of all the stuff and magic that he was made of, from the smallest details, the fairy figurines in the dining area, to the Disney-inspired animatronic displays in the movie theatre, with characters like Cinderella and Pinocchio that came to life at the touch of a button, to the nighttime spectacle, when the grounds lit up with twinkling lights, turning the weaving pathways golden and making the trees sparkle and shine.

Frozen in time: Me with one of the bronze statues from Neverland Valley, at an exhibition in Beverly Hills, April 2009.

From the zoo, we went on to the amusement park, where we rode rides like the Sea Dragon, the Chair-O-Planes, and the Ferris wheel, and the movie theatre, where we helped ourselves to free candy in the lobby, and then sat in plush, red seats watching a series of videos of Michael on the big screen. The series began with the opening of *Moonwalker*, and my tears flowed again as I reflected on my childhood self watching this film for the first time and feeling my love for Michael released, never imagining that one day I would watch it inside his kingdom, having been invited there by him only hours before.

As sunset approached, the sky darkened, producing the first raindrops of the day. We took the train to the main station, which was perched on a hilltop and housed a giant painting of Michael's beloved mother, Katherine, along with a poem he had written to her. We stepped outside to admire the giant topiary display of shrubs and flowers arranged into the shape of a clock and yellow letters that spelled out "Neverland." A rainbow arced across the sky, marking what we thought was the perfect end to the perfect day – until Joe surprised us by inviting us to have dinner in Michael's house. There, we were joined by some of the other guests, including Miko Brando, a young girl called Marie Cascio, whose family were close to Michael, and Gavin Arvizo, who we recognised from Bashir's documentary, along with his siblings.

As we left the twinkling paradise later that night, I said goodbye in my heart, only to be comforted by one final touch of magic, a road sign that we drove by on our way out. It was painted with three cherubs and the words "Goodbye for now." It was only goodbye for now, not forever, and in fact, only six months passed before I found myself stepping through those golden gates again.

*   *   *

On the night of 29 August 2003, which was Michael's forty-fifth birthday, Tick and I were among about eighty fans outside Neverland when the security guard issued an unexpected invitation to us all to go inside. It was a joy to re-enter the kingdom and to see the reactions of so many of my friends, including Tick, who were stepping inside for the first time. We didn't get to see Michael, and the access was restricted, with his house once again off-limits, but we did get to visit the lobby of the movie theatre and go on the amusement park rides.

The next day, Michael was to attend a birthday celebration, organised by an American fan club, at the Orpheum Theatre in Los Angeles. I was sharing a rental car and hotel room with Tick and Dani, the German girl who I'd visited Neverland with in February. I had a hunch that Michael would leave early to go to LA, rather than drive directly to the venue that evening, so the next morning, we woke up early and were the first people to arrive at Neverland, around 9 a.m. Sure enough, minutes later, the gate opened and the white truck limousine, followed by a black SUV, rolled out. We tossed aside our takeaway breakfasts and drove behind the SUV, down the winding Figueroa Mountain Road, along the highway, onto the 101 freeway, and all the way to the Beverly Wilshire Hotel in Beverly Hills.

Wearing party hats we'd bought for Michael's birthday event that evening, we hopped out of our car and ran to the edge of the garage, where the limousine was parked. Michael got out of the limousine, called us to him, and hugged each one of us, turning yet another of my long-held dreams into a reality. A hug, just like a photo, with Michael was something I'd long desired but never asked for, because I found it impossible to ask him for anything, though I often benefited when other people did, and will be forever grateful to them for that. My first hug, like my first photo, was initiated by Michael, making it all the more special, and it was just as heavenly as I'd always imagined it to be, like being wrapped up in a blanket of love.

The day after the party, Michael returned to Neverland, and this time, we all followed behind him in a convoy of cars. We spent the next week hanging out at the gate, playing games together, biding our time, hoping for one more opportunity to see him before we had to leave and make the long journey home. By Saturday, 6 September, there were only thirteen of us left, and Tick, Dani, and I were due to fly back to Germany that evening. We initially planned to leave at 1 p.m. and have lunch along the way, but as the time drew near, we decided to have a final picnic outside Neverland and leave thirty minutes later instead.

We were the only party among the group with cellphones that worked in the US, so we gave one of them to a French girl called Mari, who promised to press "send" on a text if anything happened while we went to the nearby town of Los Olivos to buy some food. Minutes after we'd reached the bottom of Figueroa Mountain Road, the text came through on my phone and we raced back to Neverland, all the while telling each other that Mari had probably pressed "send" by mistake, as I had done earlier in the week, when Tick had gone to the store without me, and that it was a false alarm.

When we got to the gate, the other fans were clustered around it, and just inside, sitting on a squad bike, wearing a red helmet, a blue shirt, and a pair of pyjama pants, was Michael. "Oh my God, we were almost at the store and we got a text from Mari that you were here and we came back sooo fast," I burst out. Michael laughed and said, "And you came back just like that," and clicked his fingers. We all chatted with him for another few moments and, before driving away, he told us we could all come inside Neverland "to play." We had just met Michael again, and we were going inside Neverland again; none of us could quite believe our luck, least of all Tick, Dani, and me, who would have missed everything had we left at 1 p.m., as originally planned.

None of the other fans had working cellphones, so they couldn't have called or texted us to tell us to come back. The first we would have heard of any of this would have been on our return to Europe, and how heartbroken we would have been! Now, all we would miss was our flight home that evening, just as I had in February, when I'd talked the airline into putting me on one the next day instead, something we were hopeful we could all do this time, and even if we couldn't, none of us cared; opportunities like this were virtually unheard of in the fan world, far too rare and precious to be passed up over such worldly considerations.

*   *   *

Inside Neverland, which was now becoming familiar territory, we all filed through the gates and piled onto the waiting train. We assumed the train would take us to the amusement park, so were happily surprised when it pulled up near Michael's house instead. Michael's cousin Lee invited us to visit the games arcade, and we played on the machines and engaged in water fights outside, filling up our pistols from the nearby fountains and ponds.

After about ten minutes, I noticed that some of the fans were missing, and then I spotted Lee, beckoning us to come inside the main house. He led us into a small room decorated with waxworks and paintings, and I stood admiring the pretty furnishings and saying hi to the other fans trickling inside – only then noticing Michael, sitting in an oversized armchair, with the nanny to his children, Grace Rwaramba, standing beside him.

We gathered around Michael to greet him and then sat facing him in a semi-circle, thirteen people living an impossibly rare dream, the absolute ideal, an amalgamation of the two things that most, if not all, of us had desired since childhood: 1) to meet Michael and 2) to visit Neverland Valley. This was the ultimate fan experience, and if everyone could have seen what we saw and known what we knew, it would have been considered the ultimate human experience: being with this maker of dreams, the shiniest soul on the planet, inside a dreamland of his creation.

Once we were all seated, Michael turned to Grace and asked her if she had the video camera, which she did. He said, "I want each of you to talk to the camera. Tell us how you became a fan and why... Who wants to go first?" Nobody said anything for a while, all too shy and overwhelmed I think, so I said "Mari!" because she was sitting at one end of the semi-circle. She told her story and then everyone took their turn, some feeling too emotional or having too little English to say more than a few words.

Beside Michael was a desk lamp with a long neck, and he switched it on and pointed it at each of us as we spoke, as if placing us in the spotlight. Tick and I described how we'd met on the *HIStory* tour and travelled together since then, and Michael said he'd always wondered what we did when we needed the restroom while waiting for hours at his concerts. We told him, laughing, that we just endured the discomfort of it, but that whenever he was on stage, all of that discomfort went away. Grace then asked us which countries we'd been to to see him and, as we listed them off, he said, shaking his head, "Everywhere. They've been everywhere."

After everyone had spoken, Michael asked, "What will we do now?" and I said, "Tell us a story," because he looked like a storyteller, sitting in an armchair with a group of "kids," as he had referred to us as, gathered around, gazing at him spellbound, hanging on his every word.

"Okay, I'll tell you a story," he said. "A story about Africa. You read a lot of things about Africa but they're not true. People want you to believe that it's a poor country, full of crime. Every country in the world has poverty and crime. Africa is so beautiful. Prince and Paris and I go there on holiday all the time. That's where we go. And I can tell you it's one of the most beautiful countries in the world, full of rich resources. Diamonds come from Africa. But what happened was the British went over and colonised..."

At this point, Tick and I elbowed each other playfully, as she was the only Briton among us, and Michael laughed, before continuing, "You know I don't care what colour or race you are, if you're black or white or yellow or blue or green. I don't care...But it's important that you know the history of the land. Africa's where it all began. That's where civilisation started. If you read the Bible, you can trace it all back to Africa. That's another thing: all the paintings and images you see of Jesus today depict him as a white man with a moustache and long hair. But according to the Bible, he was olive-skinned. It doesn't make a difference to me."

I said, "But it's the principle of it, right?"

He said, "That's right. If he was black, why not say he was black? Why change it?...It doesn't matter what religion you are either. But you should know that Jesus was a great prophet."

He urged us all to visit Africa one day, and Grace, who is originally from Rwanda, agreed, having applauded what Michael had said about her native land.

It was a privilege beyond measure to hear Michael speak at length, something I'd experienced as part of audiences that he'd addressed, for example at the Heal the Kids seminar in New York, but never among so few. He went on to talk about his humanitarian work and a new charity he was starting.

"We're going to call it the Follow Your Dreams charity," he said. "We want one million children from every nation to march in front of the White House for International Children's Day. We want to make that happen. On that day, kids would get to tell their parents where they want to go and what they want to do. And we're working on that. We're organising a meeting with Kofi Annan [the then Secretary-General of the United Nations]. A lot of people don't care about children as much as they say they do. Politicians and other people agree to meetings to promote themselves and further their careers. We have to make it happen together."

Michael continued, "You know, parents don't spend enough time with their kids. PlayStation has become the pacifier. Children are crying out to be loved. That's why there is so much violence in schools. It's a cry for attention. I think a Children's Day would help. I didn't have a good relationship with my father. It was all work, work, work. It's better now because he's a genius, he's a genius. But I think if there had been a Children's Day then, it would have helped. I would have remembered it. My message is to help children. But I'm not sure that people hear it."

We all said, "We hear it!"

He said, "Do you really? Sometimes, I'm not so sure. Boys are all about the beat and the rhythm. Girls listen more to the lyrics."

I told him I wished he would write more poetry because I loved his book *Dancing the Dream* so much, and he told us he was working on a large book of poems and photos, though sadly, perhaps because of the darkness that descended later that year, neither the charity nor the book he described to us that day ever came to fruition.

"I don't know why the media always says that I'm a freak and that I'm weird and that I don't want to talk to people," said Michael, in a pained voice. "Why do they say those things when they're not true?"

We responded vehemently to this and expressed our disgust at the tabloid press, and Grace said, "Every week, Michael invites a busload of sick children to spend a day at Neverland. They never write about that."

Discussing the recent documentary *Living with Michael Jackson*, Michael said, "Martin Bashir tricked us all. He tricked us all. He was so cunning."

A fan from Israel called Shay, who is one of my dearest friends to this day, showed Michael his t-shirt, which said, "Destroy Mottola, Bashir, Avram now!" referring to the journalist, the concert promoter Marcel Avram, who had sued Michael over two cancelled concerts, and the former head of Sony Tommy Mottola, who'd resigned following fan protests against him in London and New York the previous year. Michael said Mottola was an evil man and that Mariah Carey used to call him crying, telling him he was trying to destroy her career.

"Imagine you're the biggest recording artist in the world with the biggest record company in the world and the boss is trying to pull you down because he's jealous of you," he said. "But we got him out. All of you were amazing. Sony's record sales dropped dramatically. They knew it was because of you. So they had to get rid of him. They had to get him out. One day, they held a meeting and that was it, he was gone."

We spent well over an hour in that room listening to Michael speak, asking and answering questions. Finally, he got up and we followed him outside, down a long corridor, only to realise that he was on his way into a restroom, at which point we withdrew in laughter and apology. When he emerged, we followed him outside, and Tick and I asked him if he wanted to try one of our Razor scooters, which we'd abandoned at the door. He stepped onto one of them and rolled along the cobbled pathway, and we cheered him on, shouting, "Faster, faster," but he told us, laughing, that he was afraid to go too fast because he was always injuring himself.

Grace pulled up in a black van, and about half of the fans climbed into it, while the rest of us followed Michael into a black Bentley that one of his cousins was driving. He got into the front passenger seat and we climbed into the back, where I sat in the middle, on Shay's lap. Michael put on the song "Ignition" by R. Kelly, telling us that he and his cousins had busted some speakers while listening to it too loud. He promised to show us some of his awards later.

"I don't really like awards," he said. "They're competitive. That's not what art should be about."

"But you love the Bambi, right?" I said, referring to the award that he'd received in Berlin the previous November, as I recalled seeing it on the desktop in his library during my first visit to Neverland. "That's special."

"Oh," he said. "I *love* the Bambi. I love it, it's so sweet."

The car pulled up outside the movie theatre and we all climbed out.

"You know," I said, as we passed by the candy display in the lobby, "I've always thought you should open a chocolate factory, like Willy Wonka."

His eyes widened and he said in a hushed tone, "It's funny you should say that. That's my very next project. But it's a secret, it's a secret."

I beamed, thrilled to be in on the secret, though saddened later that, like the charity and the book, the project was never realised, or, if he was referring to the Hollywood movie that came out two years later, he wasn't involved in it.

Inside the lobby, Michael revealed to us a secret door hidden in the wall, and he led us through it into a room that I recognised from Bashir's documentary. It had a huge painting of him surrounded by angels, as well as recording equipment and racks of clothing that included several jackets he had worn to awards shows and other events, and the armour he'd worn over his gold pants during the opening sequence of the *HIStory* tour. Tick and I handled the armour, marvelling at our proximity to this part of our history, an item he'd worn on the tour we'd first attended as teenagers and that had become our portal into this magical world.

We trailed after Michael, squeezing between the room's cluttered contents, to the painting of him surrounded by angels, which I later discovered was titled simply *Michael* and was by the artist David Nordahl. Michael told us, "There's something hidden in the painting. You can see me doing 'Billie Jean,'" meaning the iconic pose in which he's balanced on pointed toes, with his gloved hand on his fedora. "It's an illusion. I'll give you a clue. It's below the knees." None of us understood at first what he meant and then Tick found it, the image formed by lines drawn in the foliage. "I have things hidden in all my paintings," said Michael, and congratulated Tick on her keen eye.

The rest of the fans arrived and we filed into the heart of the theatre, where, instead of sitting on the plush, red seats, most of us sat on the floor around Michael. On his invitation, I helped myself to a handful of popcorn from the bucket on his lap as we watched a series of his videos, including the *HIStory* Teaser, the full-length version of "Smooth Criminal," and clips from the *Bad* tour, on the big screen. It had been one thing to watch Michael's videos inside Neverland in February, but here I was repeating that glorious wonder while sitting next to Michael, sharing his popcorn.

When "Smooth Criminal" came on, I told him that when it was

released in 1988, two years before I watched *Moonwalker* for the first time, my brothers and I had recorded it off the television and would watch it over and over again after school. He squeezed my hand in gratitude for sharing this memory with him, and when the cat crossed over the piano, he said, laughing at his own perfectionism, "I recorded that bit six months after I'd finished the rest of the video. I decided there had to be a cat walking on the piano – six months later!" (Naturally, there were also many interactions between Michael and the other fans present, which I recorded in writing but avoid sharing now, instead focusing on my own interactions with him that day, out of respect for their privacy.)

After leaving the movie theatre, Michael climbed back into the Bentley, explaining to us that he had to take care of some business, and we waved him off, assuming that that was the last we'd see of him that day. Lee took us to the zoo, but we had only time to see the elephants and visit the reptile house before a security guard called Violet came and told us, "Mr Jackson would like you back in the house now." When we arrived, she had us line up in single file at the back door, and it swung open, revealing Michael, who had changed into black pants and a button-down shirt, holding his youngest child, eighteen-month-old Blanket, who was dressed in a velvet suit with short trousers. "He's walking now," said Michael. He put Blanket down and walked a few paces away, and Blanket toddled over and fell into his arms, as we all cooed in delight.

Michael guided us through the house, past the kitchen, where the staff greeted us, and into the living room, and Blanket toddled among us, sometimes clutching the edge of his father's trousers, other times holding our hands. We crowded around Michael as he showed us some of the photos of him with dignitaries and of his children, and

Grace told us that he had taken all of the photos of his children himself. He had also conceived of the giant paintings, many of which depicted fantasy-inspired scenes, like my favourite of all, *The Storyteller* by David Nordahl, of Michael sitting under a tree inside a magical realm, with an oversized storybook on his lap.

We stopped at each painting and Michael challenged us to find the hidden images, which included more iconic depictions of him but also his sequinned glove, his fedora, his sister Janet, and his friends Macaulay Culkin and Ryan White, an American teenager who had died of AIDS in 1990 and to whom Michael had dedicated his song "Gone Too Soon." At one of the paintings, called *Playmates for a Lonely Child*, also by David Nordahl, of a golden-haired girl communing with a fairy, we found one image after another. "Now, find the hat," said Michael, and he started to count down, "Ten, nine, eight…" I found it and pointed it out, but he continued, "Seven, six, five…" "Hey, I found it," I protested as he continued counting, and when he couldn't keep a straight face any longer, he erupted in laughter, and we all joined in.

At one point, Michael's two older children, Prince, aged six, and Paris, five, burst into the room and ran into their father's arms, and they joined us on the rest of the tour. As Michael led us further through the house, and into the library, I tried to absorb every word, every gesture, every detail, that I might hold onto it forever. Normally, my encounters with him were so brief that it was only later that I reflected on their content, but here, I found myself stepping out of the moment to observe the wonder that was unfolding, the wonder of who I was with, talking with, laughing with, brushing past as we wandered between the furnishings admiring the artwork. My mind reeled as I tried to reconcile the dualities, both in him and in me: the Michael with the Michael Jackson; the man with the megastar; the fantasy I'd been dreaming up since I was a little girl with the reality I was living; the fan that I was with the friend he was treating me as on this blessed day.

*　　*　　*

When my friends and I had visited Neverland in February, the only area of the house that had remained off-limits had been Michael's private quarters, which were behind a closed door topped with a sculpture of a boy and a girl leaning towards each other, clasping hands. The staff member Maria had told us that nobody, not even the people who worked in the house, was allowed beyond that door when Michael wasn't present. Well, Michael was our personal tour guide today, and he amazed us all by inviting us into this private world of wonders, telling us, "If you want to know what stimulates my mind, take a look around."

With expressions of delightful curiosity, we filed through the doorway and into a long corridor that led to a network of rooms, each one cluttered with paintings, photos, posters, waxworks, cardboard cut-outs, awards, clothing, toys… There was memorabilia from the world of music and movies: *Peter Pan*, *Star Wars*, *Harry Potter*, *Titanic*, and Charlie Chaplin, to name a few, and fan gifts, including paintings by a girl we knew called Mitzy. Michael had told us earlier that he kept everything we gave him in a warehouse, that it was all catalogued on a computer, and that he planned to display it in a museum one day. He reiterated that now, while showing us giant photos of babies that fans had given him and that he'd had enlarged. "You have no idea how happy you make me," he said, and Grace confirmed, "He keeps everything you give him. He reads everything. He treasures it all."

We crammed into a walk-in closet, where we recognised more of the jackets Michael had worn in public. He kept picking them off the racks and handing them to me, and I remarked about some I recognised from past performances, "Oh, they're really heavy. How do you dance with them on?" He said, "That's what you don't see when you watch me perform. You have no idea how heavy they are. But when I'm dancing, I don't think about it. I melt into the music. If you see a dancer and you see her counting, 'One, two, three,' she's not really dancing. When you dance, you become the music. You become the rhythm and forget everything else."

He showed us a leather jacket that his longtime makeup artist and friend, Karen Faye, had made for him. "She wanted to put everything I like on it," he said, pointing at its many badges and motifs. "But she was a little cheeky. Look," and he pointed at a badge of Karen herself. We giggled at that, but what evoked the biggest response was a jacket with an image of the character Peter Pan, to whom Michael was often compared, on the back, surrounded by fairy lights. "Oh, you *have* to wear this one," we all told him, to which he responded teasingly, "Will I? Will I?" provoking a chorus of impassioned pleas.

Michael was leading us back along the corridor when we came to a short stairway and he remarked, "You've been up there, right?"

"Nooo," we all said.

"Come on up then, you can see where I sleep," he joked, "my hyperbaric chamber."

This was a reference to one of the many ridiculous rumours about Michael circulated in the 1980s that claimed he slept in a hyperbaric oxygen therapy chamber, after he was photographed lying in one while visiting a treatment centre for burn victims. We followed him up to his bedroom and he dimmed the lights, making the rhinestone-embedded cover on his bed shimmer, as we all exclaimed in awe. I sat on the edge of his bed and brushed my hand across it. To think, this was where Michael lay his head every night, where I would picture him from now on, lying on a bed fit for a king, inside a room that sparkled like a jewel.

Above the bed was a painting called *Heroes, The Last Supper* by the artist Nate Giorgio. It depicted Michael sitting on a throne at a long table, flanked by eight other historical figures: Abraham Lincoln, John F. Kennedy, Thomas Edison, Albert Einstein, Walt Disney, Charlie Chaplin, Elvis Presley, and Little Richard. On the wall facing the bed was a projector screen, playing the latest *Scooby-Doo* movie. And at the foot of the bed, Tick spotted a cage, and Michael told her that there was a mouse inside, and, yes, she could hold it if she wanted to. At that, Paris flung open the cage door, plucked out the mouse, and handed it to Tick, telling her his name was Sparkles. She and Prince then teased poor Grace, saying, "See! You're the only one who's afraid of the mouse!"

Just outside the bedroom door, Michael showed us a painting of him, as he appears on the cover of the *HIStory* album, with chains attached to him, each one leading to a metal collar around the neck of the decapitated head of an enemy. Featured on it, among others, were Tommy Mottola, Martin Bashir, and attorney Gloria Allred, who had accused him of being a bad father, much to the disgust of us all.

Michael began talking about the incident that had provoked Allred's attack, when he'd been filmed holding Blanket up to an open window at the Hotel Adlon in Berlin the previous November. "I was just showing Blanket to the fans," said Michael. "But they never showed that on the TV clips. They slowed it right down, so I just looked crazy. She said I was a bad father. I would never do that, put my child at risk." It pained us to hear Michael defending himself, something he never needed to do to us, something he never should have felt he needed to do to anyone. We cut across him, in pleading tones: "We know, Michael, we know. She's a horrible woman. You're a wonderful father. We know that with all of our hearts."

Tick had told me that she wanted to show Michael her tattoo of him, which she'd got just after the *HIStory* tour, but was too shy to ask. So, as we were leaving his private quarters, I asked him if this would be possible and he said yes. He then asked Grace to get the video camera again and led us into one of the living rooms, where he sat on a sofa, with Prince on one side and Paris on the other. When Grace returned, she told Tick and me, "I recognise you guys. I've seen you *everywhere*. You know, when the security tries to push you away, Michael is always saying, 'Leave them alone. Don't push them. Let them come to me.'" We thanked her for sharing this touching insight with us, and then returned our attention to Michael, who was addressing the other fans.

"Some people want to say things," said Michael. "Grace, will you film them? One girl wanted to say something." He turned to one of the French girls. "Wasn't it you?"

She was very timid but summoned the courage to say to the camera, "Michael is better than Elvis or The Beatles."

We all cheered and applauded. Grace said, "Who's the king?" and we all shouted, "Michael Jackson!"

Michael asked who else wanted to say something, and my friend Shay stepped forward and gave an incredible performance. By imitating the sound of a drum machine with his voice, he beatboxed Michael's songs "Billie Jean" and "Smooth Criminal," and when he finished, Michael clapped hard and told him he had a great sense of rhythm. I ushered Tick forward and adjusted her shirt to uncover the tattoo on her back. Michael asked Grace to film the tattoo and Tick telling her story, which he had her do twice. Then I asked Tick to return the favour, by revealing the tattoo on my left shoulder blade.

"I got my tattoo in 1996," I said into the camera. "Back then, only bikers and big tough guys got tattoos. A young girl getting a tattoo was something unique." Then I turned to Michael and said, "I was so very proud of you, of being a fan. I wanted to show the whole world that I thought you were the Man. I wanted to show everyone how much you'd inspired me and influenced my life. I thought, what better way to do that then get your image tattooed on my body forever? I love you, Michael Jackson. I do."

My voice wavered as I spoke and my eyes pricked with tears. I had probably told Michael a hundred times or more that I loved him, screamed it at every concert, written it in every letter, punctuated every conversation with him with the words "I love you." But never before had I been so raw and open in his presence, and I think it was more the feeling than the words that provoked his response, which was to get up from the sofa, cross the room, and enfold me in the heavenly warmth of his embrace.

*   *   *

There was a perception of elitism in the fan world, an idea that those who followed the longest or the most had a greater entitlement to Michael than others, but that wasn't really valid. The only actual elitism was that this was a world reserved for those who happened to be born at the right time into the right circumstances, who had the means and the freedom to travel, and a lifestyle that enabled them to do so. Beyond that, we all began on the same footing, as strangers loving Michael from afar, and it came down to just how privileged we were – I was young and healthy and had a well-paid job and a flexible and lenient boss who allowed me to take off frequently, often at the last minute, so was in a highly privileged position; how much time you wanted to spend engaging in this world, which in my case was as much as possible;

and how fortunate you were. The weight of this final factor cannot be overstated, because seeing and meeting Michael required, first and foremost, being in the right place at the right time, something my friends and I increased our odds of achieving by being around him as much as we could and figuring out how to navigate the many obstacles between us and him, but our efforts could only go so far.

Many followers had spent weeks in the US in the fall of 2003 in the hope of meeting Michael, and enjoyed no more than a few brief exchanges with him through the open window of his limousine, while one of us lucky thirteen inside Neverland, a girl from Israel who Michael seemed particularly taken with, was on her first and, as far as I know, only trip to see him. The point is that it didn't matter who you were or where you were from or what your fan-world experience was, if any; if you happened to be at the gates of Neverland on the afternoon of 6 September 2003, then you got to spend a day with Michael Jackson. Period. We just happened to be the lucky ones.

FIVE
On trial

he darkness provoked by Martin Bashir's distorted documentary descended on Michael's world on 18 November 2003. I had recently returned from a trip to Las Vegas, where I'd watched Michael receive a Humanitarian Award at the Radio Music Awards, and my biggest concern at the time was how I was going to get the time off I would need to go to a series of concerts that my friends and I had just heard he was going to perform in Europe that winter.

When I heard the news, that investigators from the Santa Barbara County district attorney's office and sheriff's department had conducted a search of Neverland Valley in connection with allegations of child molestation, I couldn't quite absorb it. It was an hour or two later when the reality of it, and the implications for Michael, sank in and I was overwhelmed with a sense of longing, a longing to reach out to him, to go to him, to comfort him, to stop this tide of injustice, this horrific lie against him, but I knew there was nothing I could do – just as there had been nothing I could do ten years earlier, in the summer of 1993, when the news of the first allegations against Michael had broken.

It was a year after I'd seen Michael for the first time, at his *Dangerous* concert in Dublin, I was sixteen years old, and I knew immediately that the allegations of child molestation against him were based on a lie, a conviction that was substantiated by the release of a recorded phone call in which the accuser's father, Evan Chandler, had months earlier expressed his jealousy of Michael's friendship with his teenage son and threatened to destroy his career and humiliate him "beyond belief" if he didn't get what he wanted, which turned out to be a multi-million-dollar investment in his screenwriting company.

Michael's innocence was further substantiated by a 1994 *Frontline* special called "Tabloid Truth: The Michael Jackson Story," in which the journalist that broke the news story, Don Ray, said, "It's a weird feeling to think that while I didn't cause it, I didn't make it happen, I triggered it. This is the biggest story of my career to date and I'm really ashamed of it." This wasn't a fan or a friend of Michael's, this was a hard-nosed journalist, and yet even he could see through the truth to the lie and realise that, far from exposing a criminal act, he had been instrumental in destroying the good name of an innocent man.

In the end, under the advice of his lawyers, Michael settled the case out of court for an undisclosed sum of money, and the criminal investigation was closed due to a lack of evidence. Michael, who had cancelled the remainder of his *Dangerous* tour when the allegations came to light, tried to put it all behind him, but the lie, though publicly discredited, never went away, never detached itself from his name, evoking cruel jokes and snide remarks from people who seemed to think it was clever or witty to attack him, particularly in the presence of those who held him in high esteem.

That initial lie made Michael an easy target of public mockery and of devious people like Martin Bashir, who clearly set out to make a documentary that was contentious and controversial, so instead of presenting Michael as he truly was, he manipulated the many hours of footage and added a sleazy voiceover to suggest wrongdoing where there was none. This gave the Santa Barbara District Attorney, Tom Sneddon, who had tried and failed to prosecute Michael in 1993, the ammunition he needed to go after him again, which he did with rabid enthusiasm, enlisting seventy officers, an excessive number by any standards, in his search of Neverland, and spending more than $3 million of taxpayers' money in an effort to secure a conviction in a groundless criminal case.

The accuser in this case, who Hollywood actor and comedian Chris Tucker would describe as "smart" and "cunning" at the 2005 criminal trial against Michael, was a minor, so his name wasn't publicly released, but we soon discovered it to be thirteen-year-old Gavin Arvizo, a revelation that cast a shadow over my first visit to Neverland in February 2003, during which my friends and I had watched music videos with Gavin and his siblings in the theatre, seen them playing alongside us on the grounds, and had dinner with them in the house.

One of Michael's lawyers, Brian Oxman, later interviewed us about our observations on that day and added our names to the defence witness list because Gavin's mother, Janet Arvizo, was now claiming that her children were being held at Neverland against their will during that time, one of many ludicrous claims that was disproven at the trial. We could all attest that Gavin and his siblings had clearly had the run of the place, as well as unrestricted access to outsiders who they, theoretically, could have turned to for help. None of us were called to testify at the trial but a guest list of our names was presented as evidence that Michael had continued to invite visitors to Neverland during this period of alleged imprisonment.

*   *   *

There is no comparison between my early, carefree years in Michael's world and the stretch of time between November 2003, when news of the raid on Neverland broke, and June 2005, when the trial ended, but there were two events that offered a reprieve to Michael and to my friends and me. The first was a support rally organised by Grace Rwaramba at Neverland in December 2003, named after Michael's song "You Are Not Alone." Michael's cousin Lee extended an invitation to seven of us on Michael's behalf, and we flew to California, seven girls representing five countries: one from Ireland, one from England, one from Germany, one from Sweden, and three from Spain. We stayed with Lee's family, in two charming log cabins, and on the morning of 20 December, we entered Neverland with about six hundred other invited guests.

We boarded an open-air bus that carried us through the grounds, where many of the zoo animals roamed freely with their carers. They included the eighteen-foot-long albino python Madonna, who we came across slinking along a path, and who two of us held in our arms, marvelling at the power of her body. We stopped by the house, where we saw Michael's mother, Katherine, and some of his siblings, and then we went to the movie theatre, where we did recorded interviews, talking about who we were, how we had come to know Michael, and what we wanted the world to know about him, which was of course that he was innocent, but also that he was kind and good, or as my German friend Dani so succinctly put it: "If people could see for a moment the Michael that we know, they would totally change their opinion of him."

After soaring and spinning through the air at the amusement park, we enjoyed a lunch buffet and then went to check out the production area near the main house, where a stage had been set up. Projected onto the back of the stage was an image depicted in one of the paintings in Michael's house, *Field of Dreams* by David Nordahl, in which Michael is walking across a hill leading a trail of children, who represent all of the nations of the world. It was one of the paintings Michael had shown to thirteen of us during our visit in September, a day of lightheartedness that seemed to belong to the distant past now, because as wonderful as it was that we were all gathered in love and support of Michael, it was in response to an evil force that threatened to annihilate his world.

My friends and I spotted Michael's makeup artist, Karen Faye, and costume designer, Michael Bush, by the main house, and we followed them to a nearby guesthouse, one of two at Neverland. A few minutes later, the black Bentley pulled up and Michael climbed out. We greeted him as he went inside, and when he emerged, wearing a light blue, sequinned shirt, we walked with him to the production area, taking turns holding his hand and exchanging loving words with him, while everyone else, including his family members, vied for his attention as well. It was then that I realised that Michael wasn't the focal point only among fans but among people from all areas of his life; even his relatives seemed to be in awe of him, and who could blame them for that?

When he reached the stage, Michael sat on a sofa in a cordoned-off section at the front, with his mother, Katherine, on his right, and his father, Joseph, on his left, and his other family members gathered around them. We sat just behind them, to the left, and the show soon commenced, with a choir performing Michael's song "Will You Be There." This song is from the *Dangerous* album, released in late 1991, almost two years before the first allegations came to light, and it seems strangely prophetic. In the final verses, Michael asks, in a spoken rather than a singing voice, if we'll be there, if we'll still care, during his darkest of times. As the choir performed these lines, my tears, which had been welling up all day, spilled over, and Katherine too began to cry. Michael took her hand and his expression wavered, as he visibly fought to hold back tears himself.

Alone and in groups, family members, friends, and current and former employees, including the bodyguard Mike LaPerruque, took to the stage, and many of them sang, recited poetry, and talked about how Michael had touched their lives. Some of Michael's young friends had suffered from accidents or illnesses, like the accuser Gavin Arvizo, a former cancer patient who had credited Michael with saving his life. A burn victim talked about the profound impact Michael had had on him, and how he'd given him the strength to face the world following his injuries. Another young guy said he'd had a nervous disorder but learned to walk again, thanks to Michael's help and influence.

One speaker recited the poem "Footprints in the Sand," by Margaret Fishback Powers, about a person walking with God along a beach, which serves as an analogy for life. During happier times, they see two sets of footprints in the sand, but during difficult times, they see only one, and God explains, as if in reply to Michael's plea in "Will You Be There," "During your times of trial and suffering, when you see only one set of footprints, it was then that I carried you."

Grace, who was the event's main organiser, told the audience that after the allegations were publicised, she'd been bombarded with phone calls from people pledging their love and support to Michael, and asking her to pass on their prayers and condolences to him. She said she'd decided to organise this day as a positive one for Michael, that there were a *lot* more people who'd wanted to be there but that she'd had to limit the numbers or it wouldn't have been possible. She said, "When any friend is going through a tough time, you go to their home to be with them. That's what we're all doing now. We are all here because we love Michael." We cried out in agreement, and the cry grew louder and louder, rising in pitch and fervour. Michael was characteristically embarrassed, hiding his face in his hands, until those sitting closest to him pulled him to his feet, and he finally seemed to accept the wave of love and allow it to wash over him.

*   *   *

It was just over three months later, on 1 April 2004, that I once again had the privilege of observing Michael at a celebratory occasion where he was treated with dignity, respect, and love. It was at the Ethiopian Embassy in Washington, D.C., where he was presented with the Humanitarian Award by the African Ambassadors' Spouses Association. Fans from near and afar travelled to Washington, D.C. for the event, but only four of us made it inside the embassy, as I used my media credentials to gain access for three of my friends from Spain and me.

At the embassy, my friends and I joined the other media representatives on the upper-floor balcony, which looked out over a room with a stage at one end. By this time, Michael's old security team had been replaced by members of the African American organisation the Nation of Islam (NOI), and when they arrived, they combed the place thoroughly, opening closet doors and checking behind curtains. Some of them recognised us as fans, which caused a bit of a ruckus among the journalists, and we had to fight to keep our spots at the front of the growing crowd.

Around 9 p.m., Michael arrived and took to the stage, and, as usual, the place erupted. After it had quietened down, an American woman near us shrieked in excitement. Michael glanced up and one of my friends shouted, "Up here." He saw us then and responded by pointing at us, flashing us the peace sign, blowing us kisses, and gesturing to us to come down. We had told some of the people on the balcony that we travelled the world to see Michael and that he knew us, but they were still astounded by his response. A cluster of photographers gathered behind us, because they knew they'd get good photographs of him from there, looking in their direction, and *The Washington Post* even mentioned in an article the next day four female fans on the balcony to whom Michael had been blowing kisses.

Michael kept gesturing to us to come down, and we tried to gesture that we couldn't, that we weren't allowed. Then we gestured to him to come up, making him laugh. Throughout the ceremony, as he sat on the stage while people gave speeches and sang and danced in his honour, he intermittently engaged with us, sometimes just staring lovingly at each of us in turn.

Towards the end of the ceremony, a choir of children sang Michael's song "Heal the World," after which they crowded around him, drawn to him as all children were, as my friends and I had been since childhood. He was presented with the award, which was in the form of a golden elephant, just as sweet and surely as treasured as his Bambi Award, which was in the form of a golden fawn. Michael took to the podium to say a few words, as did Grace, who was originally from Africa and, as was evident during my September visit to Neverland, took great pride in her native land.

As soon as the ceremony ended and Michael left the stage, my friends and I ran to the stairway, but the NOI guards there wouldn't allow us past. We returned to the balcony, leaned over, and called to Michael, who gestured to us once again to come down. We explained to the NOI guards that he was calling us to him, but it did no good, and we were certain that they would hold us there until Michael had departed the building, but suddenly, they left and we ran down the stairs, followed by everyone around us.

We discovered that Michael was in a small room, taking photographs with ambassadors and other dignitaries, and we waited outside it, in the hope that we would get a chance to say hi to him as he left. Grace came out of the room and I asked her if she remembered me, and she said that she did. She then asked me how I'd got there, probably, I realised in retrospect, meaning how I'd got inside the embassy, but I misunderstood and said I'd flown in from Germany that day.

My friends and I explained that Michael had seen us on the balcony and that he'd been calling us to him but that the security guards hadn't allowed us to go down the stairs. She said, "I'll make sure you get to say hello to him." She then turned to a member of the Secret Service, which was also present, and said we were to go inside the room but he shook his head, no. So, instead she approached a member of the NOI and said, "These four girls are Michael's very special fans. He wants to talk to them. They are to go inside the room," and to our enormous relief, he said, "Sure, no problem. Come through here, girls."

With our hearts hammering, we waited alone at the door to the room, as other people tried and failed to talk their way past the guards. The door opened and we saw Michael inside, posing for a photograph with a man in a suit. He turned to us and his face lit up, and as the other people in the room left, we filed in and he opened his arms to us and hugged us each in turn.

"How's Germany?" he asked, no doubt having heard from Grace that this is where we'd travelled from, and one of the girls, Sara, who sadly passed away at a tragically young age, answered with characteristic wit, "Germany's fine but we're from Spain," making us all laugh. I then explained the confusion, and we congratulated him on his award and told him how much we loved him, a sentiment that he returned with sweetness and affection, before posing with us for a photograph. Later, as he left the room, he again took our hands and pulled us to him, telling us over and over again how much he loved us, as we responded in kind.

Nothing in the universe compared to the joy of being in Michael's presence, of being held by him, of being loved by him, but throughout this darker phase, the need to convey my love to him, to hold him rather than be held by him, to give rather than receive, was greater than it had ever been, and I am beyond grateful to Grace for the opportunity to deliver all that my heart held to him directly in person that night, hopeful that, if only for a moment, the love of my friends and I alleviated the turmoil and anguish that he was going through, in some small way.

*　　*　　*

Some of my friends had been to the first trial-related hearing that Michael had attended, which was an arraignment in January 2004 at the Santa Barbara County Courthouse in Santa Maria, about thirty miles northwest of Neverland Valley. After leaving the courthouse, Michael had got on top of his SUV to thank his fans for their support and to show them that he was holding strong, that we were all going to overcome this injustice together, and then he had opened the gates to Neverland to everyone, as he'd done on his birthday the previous year and would do again after a hearing the following September. The first hearing I attended, however, was the second that he attended, on 30 April 2004, a few weeks after I'd seen him in happier circumstances in Washington, D.C., and it made the nightmare that he was enduring real to me in a new and undeniable way.

Instead of gathering at a concert venue or Michael's hotel or the gates of Neverland, as we normally did, my friends and I, along with hundreds of other fans, gathered in the early hours of the morning at the courthouse in Santa Maria, a concrete building secured by armed police officers and chain-link fencing that had been erected specifically to control the crowds that the trial would inevitably attract. I had acquired a media pass to the courthouse, something I would continue to do throughout the trial, while the other fans had to enter a daily lottery to compete for one of the sixty seats inside the courtroom that were reserved for members of the public. I filed into the courtroom with the other journalists and sat in the media seating, from where I exchanged glances of solidarity with my friends across the aisle.

Members of Michael's family, including his parents, Katherine and Joseph, arrived and took their seats in the front rows, and they were soon followed by Michael, wearing a black suit with a red tie and a red armband. Looking sombre but strong, he walked down the aisle, past the rows of family members, fans, journalists, and members of the public, and sat beside his new lawyer, Thomas Mesereau, a man who would become a hero to many for his steadfast loyalty to Michael, his gentle but firm demeanour, and his ability to cut through the lies and contradictions presented by the prosecution team to uncover the truth. Michael sat on Mesereau's left, and his antithesis, District Attorney Tom Sneddon, sat on the right, and after the judge entered the room and took a seat behind a raised bench, the court session, during which Mesereau pleaded not guilty to all charges against Michael, got underway.

As I sat observing the proceedings, it occurred to me that this was much more than a battle between Michael Jackson and Tom Sneddon; it was a battle between good and evil, one that was playing out inside this courthouse, through a justice system that often fell short of what it aspired to embody and achieve, by prosecuting, and in doing so persecuting, the innocent, while the guilty faced no consequences for the crime they'd committed, in this case the public damnation and humiliation of an innocent man. I also came to understand, through the events leading up to the trial, that Michael was such a powerful force of goodness in the world that he had become a focus of light and darkness in equal measure, that just as millions connected to him through love, others preyed on him, feeding their desire to possess him and, failing that, to destroy him. This was the basis of a very lengthy letter that I gave to Michael during the trial in 2005, and he told me a few days later that he was keeping it by his bedside and reading a few pages of it every night.

The next hearing that I attended was almost five months later, on 17 September 2004, and this time Michael arrived dressed all in white, a colour that many of his fans would wear at the trial as a symbol of his innocence. At the hearing, Gavin's mother, Janet Arvizo, took to the stand to give a testimony that was often incoherent and nonsensical, evoking sniggers in the courtroom. This was Sneddon's star witness, someone he'd built his whole case around, and she came across as evasive, hostile, and unhinged, remarking several times, "I'm looking in my mind."

It would emerge during the 2005 trial that Janet Arvizo had committed perjury in an earlier case, a crime she admitted to under oath, and defrauded the welfare system of about $18,000, a crime she would be convicted of the following year. Equally revealing was Gavin's testimony at the trial, during which he admitted that he had felt angry at Michael for distancing himself from him and his family following the release of Martin Bashir's documentary, at which point they had begun working with the District Attorney Tom Sneddon – who, by the way, had approached them, and not the other way around – to build his case, which was based on the absurd premise that Michael had begun abusing Gavin *after* the release of the documentary, while he was under increased scrutiny.

*　　*　　*

This was not only a dark time in Michael's world, it was also a challenging time in my own life in relation to the fan world, in large part because after our visit to Neverland in September 2003, Tick had made the difficult decision to stop following Michael. Her reason was twofold: she wanted to return to England to complete the diploma that she had abandoned after the tour, thereby giving up on her dream career, but also, she felt that our visit to Neverland was the ultimate fan experience, never to be surpassed. I understood and accepted her decision but I missed her terribly, primarily because of our friendship but also because she could drive and I could not, and so now I had to rely on other people when a car was a necessary component of a trip, as it always was in California and would be throughout the trial.

The loss of Tick had exposed me to fan politics, which I'd always been aware of but never really engaged in or been affected by, and, perhaps owing to the wave of good fortune that had granted me several rare encounters in recent months (at Neverland in September and December, and in Washington, D.C. in April) as well as my guaranteed access to the courthouse, I had found myself becoming a target of jealousy and hostility. I thought about withdrawing somewhat from the fan world, as many others had done due to fan politics, but decided instead that it was time for me to become fully independent, so that I could navigate my own way forward. I began taking driving lessons and, a few months later, I made the biggest decision of my life, one that would shape, for better or worse, all that was to come.

The trial, which I wanted to attend for weeks at a time, and not the few days here and there that my job would allow, was the catalyst for my decision, but it wasn't the reason for it. By early 2005, I had been living in Munich for three years, had a job I loved, writing for a teen magazine, copies of which I would often give to Michael and that he'd told me he loved, and had a wide circle of friends. But ever since I'd visited Los Angeles for the first time, in February 2002, I'd dreamt of living there, and I knew that if I didn't make the decision to move there now, I never would.

For weeks, I stood at a crossroads, looking out at two paths, agonising over which one to take. Would I stay in Munich, where I had a secure job, a stable income, and a solid circle of friends, or would I move to LA, a city where I knew not a single soul and would have to work as a freelance writer, a position that offered little to no financial security? It was a choice between my head and my heart, between logic and emotion, between what was known and what was unknown, between the reality I was living and the dream I longed to fulfil. In the end, I decided to throw caution to the wind and move to LA, and I embarked on a path that would eventually lead me deeper into Michael's world, into Michael's heart, than I had ever thought possible, except, perhaps, in my most fanciful of dreams.

*   *   *

By the time I had packed up my life, secured the paperwork I needed, and arrived at Los Angeles International Airport, it was the end of April and the trial, which had begun two months earlier, was well underway. All throughout May and into June, every day that the court was in session, I woke up before dawn and drove from the family home where I was renting a room in Santa Ynez, near Neverland Valley, to the courthouse in Santa Maria to secure one of the daily media passes that were handed out on a first come, first serve basis.

The courtroom had about one hundred seats for onlookers that were divided into three sections, and I always sat on the end of a row reserved for media, on the edge of the aisle that Michael walked along while entering and leaving the courtroom. At the end of each session, all of the other journalists would leave, presumably in many cases to file reports, and I would remain seated there alone until Michael left, while the rest of the fans sat in the public seating across the way. None of us were allowed to speak to Michael in the courtroom but he would often give me a loving stare and squeeze my shoulder on his way out.

I'd always known that Michael was strong but it was during the trial, when he was at his most vulnerable, that his strength and generosity of spirit shone brighter than ever. Every morning that the court was in session, he had to say goodbye to his three children, from whom he was trying to keep hidden the ordeal that he was going through, climb into the back of a black SUV, and make the thirty-minute journey from Neverland to the courthouse in Santa Maria. There, he had to subject himself to the gaze of the media as he made his way into the courtroom and through a set of metal detectors, while armed police officers stood by, looking on.

Inside the courtroom, Michael had to sit for hours beside Tom Sneddon, the monster responsible for this mindless fiasco, and listen in silence as he and his co-counsel, Ron Zonen, tried to twist the minds of the twelve jury members against him, prohibited from uttering a word in his defence. Both inside the courtroom and in the court of public opinion, he had to endure the humiliation of hearing his name associated with a crime that many consider to be worse than murder, that was as appalling and repulsive to him as it is to any sane and normal human being. And all the while, he faced the terrifying possibility, however unlikely, that at the end of all of this, he would be convicted, led away from the courthouse in handcuffs, and confined for over a decade to a prison cell, perhaps never to see his children again.

This synopsis offers only a glimpse into the horror that Michael was enduring, and yet, throughout this terrible ordeal, he went out of his way to acknowledge and thank the fans who were there for him through it all. Every time he arrived at or left the courthouse, he would stop to wave to those pressed up against the chain-link fencing outside, many of them holding banners declaring his innocence and castigating Sneddon, who was commonly depicted wearing devil horns, and his cohorts TV journalists Diane Diamond and Nancy Grace, aka Nancy Disgrace, who seemed to have some kind of sick obsession with Michael and take immense pleasure in spewing hatred against him.

Whenever Michael returned to Neverland, he would stop outside the gates and roll down the window of his SUV to talk to the fans, and one day in April, he invited all sixty or so inside and greeted them there. At a time when he had everything to lose, he continued to give, and he would have continued to give until there was nothing left; this was simply his nature.

*   *   *

As a member of the media, I got to observe the attitude of journalists towards the case from ground zero, so to speak. During breaks between court sessions, I would often hang out in the media area by the courthouse. One day, I had a conversation with a young journalist from a British tabloid who told me that she had been very busy during the first half of the trial, while the prosecution team had presented their case, as this had resulted in many sensational headlines, but that her editor was far less interested in the case now being presented by the defence team. When I asked her if she didn't think that this was very unbalanced, she said that yes, it probably was. On another occasion, I overheard a reporter remarking that the prosecution had failed to present a compelling case and that an acquittal seemed inevitable, and yet I saw him on television that night promoting the opposite viewpoint.

Throughout the trial, reporters skewed their coverage to sway public opinion against Michael. They emphasised any statements made against him in the courtroom, while ignoring evidence to the contrary, including the cross-examination from his lawyer that exposed the lies for what they were. This resulted in damning statements about Michael being presented as bold headlines, which then seeped into the public consciousness as truth, without context or contradiction.

Regardless of their personal opinion, as substantiated by my observation, journalists promoted the idea that a conviction was inevitable, devoting hours of airtime and reams of newspaper in the final days of the trial to detailing the process Michael would be subjected to as a newly condemned convict, the cell where he would be contained, and the treatment that he would receive. This fantasy-fuelled reporting fed the public appetite for sensationalism, and solidified the perception of Michael's guilt that the media had promoted, while further degrading and defaming an innocent man.

A Santa Maria local I befriended during the trial told me that when he'd first heard of the allegations, he'd been ninety per cent sure that Michael was guilty, because no smoke without fire, right? However, after attending several court sessions, his opinion had begun to sway, and by the time I met him, he was close to one hundred per cent sure that Michael was innocent and that Tom Sneddon had a personal vendetta against him – something he'd concluded without knowing very much about either party to begin with but by simply attending a few court sessions here and there, whenever he'd won entry through the public lottery.

*   *   *

Some of the court sessions I attended, particularly those involving pages and pages of documents that were discussed in minute detail, were mind-numbingly boring. Others, however, played out like scenes from a crime drama, with witnesses giving powerful testimony in favour of Michael, after which Sneddon or his co-counsel would try to undermine them, after which Michael's lawyer, Mesereau, would deliver a blow to their counterargument and invariably win the day. The most memorable episode from the over one hundred hours of procedure and testimony that I sat through, from the first hearing I went to in April 2004 to the end of the closing arguments on 3 June 2005, involved an exchange between Sneddon and the final witness to take the stand, actor and comedian Chris Tucker.

Chris gave a damning testimony against the Arvizo family, telling the court that he had distanced himself from them after they'd asked him for money and behaved in a disrespectful manner on a film set, and that he'd warned Michael to stay away from the accuser's mother, Janet. "I told him to watch out for [the mother] because I felt suspicious," he said. "You need to watch out. Be careful." During cross-examination, Sneddon showed Chris a photograph of him with the Arvizo family. Chris said, "That's a nice photograph. Can I get it after the trial?" to which Sneddon responded, "That depends on whether you're a good boy or not."

There was an audible gasp in the courtroom, followed by an uncomfortable silence as Chris glared at Sneddon, whose reference to him as a "boy" had not only been highly inappropriate but also come across as overtly racist. Considering Chris's celebrity status, I expected this interaction to be the lead story that evening, but it barely got a mention on some networks and nowhere near the level of coverage I'd thought it would receive. News editors were interested in scandals about Michael, however fabricated, not the man who had brought him to trial.

The most memorable court session of all, however, occurred almost three weeks later, on 13 June. I was sitting at a coffee shop behind the courthouse around noon, waiting, as I had been for days, with the other fans and journalists, when the news broke that the jury had reached a verdict. My throat dried up and my heartbeat quickened. The verdict was not only the central point of the biggest media story of the decade, it was also the defining moment of Michael's life. The wait for it had been almost unbearable, and now that it was here, I felt terrified. I knew that innocence was no guarantee of justice; the fact that the case had gone all the way to trial, all the way to verdict day, was testament to that.

I lined up with the other journalists and we filed inside the courtroom, where I sat in my usual spot, at the end of a row. As the public seating filled, I spotted some of my friends. They were crying silently but I wasn't able to shed a tear; I was frozen in terror. I'd had a vivid nightmare a few nights earlier in which the jury had returned a guilty verdict. They'd entered the room with their eyes averted and some of them had started crying. When we'd asked them what was wrong, they'd told us, "We're sorry. We know he's a good man, but we had to find him guilty." We'd all erupted and I'd woken up sobbing, chilled to the bone.

What would I do if such a scenario played out in real life? What would I do if they took Michael away? What would any of us do? How could we go on with our lives, knowing that this gentle soul was locked away in a prison cell, accused of the most deplorable crime? I hadn't asked to love Michael. I hadn't asked to care this much. I hadn't asked to be caught up in this drama, to put my happiness in the hands of twelve strangers, any more than he had. My only choice had been whether to try to ignore my love for him or to embrace it. I had chosen the latter and there was no turning back now. If they found Michael guilty and took him away, I would never know peace again.

With the tension at breaking point, Michael arrived. He had been losing weight throughout the trial and on this, the final day, he appeared frail and fragile. His expression, as he entered the courtroom, wearing a black suit that hung loosely on his slight frame, was harrowing and haunted, that of a man who finds himself alone in the face of judgment. Nothing in the world, not his fame, not his wealth, not his loved ones, not the devotion of his fans, not even his innocence, could spare him from the verdict that was about to be delivered, one that would either strip him of all that he was, effectively ending his life, or finally set him free from this senseless ordeal, though wronged and wounded, free at last.

Courthouse police lined the back of the courtroom, and riot police were gathered outside, batons in hand. If Michael was found guilty, nobody expected him to be taken away without a fight. The judge entered the courtroom and delivered a short speech, warning against any emotional outbursts. When the jury filed inside, they didn't make eye contact with Michael. People always said that this was a bad sign, that it meant that they couldn't look the defendant in the eye because they were about to send him to prison. My sense of panic rose. I didn't want to be here. I was too afraid of what was to come. And then it came, and it was such an enormous relief.

The judge read out each charge and then asked the jury foreman for the verdict. Every time, the foreman responded, "Not guilty," and every time, a cheer went up from the fans outside and the tension inside the courtroom eased a little bit more. The jury might have had their own prejudices against Michael, as so many Americans did, but they had sat in that courtroom every day listening to the actual testimony, the arguments of the prosecution and the powerful rebuttals, not the distorted version presented by the media. Of course, they had found him not guilty, not guilty of all fourteen of the trumped up charges that Sneddon, in his desperation to convict, had brought against him. It would have been impossible for any twelve right-minded human beings to do otherwise.

Most of my friends celebrated the acquittal that evening, but I didn't join them. I didn't feel like celebrating. While I was enormously relieved, I was also angry, angry that Michael had had to endure more than a year and a half of humiliation, just to have twelve strangers publicly acknowledge what we'd known all along, that he was an innocent man. As soon as I left the courtroom, I called my mother in Ireland, who'd been following the events on the news, and told her how I felt.

Although I'd just moved to America, I wanted Michael to leave, to take his children and go far away, to try to heal and find peace again. Going through the trial and facing the prospect of losing him had made me more selfless. I'd have given him up right then, given up ever seeing him again, in exchange for the knowledge that he was free and happy and safe with his children, who were his world as he was mine. "I'm so glad it's over," I told my mum towards the end of our conversation, "but it should never have happened. I think I like the world a little less now."

In later years, I never asked Michael about the trial because I never wanted to turn his attention to such darkness, but he brought it up a few times. During a late-night conversation in September 2008, he told me, "What I went through, it just showed me that there's so much evil in the world, but there's also so much beauty. You were there for me. I wrote a song about you, the fans, how you were there for me in my darkest hour, in my deepest despair…I have written a song about all of you, how much you helped me, what you do for me."

He also said, "My mother always told me, Katherine always told me that. She used to look at me across the room and say, 'You're just like me. You're going to get hurt. You're going to get used. There are people who are going to use you.' I didn't know there were people in the world like that, so evil. I thought that was just in the movies. I didn't know they existed in real life. I trust people. I always see the best in people. I can be so naïve. So during the trial, there were evil people, but there were also so many beautiful people that came out, beautiful people like you."

Of course, it was Michael's beauty, his heart, his soul, his spirit, that drew us all to him, and, though he could never accept it, I always told him as such.

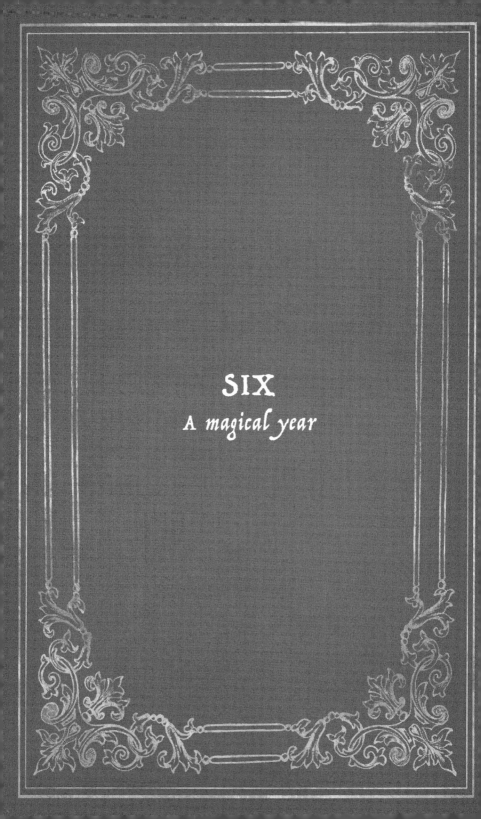

SIX

A magical year

very step I took towards Michael was infused with magic, and that magic intensified in 2007, a year when, more than ever before, I felt the universe was delivering me to him on a wave of pink, fluffy clouds. By the start of that year, I had been living in Los Angeles for almost a year and a half, having relocated there from Santa Ynez shortly after the trial. During that time, I had seen Michael only once, in London in November 2006, when he went there to receive the Diamond Award at the World Music Awards.

After the trial ended, in June 2005, Michael left Neverland Valley almost immediately and stayed with his friend and spiritual guru Deepak Chopra for a week in San Diego, before relocating to Bahrain. During my absence from his world, he made short, unannounced visits to London, Berlin, and Paris, and although many of my friends saw him on these occasions, I did not, both because last-minute flights from the US to Europe were far more expensive than they were the other way around, and because I knew that by the time I arrived, he would most likely have departed, as he only ever stayed for a short while. Michael also made an appearance in Tokyo, Japan, in May 2006, to receive the Legend Award at the MTV Video Music Awards, and I was about to book a flight there when I realised, to my dismay, that my passport was about to expire.

Then, a month later, in June 2006, Michael flew into Cork Airport on a flight from Paris, amid reports that he would remain in

Ireland for an undetermined period of time. I couldn't believe it; here I was, more than five thousand miles away in LA, and there he was, in my native county, where I'd grown up in the countryside, imagining the scenarios that had become my most precious memories. Now, here was my opportunity to see him in the land where my journey towards him, through dreams and imaginings, had begun.

I booked the next flight to Ireland, and I spent the next two weeks driving around the country, alone or with my dear friend Pedro from Spain, hoping to cross paths with him, but to no avail. It seemed that the wave of good fortune that had carried me to him so many times in the past had finally run dry, and when I re-entered his world, later that year in London, where I met him several times in the lobby of his hotel, my friends told me that the same was true for everyone.

They said that Michael had changed, become more like the Michael of past eras, when his shyness had kept him out of reach, but for very different reasons. He had become more withdrawn, and therefore difficult to meet, almost certainly because of the trauma of the trial and the betrayal that it had revealed, not only by the Arvizo family, but also by other friends and associates. He had become more wary, they told me, less open and trusting, and the glory days of the early 2000s, when he'd been at his most accessible, were no more. While I felt deeply saddened by the impact of the trial on Michael, I also felt immense gratitude for the memories he'd gifted to me, which seemed all the more precious now.

From London, I travelled to my home in County Cork for Christmas, hoping that Michael would also return to Ireland so that we could at least be in the same country over the holidays, but alas, that wasn't to be. The next report that I heard about him was that he'd flown into Las Vegas a couple of days before Christmas, accompanied by his three children.

It was one thing to think that my wave of good fortune had run dry, but now I couldn't help wondering if it had been replaced by a wave of misfortune. After the trial, I had gone almost a year and a half, the longest since after the *HIStory* tour, without seeing Michael, and now, once again, I was at my home on one side of the world, in Ireland, while he was in proximity of my home on the other side of the world, in LA, which is only a few hours' drive from Las Vegas. I was certain that by the time I returned to LA, he would have moved on, but this is where my misfortune ended and my wave of fortune returned, bigger and brighter than ever before.

*   *   *

In the weeks following Michael's arrival in Las Vegas, there were reports of him at various restaurants, shows, and other places on the Strip, a four-mile stretch of resort hotels and casinos at the heart of the city. So, after returning to LA, I decided to drive to Vegas on the first Friday in February, in the hope of running into him there. I knew that my chances of seeing him were one in a million; I didn't even know for sure that he was in Vegas that weekend, let alone if he had any intention of going out, and if so, where to, but I had to try. Although I had failed to see him in Ireland, I'd at least opened myself to the possibility by going there, knowing that I would regret it otherwise and always wonder what might have been. Besides, some part of me believed that in order to see Michael, I needed to prove to the universe how much I wanted it, a belief in keeping with my perception that his world, or at least my experience of it, was governed by such forces in a particularly powerful and apparent way.

On the previous weekend, Michael had been spotted at the

Wing Lei, a Chinese restaurant at the Wynn, so I decided to start there. The Wynn was a relatively new resort at that time, and I had been there only once before. I dropped my car off with the valet at the front entrance and then wandered through the casino and along a maze of corridors, getting utterly lost and doubling back on myself several times, before finally finding the restaurant, an upscale venue at the end of a plush corridor. I walked inside and looked around, but saw no sign of Michael or his entourage. I returned to the corridor and was leaving through a glass exit door (a door that was removed a few years later, during a revamp), trying to decide which location to check out next, when I had what I can say, without reservation, was the most surreal experience of my life.

There, walking towards me, all alone, looking like he'd just stepped out of a music video, or one of the posters still lining my bedroom walls in Ireland, was Michael Jackson. For a moment, my mind could not process the reality of the situation, and I fully believed that I was fast asleep, dreaming, not standing in the real world, being approached by a man I'd been told throughout my teenage years I would never meet. A wave of disappointment washed over me, accompanied by the thought, "Oh no, this is a dream. I thought it was really happening but it's just a dream." Then, my mind shifted, I absorbed the reality of the wonder that was unfolding, and the feeling of disappointment was replaced by profound awe.

A few people were standing outside smoking and, as Michael walked up the path to the door, they said, as casually as can be, "Hi, Michael," and he glanced up and said, "Hi," to each of them in return. Then, as he opened the door to step through, I said, in a breathless voice, "Hi, Michael." He glanced at me and then did a double take, and his face lit up in a smile as he drew me to him in an embrace. Later, when reliving our encounter, I delighted in this detail in particular, in his instant recognition of and response to me, as ever since the disappointment in Monte Carlo, when he'd failed to recognise me alone, without Tick, I had doubted that he would know me outside of the context of the fan world, this despite the many encounters I'd had with him since then.

We chatted for a few minutes and I gave him a letter I'd written to him, and when he left the restaurant later, with a group of young Asian people, he pulled me to him again and we walked outside holding hands. We talked about his upcoming trip to Tokyo, and he said he was really happy that I was going to be there. Before climbing into the back of a black SUV, he stroked my cheek affectionately and then he waved to me through the open window, telling me, "I love you. I love you so much. God bless you," as I responded in kind.

This encounter represented another first for me, because it was my first time seeing Michael alone, in both senses of that phrase; he was all alone and I was all alone, a combination of circumstances that only one other fan I knew had ever experienced. It was also my most unlikely encounter, because had I arrived even a minute earlier or later, I would have left without knowing he was there. Once inside the restaurant, he and his bodyguard, Basheer Muhammad – who had turned up a few minutes later, presumably having been delayed outside – disappeared behind a red curtain, into a VIP section, out of view from the other guests. So, seeing him that evening necessitated not only deciding, of all the locations where he'd been seen in recent weeks, to head first to the Wing Lei, but also wandering through the resort for the precise amount of time that I had, only to reach the restaurant moments before his arrival.

*   *   *

When I wasn't engaging in Michael's world, I was perfectly content, particularly since moving to LA, which I had longed to call home from my first visit. But whenever an opportunity to see Michael presented itself, I seized it, as I knew there was no guarantee of another, certainly not any time soon. As fans, we never knew if or when he would make another public appearance or we might hear where he was, be that Neverland, Bahrain, (where no fan I knew ever got to see him, though at least a couple tried!), or Las Vegas, or when he might decide to retreat from the world altogether and live out his life alone with his children, as he had every right to do and which part of me wished he would do, to protect himself from future harm. So, whenever I heard where he was and had the means to go to him, I dropped everything and I went.

The next time I saw Michael was a month later in Tokyo, where he went to attend a VIP party at which guests who paid $3,500 were guaranteed a meet and greet with him, with all of his proceeds going to charity. He also went to a fan party, tickets to which were far more affordable, at around $30 I think. I stayed with four other girls from Europe (the UK, Spain, and Holland) at the same hotel as Michael, the Four Seasons, and we met him there several times. On the evening before the VIP party, we heard from his entourage that he was going to Disneyland, so we took the train there and, after failing to find any trace of him, slipped through a door into the backstage area.

There we were, a gaggle of giggling girls, sneaking through the shadows, searching for Michael's convoy of cars, and then we saw them and we took off after them. The second one, a minivan with a sliding door, stopped and waited for us, and the entourage members inside invited us on board. One of them was a make-up artist called Lynda Parrish, who had relayed to one of my friends remarks Michael had made about us a day or two earlier, in which he'd referred to us as "my girls," making us all squeal. Lynda seemed fascinated by our stories and told us that we were not what people expected his fans to be, least of all those who travelled everywhere to see him, so smart and pretty and accomplished.

Michael's car pulled up at the backstage entrance to a couple of rides, and we filed out to greet him. At one point, the park's manager told his security team that we had to leave, as of course we weren't supposed to be there, but we begged him to allow us to stay, promising him we would approach Michael only if he called us to him, and, perhaps moved by our expressions of intense pleading, he relented. Michael emerged and we gathered around to greet him, before accompanying him on to the Peter Pan ride.

This was another fantasy made reality, because if there was any place apart from Neverland Valley that a fan would want to be with Michael, it was Disneyland, a theme park in keeping with his spirit, and if there was any ride they'd want to join him on, it was Peter Pan's Flight, named after a character to which Michael was often compared because of his childlike nature – not to be confused with childish, because there was nothing childish about Michael, but childlike in the sense that he possessed a purity and innocence that most people lose as they leave childhood behind. It was truly magical to sit in a carriage behind him and soar through a galaxy of stars and storybook depictions that reflected his soul's content.

*　　*　　*

There was no way any of us could afford the $3,500 tickets to the VIP party the following evening, but there was also no way we could miss seeing Michael there, so we employed our usual trick of using duplicate passes to gain entry to the venue. We couldn't participate in the actual meet and greet, because we lacked the necessary ticket, so we settled for watching it unfold through a large window, from an upstairs area. We watched one person after another enter the room and light up at the sight of Michael, and then tentatively approach him to exchange a few words and pose for a photograph, some shedding tears of joy as he held them in his arms.

After the meet and greet ended, Michael emerged onto the floor of the venue. My friends went one way and I went another, because, at the last moment, I noticed that the stairway nearest to us was no longer guarded by the security man who had been stationed there all evening. I hurried down this stairway and across the floor of the venue to where Michael was now sitting, at a round table with other dignitaries. I stood opposite him, waiting for him to see and acknowledge me, as he always did. His eyes landed on me, but instead of just waving and pointing at me, he got up from his seat, came around the table, and enfolded me in his arms, and, as I only realised later, when I watched a video clip of our embrace, the entire venue erupted in a chorus of "aww."

Michael held me then for the longest time, longer than ever before, longer than ever since; as one of my friends put it later, the hug "just went on and on and on." From the moment he enfolded me, everything and everyone fell away, and it was just him and me, floating through a heavenly cloud, spinning through a higher dimension, one that he was connected to in a way that nobody else was, that he connected us to through the love and light that radiated from his soul.

He held me tight, stroking my hair, whispering sweet words in my ear as I implored him to accept all of the love that my heart contained. "Do you know how much I love you, Michael, how much we all love you?" "Nooo," he said in a pained voice that made my heart ache, for he really didn't; he was too humble to know, to accept, to absorb that which he inspired. Through that hug, I experienced the deepest connection to Michael that I had ever known, and it set the tone for all that was to come, which was the most magical year of my life, up to that point at least.

*　　*　　*

From Tokyo, Michael flew to London and I flew home to Los Angeles, and about a week later, he departed London on a flight to Los Angeles International Airport. I didn't know if he would exit at the airport or take a connecting flight to Las Vegas or another destination, but I went there anyway, in the hope that he would emerge. Between my encounters with Michael, be they months, weeks, days, or even just hours apart, I loved nothing more than to daydream, to re-enter and re-experience the moments I'd shared with him, and to imagine what might yet be to come. While counting down the hours to his arrival at the airport, I channelled all of my energy into an imaginary scenario in which he emerged and enfolded me in his arms, before inviting me into his car, and lo and behold, as impossible as it sounds, reality mirrored almost exactly what my imagination had conceived.

On arrival at the airport, I met up with my friend Edina, who lived in Central California and who I'd told about Michael's possible emergence at the airport. We waited outside the arrivals area of the international terminal, where we saw Michael's black SUV and a few of his security guards. One of the guards told us that they were there just to collect Michael's luggage and that he would exit upstairs, on the departures level.

We weren't sure whether or not to believe him and were agonising over what to do when, all of a sudden, Michael emerged, with his three children, his bodyguard, Basheer, and a few members of airport security. We approached but he had his back to us, so I gently called his name: "Michael." He turned around and, just as I'd imagined, as captured by a series of paparazzi photographs, his face lit up as he drew me to him and wrapped his arms around me. "How did you know I'd be here?" he asked in amazement. "How did you *know*?" I explained that my friends had told me that he'd left London on a flight to LA, and he told me how happy he was to see me and how much he loved me. He then hugged Edina and, when he turned back around, I handed him letters from my friends and me, along with a single red rose.

Edina and I walked with Michael to the SUV, as paparazzi snapped photos of him, and an autograph collector I later came to know as Bryan from Canada handed him albums to sign. He and his children sat into the SUV, and Edina and I went to the back window to try to talk to him through it. I chattered a little, not sure if he could hear me or not, while he continued to sign albums for Bryan. Paris kept waving at me and pointing, and I waved back. Then Michael started laughing and saying something to me, but I couldn't hear him. He gestured to me to go to the front window on the driver's side, which was cracked open a little, so I did, and I could see him more clearly from there.

He kept saying something to me but all I could hear now was "...autograph."

I said, "Oh, you don't need to give me an autograph," in a baffled tone.

He leaned forward and said something again, but this time, all I heard was, "Paris...autograph," and I wondered, in a state of ever greater confusion, if Paris wanted to give me an autograph. Then he said to me, "Open the door."

I said, "What? Open the door?"

He said, "Yes, come in!"

I put my hand on the door handle but then I hesitated. I was too scared to open it because of Basheer, who was by far the most intimidating bodyguard I'd ever encountered. I said, "Oh Michael, I can't. I'm going to get in so much trouble."

"No, you won't get in trouble," he said. "Come on, open it, come in."

Then, to my relief, Basheer appeared and I told him, "He wants me to open the door."

He said, "I'll ask him." Basheer leaned in to the car to talk to Michael, then came out and said, "Okay, go on in."

He opened the door for me, I sat into the front seat, and he closed the door behind me, cocooning me alone with Michael and his three children.

"Paris thought you wanted an autograph," said Michael, as if that was the craziest idea in the world.

"Oh no," I said, beaming. "I don't want an autograph from your daddy. I don't want anything from him. I just want to give him lots of love and cuddles and make him feel really happy."

"You see," said Michael to Paris. Then he said to me, "I want to hold you again, come here."

He got up and leaned over the front seat and I leaned into him in another embrace. We exchanged more loving words, and when I sat back down, he stroked my arm with the back of his hand. Then he asked me, "Where are you from again?" because as he later told me, he was great at remembering faces but not so much names and other details. What followed was the first of several conversations we had that year about Ireland and the time that he and his children had spent there.

"I *love* Ireland," he said. "It has such a special place in my heart and it always will. There's a magic to it that I adore."

Paris said, "Tell her about the castle, Daddy," and Michael said, sharing her enthusiasm, "Oh yes, we had this great castle up in the hills, and we went horseback riding all the time out in the countryside and for long walks."

Left to right: Paris, Michael, and me at Los Angeles International Airport, March 2007. Michael is holding a red rose that I gave him, and is signing autographs for the autograph collector Bryan. (Photo: Bauer-Griffin)

We talked about the country's mythology and folklore, with the two older children chiming in, and then Michael said, with obvious disappointment, "We couldn't live there though. We couldn't find a house. We looked for such a long time."

I said, "Well, you could have stayed at my house. I would have taken good care of you all."

"Oh, I know you would have," he said, stroking my arm again, and Prince chuckled and said, "Next time!"

Michael told me that Las Vegas was home "for now" and that I should come by and see him there, because it always made him very happy to see me, and, with flutters of joy, I promised him that I would.

After some more sweet exchanges and another embrace, I bade Michael and his three children goodnight, and a short time later, a limousine with Nevada licence plates that I had spotted earlier, parked outside the departures area on the upper level, arrived, and they got into it. The security guard had been telling the truth! Michael wasn't supposed to come out here but on the upper level, and had he done so, Edina and I would likely have missed seeing him altogether, making my encounter with him all the more magical in my mind. I felt like I had been sprinkled with fairy dust, because in the space of just over a month, I had had the three most intimate and amazing encounters with him of my life.

The next day, I awoke to emails from friends in Europe, telling me they'd seen the most beautiful photographs of Michael and me online, hugging and beaming with delight. Up until then, I was the only follower I knew who didn't have a single photograph alone with Michael, mainly because, as much as I'd always longed for such a treasure, I'd never felt comfortable asking him for one. So, all of my photos with Michael were with other fans as well: Tick in London, four girls in the limousine at Neverland, three Spanish girls in Washington, D.C.… But now, I had the most stunning series of photographs of us together and I gazed at them spellbound, overwhelmed by the expression of joy on Michael's face as he held me in his arms.

Michael and me hugging at Los Angeles International Airport, March 2007.
(Photos: Bauer-Griffin)

*   *   *

By now, I knew the address of Michael's house in Las Vegas, owing to an American friend who had given me the address while swearing me to secrecy, though he had agreed that I could share it with my best friend within the fan world, Dani from Germany. After seeing Michael at the airport, I waited no more than about a week before driving to Las Vegas, as I had no idea how long he would stay in this rented property and didn't want to miss the opportunity to see him there. I had flown thousands of miles across the world to see him so many times in the past, and now here he was, virtually on my doorstep, and I had an open invitation to go and see him any time.

After checking into a hotel on the north end of the Strip, I drove to the house, which was only about ten minutes away, but on arrival there, I was at a loss as to what to do. The gated mansion was on a street corner in a quiet residential area, and there was no sign that it was occupied, much less by the biggest star on the planet. I drove half a block away and sat in my car, feeling awkward and uncomfortable.

I didn't frequent online fan forums but many of my friends did, and so I knew there were often discussions about followers, and that commentators were often highly critical of us. Some went so far as to accuse us of being "stalkers," because while they knew how much we followed Michael, they didn't know, or believe, how much he encouraged it. Yet, this was the first time I felt out of place in Michael's world, and I likely would have left and never returned, at least not alone, had it not been for Dani. She reminded me that Michael had invited me to be there, that I had been given a golden opportunity, and that I'd be foolish to squander it.

I spent the last day of my visit exploring the Strip and, as evening approached, I dropped by the Palms Casino Resort, where Michael was known to go to the movie theatre on weekends. As I entered the parking garage, my heart skipped a beat, because parked in the reserved section by the entrance was Michael's pair of black SUVs. I bought a ticket and was wandering the corridors of the movie theatre, hoping to catch Michael on his way out, when the door to one of the screening rooms sprung open and his bodyguard, Basheer, began walking towards me.

I froze, wishing the ground would open up beneath me, and then began backing away. I still felt unsure about being there, and I didn't want Basheer to yell at me; he was a very scary guy. Perhaps softened by my obvious fear, he held up a hand in a reassuring manner and said, "It's okay. I just want to talk to you. Come here for a minute," which I reluctantly did. He said, "Look, we know you come by the house and he's fine with that. You can come by any time and give him your letters. But right now, I'm in charge of his security. I need to get him in and out without stopping, you understand?" I nodded: yes, I understood. He told me that I could wait at the house instead, and I thanked him and walked away in a swirl of thoughts and feelings.

I was stunned that he knew I'd come by the house, as I'd always parked half a block away and never even got out of my car; so much for my stealth! But I was happy that he'd said I could come by any time; I would no longer have to hide (or try to hide rather!) or feel awkward. At the same time, I wasn't sure whether or not to trust him, as security guards in general had a history of lying to fans. Here, inside the theatre, I had a guaranteed opportunity to see Michael, whereas back at the house, I had no idea if his car would stop or drive right in, as it was unlikely that he would see me, standing outside in the dark. Still, I had given Basheer my word, so I had no choice but to keep it.

This time, when I arrived at the house, which was on the corner of Monte Cristo Way and Tara Avenue in the Spring Valley neighbourhood, I parked directly across from it and got out of my car.

The street was dark and empty, and I paced up and down nervously until I saw the beam of a flashlight behind the gate and heard the crackle of a walkie-talkie. Then a male voice began talking, presumably to Basheer, and said, "There's a young lady here waiting to see you." My heart skipped a beat and, moments later, a set of headlights turned the corner from the main street of Sahara Ave onto Monte Cristo. The SUV pulled up, the back window rolled down, and Michael reached out and took my hand in his, caressing it as we exchanged words of love and affection, melting away any remaining doubts that I had about being there.

*   *   *

After that night, I felt free to embrace this opportunity to see Michael, this gift from the universe, and a few weeks later, I rented a room and began living in Las Vegas and dropping by the house whenever I could. I did share the address with another couple of fans, partly because I didn't have the heart to keep it to myself, and partly because I was so bored of waiting alone and longed for their company. One of the fans was Edina, who still lived in Central California and would drive over for a couple of weekends every month, and the other was Melissa,* a follower from England who I'd first met on a ferry from Belgium to England during the *HIStory* tour, and who Michael adored; she moved to Vegas at the end of April, so she could take full advantage of this opportunity as well.

Alone and with my friends, I had many amazing encounters with Michael in Las Vegas that late spring and early summer, but there are a few that stand out, for varying reasons. The first of these was on Paris's birthday, and it stands out not so much for my interactions with Michael, which were brief but lovely, but for the opportunity it presented to observe the reaction of strangers to him, which was always a joy to do.

*Not her real name

Michael often took his children toy shopping on their birthdays, so it wasn't surprising when he and Paris went to the toy store FAO Schwarz at Caesars Palace on her ninth birthday, which was on 3 April 2007. Afterwards, they went for lunch at the Wing Lei restaurant at the Wynn and, as they left, I greeted them and gave Paris a pink Hello Kitty purse and a birthday card. They both thanked me and Michael, while squeezing my hand, told me repeatedly that he loved me and that I was "so sweet."

Me trailing behind Michael and Paris as they wandered through the Wynn resort in Las Vegas, accompanied by a team of bodyguards, on the afternoon of Paris's ninth birthday, April 2007. (Photo: Bauer-Griffin)

Michael said hi to a few other people and posed for photographs with them, and then he and Paris began strolling through the resort together. He beckoned to me to join them, and so I trailed behind, not wanting to intrude on Paris's special day but overjoyed at the opportunity to spend more time around him. As we walked through the casino into the shopping plaza, I watched people's jaws drop and eyes widen as they realised who was in their midst. Several people approached him to shake his hand, and one older guy told him that he'd seen him in Gary, which is the city where Michael grew up, in the state of Indiana, when Michael was just seven years old.

The world often seemed to me like a cruel place for Michael, because of the mean and disrespectful things people often said about him in the media, and occasionally to my friends and me in person. However, throughout the time that I travelled to see Michael, I only ever saw people responding to him positively in real life, and one time, at the first of his two concerts at Madison Square Garden in New York in September 2001, I witnessed a group of journalists behaving like the most frenzied of fans.

Marlon Brando, Samuel L. Jackson, Whitney Houston, Ray Charles, Destiny's Child, Usher, and Chris Tucker were among the stars who participated in that concert, and when they took to the red carpet, where Tick and I stood pressed against the railing, the journalists around us took their photos and asked them questions. As the evening wore on, some of the journalists began speculating about whether Michael would make an appearance there, which they all agreed was highly unlikely, and a few of them made snide remarks about him, which Tick and I countered. Well, Michael's limousine did pull up at the end of the red carpet, and when he stepped out, with Elizabeth Taylor, the journalists erupted with greater fervour than they'd displayed all evening, reaching out towards him, shouting his name, and pleading for his attention.

I observed similar hypocrisy the first time I walked through a

Las Vegas resort with Michael, which was with a group of other followers in October 2003, when he was in the city to receive the Humanitarian Award at the Radio Music Awards. At one point, my friends and I were waiting at the bottom of an escalator, because we knew he was coming that way, when we heard someone saying they'd heard he was in the resort and then making a derisive comment about him while rolling their eyes. Yet, as soon as Michael appeared, that same person began calling his name and pushing through the crowd to reach him.

It was fashionable, perhaps due to the level of his status and the false allegations against him, to have a cynical and condescending attitude towards Michael (and his fans), but when people saw him in person, their cynicism fell away and they revealed their true feelings. I think that most people knew intuitively that Michael was special, that he belonged more to a higher dimension and less to this world than the rest of us do, which is why even the most cynical of New York journalists responded the way that they did, as stunned and excited to see him in real life as I had been as a teenage girl, and still was and always would be, never for a moment losing that sense of his ethereality.

*   *   *

Of all of my earthly possessions, my most treasured by far are my photographs with Michael and the sweet letters and notes that he wrote to me – to me alone or to my friends and me. I received the first of these in April 2004, when after the court hearing in Santa Maria, five of my friends and I caught up with Michael at a nearby gas station. We talked to him through the open window of a private bus, and he wrote us a message in red ink that ended with the words, "I am yours forever," and invited us to spend the afternoon inside Neverland.

The next time I received anything in writing from Michael

was in Las Vegas in late May 2007. Edina, Melissa, and I met Michael several times that day, first at the Palms resort and then at his house, where he chatted to us through the open window of his SUV while holding our hands in turn. A few minutes later, one of the security guards came out and gave us three notes that Michael had written to us, expressing his love and thanking us for being there.

That evening, another guard came out, this time with a full-length letter from Michael. This letter was folded in three and taped to one side was a gold sparkly twig from the Christmas tree that stood inside the front door of his house. Written across the folded sheet of paper, in Michael's flowing, cursive handwriting, which throughout the letter displayed a random assortment of upper- and lowercase letters, a few underlined words, and one minor misspelling, was:

"Never stop wishing or dreaming, for this is where the magic begins. M.J. Believe."

We carefully unfolded the white sheet of paper to read the message he'd penned inside, which went as follows:

"Thank you for making us so happy, your gifts were very thoughtful, your [you're] the reason why I live each day. I love you <u>all</u> soo much, may all your days be filled with joy, love and most of all <u>peace</u> of mind and <u>heart</u>. Keep the child inside you alive forever. I look so forward to the future. Love Michael Jackson and family 2007."

I had so many sweet words from Michael contained in my heart, but it was special to receive them in writing, where they formed a tangible and permanent record of his expression and love.

*   *   *

One of the last times I saw Michael that summer was in early

June, shortly before he left Las Vegas and relocated to the east coast of the US. I was with Melissa and Dani, who'd finally made it over from Germany for a visit, waiting by the black truck limousine parked at the side of his house. My brother, who was travelling through New Zealand, called, and I was still talking to him when Michael and his three children, along with their nanny, Grace, and another security guard, came out and got into the back of the limousine, and Basheer sat into the driver's seat. Michael invited us to join him, and we filed inside the main cabin and sat down, Dani and me across from him, and Melissa to the right of him and Paris.

My brother was listening to all of this unfold, and I asked Michael to say hi to him, which he did, and they chatted on the phone for a few moments. Then Michael buckled up the seatbelts of his three children and we drove away from the house, meandering through the streets in what Michael explained to us was a test drive, as he was trying to decide whether to purchase the limousine or not: I guess he decided not to, as I never saw it again after he left that house, a week or so later.

Along the back of the limo was a series of fibre optic lights, and hip-hop music played through the speakers, making me feel like we were inside a private nightclub together. Michael bopped along to the music and we did too while chatting with him, drifting from one topic to another. We talked about the upcoming BET Awards (Michael was still deciding whether to attend or not; he didn't in the end.), living in Las Vegas (He asked me where I lived and how I liked it.), the Strip (He said he'd designed several of the attractions and that his favourite resort was the Venetian.), Neverland Valley (He said that he'd never live there again but that he'd also never sell it.)...

At one point, we talked about his music. He asked us what our favourite song from his *Invincible* album was.

"'Break of Dawn,'" said Melissa.

"I don't have any favourites," said Dani.

"It depends on my mood," I said. "At the gym, I want something fast, but when I'm going to sleep, I want something mellow."

"What's your favourite when you're sleeping?" he asked.

"'Speechless,'" I said, without a moment's hesitation.

He reached across and took my hand. "Thank you for saying that. I put my heart and soul into it."

"I know," I said, lost in his gaze. "I can feel it. It gives me shivers down my spine."

Then Melissa asked him about the meaning behind the song "You Are My Life," and as they were discussing it, Dani said to Michael, "You are my life," and he leaned across and caressed her cheek, something he did to all three of us during that car ride, interspersing our conversation with gestures of tender affection. There were also sweet moments between him and his children, like when Paris asked him if she could have a cookie when they got home and he said he'd have to think about it, or when she knelt down on the floor to retrieve something and he told her, "Brace yourself!" before helping her back up and strapping her back in. At one point, he started laughing and I asked him, "What are you laughing at, Michael?" He said, "Blanket. He's so funny. I love my baby," and he cradled his son's face and kissed him on the head.

Towards the end of the journey, Michael asked us if we were keeping safe and we told him that we were but that there was this group of guys who kept harassing us at his house, driving by at night and throwing water balloons at us, or sounding an air horn to frighten us. He asked us if it was funny and we said it was at first but not anymore. "Once is fun but you have to know when to stop," he said, then reassured us, "Don't worry, we'll get them, we'll get them!" and sure enough, the next time they came by, his security guards took off after them in their car.

That limousine ride represented another first for me, as it did for all three of us, but an even more cherished first came at the end of the evening, when he hugged each one of us goodnight. As he held me in his arms, he kissed me for the first time, softly and sweetly on the cheek. And later, he sent out another beautiful letter to us, along with another sprig from his Christmas tree and a bag of ice pops for us to enjoy.

As we sat eating the ice pops and going over every detail of our car ride with Michael, the security guard who'd been sitting at the far end of the limousine with Grace came out to say hi. "He must really trust you guys," he said in amazement, "because he's really careful about who he allows around his children. I'm a huge fan too and I wish I could be like that around him, but we're not allowed to even talk to him unless he talks to us first." It had never occurred to me that a member of Michael's security team, who worked out of a trailer beside his house, might be envious of us, and it made me appreciate all the more how privileged we were and the special bond that we shared with him.

The only negative experience any of us had while waiting to see Michael at that house in Las Vegas was some mild harassment from a few of the neighbours, from the guys we told Michael about and from a woman who'd rudely accused one of the girls of being a gold digger while driving past in her car. We were so immersed in our little bubble of a world that it always felt odd when people peered in and misinterpreted what they saw, whether that was online fans calling us stalkers, or strangers assuming we must be groupies or gold diggers, because why else would anyone wait for hours on end to see a celebrity?

What such people seemed unable to grasp was the purity of our motive, which was simply to be there, to love him and, at the most, though it always felt like a miracle to me, to be loved by him in return, and that it was his love, his expression, his gratitude that held us there, that we wanted to be there only because he wanted us to be there, as he told us repeatedly. On two separate occasions in 2007, he told Melissa and me that when he looked out his window and saw us waiting outside his house, it made him feel less lonely, it made him feel loved, and that, above all else, was what we were there to do, what we were born to do I believe.

*　　*　　*

By the time Michael left Las Vegas in June 2007, I had made several new friends in the city and was enjoying the gated community where I lived, which included a private gym and a pool (amenities that would have cost a fortune in Los Angeles!), so I decided to stay, while also continuing to rent my place in LA. Michael remained on the east coast of the US until early November, when he flew to LA to attend the sixty-sixth birthday celebration of Jesse Jackson, a civil rights activist, minister, and politician who had been a staunch supporter of Michael's throughout the 2005 trial.

I acquired a media pass to the event's red carpet area, which was inside the Beverly Hilton Hotel, and met two of my friends from Europe there. Around 8 p.m., Michael arrived, and the three of us greeted him and handed him our letters, after which I used my media pass to gain entry to the red carpet area. When Michael saw me, he reached out and squeezed my hand, and then he took a step back and told me, "You look great!" He continued into the central area, where he posed for the photographers, and I went around them to wait at the other end. Michael saw me again and this time he called me to him but before I could reach him, his entourage swarmed around him and swept him away.

I didn't have a ticket to the event, which cost $700, and my media pass didn't allow access to it, but somehow I made it inside, perhaps mistaken in all of the chaos as part of Michael's entourage, and so did my two friends. We walked with Michael down two flights of stairs and across the floor of the auditorium, where he took a seat at a round table near the front of the stage. We stood opposite him, as I had done so many months ago in Tokyo, and he waved and pointed at us. Then one of the girls noticed Berry Gordy sitting next to him. Berry was the founder of Motown, the record label that had signed up Michael and his brothers, as The Jackson 5, in 1968, the year Michael had turned ten years old. "We love you, Berry!" we said, and Michael beamed and nodded in approval.

The bodyguard Mike LaPerruque, who I hadn't seen since around the time of the trial, was standing to Michael's right, and Jesse Jackson was standing to his left, so we decided to go around the table to the left, thinking it would be easier to reach Michael from there, but Jesse and a woman we didn't recognise kept blocking our way. One of the girls managed to lean in and ask Michael if we could have a photo with Berry and he told her that that was an "awesome idea," but we still couldn't get to him. We were about to give up when I caught Michael's eye again and he said, "Come here, come here, come here." I felt a pair of hands clutching my elbows, and I was certain they were going to steer me away from the table once and for all, but instead they pulled me through the wall of people and delivered me to Michael.

Michael grabbed my arm and pulled me down next to him, bopping up and down like an excited child. He asked me if I had a camera, and for once, I did. I gave it to him and he gave it to some other guy at the table, and Berry Gordy put his arm around me to pose for a photo. The guy was just about to take it when I noticed that the two girls were still stuck on the other side of Jesse Jackson. "Where are the girls?" I said, and finally, the people around them parted, allowing them to slip through.

I wasn't sure if Michael was going to be in the photo or not because he was leaning away a little, so I put my hand on his arm and said, "Come on Michael, you too." He leaned in then and the guy took the photo, of Michael, Berry, and my two friends and me, all beaming into the camera. Then he handed the camera back to me, and I switched it to view mode to show Michael. "Oh Michael, look at it, it's so beautiful," I said, and he took the camera to see it and said several times, "That's a classic!" He asked me to give him a copy of the photo, and the next time I saw him, a month later in Las Vegas, I did.

*   *   *

Prior to 2007, if anyone had asked me what my most amazing time with Michael was, the answer would have been obvious: it was the day that I spent with him at Neverland Valley in September 2003. But as the magical year that was 2007 unfolded, it became increasingly difficult to speak in terms of superlatives, to pinpoint the encounters that surpassed all others, a trend that would continue throughout the rest of my time within Michael's world. Yet, certainly one of my most magical encounters was the final one of that year, which was the culmination of a wave of enchantment that had swept into my life about a week earlier, when I'd received a lovely surprise in the mail: a photograph of Michael and me hugging at Los Angeles International Airport that I'd given to him earlier that year, with a message from him written across it. I'd never before received anything in the mail from Michael, and I'd also never before seen my name written in his handwriting, making this unexpected gift my most cherished to date.

I was planning to go to Ireland for Christmas, as I did every year, and what I wished for more than anything was to reach out to

Michael one more time, to thank him for giving me the most magical year of my life. It was the first week of December and I was in Las Vegas and he was in Los Angeles, and I didn't have time to go to LA before I left for Ireland, making the prospect of connecting with him one more time seem slim, bordering on impossible. Nonetheless, I decided to go Christmas shopping for him and his three children, hoping that the act of doing so would release my intentions into the universe, where some greater power might see them met. I wished and prayed, much as I had been doing since I was a young girl in the Irish countryside, gazing up at the stars, and what do you know, a few days later, Michael arrived in Henderson, just south of Las Vegas, and checked into the Green Valley Ranch resort.

With two gift bags, containing beautifully illustrated books for the children and a Pinocchio marionette for Michael, all neatly wrapped and decorated, I drove to the Green Valley Ranch. I had planned to drop the gifts off at the front desk but then I spotted a security guard called Bill, who I recognised from the house in Las Vegas, getting out of his jeep. Bill disappeared inside the hotel before I could speak with him, so I decided to leave him a note, explaining to him who I was and why I was there. I asked him if I could please give him my gifts for Michael, and told him I would be parked by the resort's shopping plaza all day and could come and meet him any time. Then I slipped the note under his windshield wiper and spent the day Christmas shopping at the nearby plaza, feeling unusually floaty, as if I knew deep down that beyond the festive spirit, some deeper strain of magic was in the air.

At 6 p.m., the stores closed and I returned to my car, disappointed that Bill hadn't called but hoping that he still would, at which point I could return, as my home was a mere thirty-minute drive away. I was about to leave when a jeep that looked like Bill's arrived, circled the parking lot, and then parked across from me. Nevada didn't require vehicles to have front licence plates (unlike California), so I wasn't sure if it was Bill's jeep (which had a personalised and therefore memorable licence plate) and assumed that it was not, that it was merely a coincidence.

The door opened and, to my delight, Bill stepped out, smiling at me. I leapt out, shook his hand, and thanked him for coming, and he told me that he'd shown the note to Michael and that he'd said he knew me and agreed to my request. I gave the gifts to Bill, thanking him again, and returned to my car. I was still sitting there, busying myself on my phone, when I heard the honk of a horn and glanced up. The sound was coming from the jeep and waving out its back window was a hand I'd recognise anywhere. It was Michael's hand; it was Michael!

I leapt out of the car again, my heart exploding in happiness, and when I looked inside the jeep, I saw that Michael was sitting on the back seat with his three children, all beaming out at me. I may have been standing on concrete ground in a parking lot that evening, but throughout my time with Michael, I felt like I was floating inside a puff of fairy dust, an illusion reinforced by the carol singing in the distance and the starry sky above, but most of all by the touch of Michael's hand, wrapped around mine, the depth of love in his eyes, and the melodious sound as he spoke my name for the first time in my presence, wrapping his voice around each syllable, making my heart sing.

"Thank you so much for the beautiful gifts, Talitha," he said, in his soft, silvery voice. "You are so thoughtful and kind." He had the children thank me too, and I, in turn, thanked him for the signed photograph, which he told me that he'd sent because he'd wanted me to know that he was thinking about me. After some more sweet exchanges, the conversation flowed, as it always did between us, and the two older children joined in, telling me about the movies they'd seen recently and their beloved pets, a chocolate Labrador called Kenya, who I'd seen at the house in Las Vegas, and an orange tabby cat called Kaity (as spelt on a photo of her that Paris gave me the following year), who they'd acquired since then.

"Michael, are you still afraid of the dog?" I asked, and both he and Bill burst out laughing.

"How did you know that?" asked Michael.

"Oh, I've known that for ages," I said. "You said it in an interview once. It surprised me because you love animals."

"See, she remembers everything!" he said to Bill. "It's true. I'm terrified of dogs. But this one is the best breed for children. He's a chocolate Labrador. They're the best breed. You can even have them around babies. They're very gentle."

He asked me what I was doing for Christmas, and when I told him I was going to Ireland, he and the children began reminiscing about their time there again. I told Michael I could see how the beauty of the countryside might remind him of Neverland, which is in the mountains, surrounded by forests.

"Oh, but it's more beautiful than Neverland," said Michael. "Much more beautiful."

"Is it really? In what way?"

"Just the forestry there, it's so special. I never saw anything like it."

"And that house you stayed at…"

"It is so beautiful on the inside. I will take you there someday."

"Okay, Michael, I'm going to hold you to that!"

"Do! You are always welcome," he said, squeezing my hand. "You know," he continued, "I always felt a special affinity to Ireland, even before I ever went there. How could you not love that beautiful, emerald island? It's so green and luscious and has such beautiful forestry. And I love all the folklore and fairies and elves and leprechauns."

Then he and Paris and I had a discussion about Irish folklore and banshees. And later, Michael returned to the topic, telling me, and I assumed he was talking about when he went to Ireland in 1988, during the *Bad* tour, to perform a concert in Cork, "Our first time in Ireland, everyone was so warm and friendly and welcoming. From the moment we stepped off the plane, they were lining the roads, farmers and workers. Oh, it was incredible!"

The conversation went on and on and on, and I felt like I was going to explode into a million pieces if he said my name or held my hand or stroked my cheek or told me how much he loved me one more time. We talked about Christmas and the Bible and dreams and energy and the projects he was working on and his plans for the future. I became tearful as I told him how much he'd inspired me as a young girl, reaching across the universe through his creative endeavours, and he became all the more affectionate as I shared this with him.

He told me that he'd written a song about his fans and how we make him feel, how deeply we touch his heart, and later he said, "I remember everything you all do for me, the cakes and the candies and all the letters and the tea on the card when we were all sick in Tokyo. I remember everything." The card he was referring to was one that the four girls I had stayed with in Tokyo and I had made after we'd heard, towards the end of our visit to Japan, that he had caught a cold. It was a handmade card with a photograph of us on the front, sitting on the bed in our hotel room holding three signs that said "Get" "Well" "Soon." Inside, we'd attached sachets of tea and honey, and written a message of love and good wishes to him, and then we'd given the card to the security guards stationed outside his hotel room on the floor above.

That was nine months ago, and Michael still remembered that card, enough to bring it up in conversation, knowing that I was one of the girls involved. I contemplated that later, imagining how many cards and letters and gifts he must have received since then, especially during his two visits to London, where he'd gone in March of that year and again in May, as well as all of the places he'd visited and all of the people he'd met and all of the new memories he'd formed, and yet still, he'd held in the forefront of his mind that simple little card, fashioned out of a piece of cardboard folded in two.

Ever since I'd felt my love for Michael released, at the age of thirteen, he had always been magical to me, and this was the first time I expressed that to him in person, as opposed to in letters, to which most of my expression to him over the years had been confined. I asked him and his children if they'd seen the movie *Enchanted*, and they all responded enthusiastically, talking over each other as they told me how much they loved it.

"I knew you would all love it," I said. "I loved it too. It was like stepping into a fairy tale. I wish I could live in Andalasia [the magical kingdom in the movie]. Well, I kind of do. I mean, you're my fairy tale, Michael."

"Oooh," said Michael, and he brushed my cheek with his hand, making me flutter.

"You are," I said. "I remember when I was really little, I didn't think you were real. I thought there was Santa and Peter Pan and Michael Jackson. I mean, real yes, but living in another dimension. Not like in the real world. You were too magical to live in the real world."

"Aw, do you hear that?" he said to his children. "That is so beautiful. You are very sweet," he said, while stroking my cheek again.

At one point, the bodyguard Bill asked me how I'd known they were coming to the parking lot to find me, and I said, I hadn't known it at all; at least as far as I'd known, I hadn't known, but maybe on some deeper level, I had, just as I'd known without knowing to go to the Wing Lei restaurant at the Wynn in February, where I'd seen Michael for the first time that year.

"See," said Michael to Bill. "She's clairvoyant. I told you."

"I am," I said. "Really. When it comes to you, I have this sixth sense. I just follow the energy."

Before parting, Michael told me that he was going to put my gifts under the tree, and that he and his children would open them on Christmas morning, leaving me with a beautiful image to envision as I spent the holidays with my family in Ireland. As the jeep moved away, it drove over a concrete bumper stop and I heard Michael's laughter ring out as he waved once more out the window, to assure me that he was okay.

He was okay and I was in heaven, because for the first time in my life, I hadn't gone to him; he had come to me, sought me out in a parking lot under a starlit sky, and that final encounter of that magical year left me feeling more deeply loved and blessed than ever before, bursting with joy and gratitude.

SEVEN

Heaven on earth

f I were to convey in physical form the essence of the final weeks I spent inside Michael's world in Las Vegas, in September and October 2008, I would do so as a scene inside a snow globe. Central to the scene, rained down upon by a shower of silver sparkles, would be a Spanish Mediterranean style mansion on a quiet residential street. In the terrace would stand a man wearing black loafers and a fedora, and three children, two boys and a girl. Perhaps the children would be engaged in a game of tag, or steadying themselves on bicycles fitted with training wheels, or playing with their beloved dog, Kenya, as the man, their father, looked on lovingly. Outside, to the right of the house, would sit a young woman under a tree penning a poem about the man, called 'Loving an Angel,' and across the street would be her friends, waiting, as she was, for this man, this maker of dreams, to emerge.

I don't doubt the accounts of my friends who told me that following the trial, Michael seemed to have become somewhat withdrawn, because throughout the time he lived in Las Vegas, I too observed a transformation, a strengthening of the spirit, a greater urge to reach out and connect. While my encounters and those of my friends at his home in 2007 were by and large brief and sporadic, those in 2008 were far more frequent, longer, and more emotionally charged. It was during this time that I began to record in writing every moment that I spent with him, mainly thanks to my friend Dani, who begged me to share every detail with her, that she might experience it from afar. Not only did I write long descriptive passages and every word of dialogue between him and me and his children and anyone else present, I also wrote a few words each day on the pages of a calendar, summing up its content.

"Met MJ, asked for my number," is my first calendar notation, on 3 September, while another, a couple of weeks later, reads, "Met MJ and kids alone, long chat," and another, "Met MJ once fast, second time looong and amazing, stroking my face. Angel," a reference to an encounter during which he kept caressing my cheek and saying things like, "God, you're so sweet," and "I love you *so* much," and calling me his "little angel." My final summation from that period in Las Vegas is on 20 October, when I met him with my friend from England Joanna and a local teenager called Hayley, as he left the house for the final time, to relocate to Los Angeles.

"Twenty-eight meetings since beginning Sept," says the following day's entry, meaning that in a span of seven weeks, I'd had twenty-eight encounters with Michael, some of them alone, others with fans visiting from Europe or those who lived locally, most of them outside the gates of his home but a couple on the grounds of his property, and one at the Palms resort, where my friend CJ and I watched a private screening of the movie *Fly Me To The Moon* with him and his children, during which we all wore big, goofy 3D glasses and he laughed loudly, and after which he held me for what felt like a blissful eternity before inviting us into his SUV for a chat.

But it wasn't the quantity or the duration of the encounters that makes this, in my mind, my most heavenly stretch of time inside Michael's world, so much as it was the quality of the experience. Michael seemed happier and more open, presumably as he continued to heal from the trauma of the trial, and I was happier and more open too. Ever since the age of thirteen, I'd been told that I would never get anywhere near Michael, and after I'd disproven this assertion, that I was wasting my time and money in going to see him, and that I would never mean anything to him.

Part of me had absorbed these judgements and made them my own, and during my early years in his world, I had felt slightly guarded around him and struggled to express in person how I felt about him, beyond telling him that I loved him. However, as I'd spent more time with him, those judgements had fallen away, only to be banished entirely by the magical year that was 2007 and the many opportunities it had offered to experience Michael's love directly, alone and in private, where no question of its authenticity could remain.

Michael's presence was so disarming that the more time I spent with him, the more open I became, and by the fall of 2008, I was in a sense transparent, at least in his eyes. On 12 September, four of us were chatting with him about art and movies and music, when he stopped mid-conversation, turned to me, and said, "I know all the love you have for me in your heart. I can feel that," and then he caressed my cheek and I leaned into him, as though resting on the softest pillow. I didn't want to hide anymore. I wanted him to see, and he did. He saw and he responded with an outpouring of love that was so overwhelming that at times I felt like I could hardly take the force of it, and I wrote about that feeling as best I could, about how every time he looked at me, it was like being kissed by an angel, and to be loved by him was to feel the light of heaven shining upon my face.

*   *   *

Before I got to experience heaven on earth, however, I had to overcome a rather unpleasant obstacle. Over the years, Michael's bodyguards and other security personnel had come and gone, and there was often an awkward phase, when they overreacted to the presence of fans, until they saw his response to us and came to accept our place in his world. I had never had a problem with any of his staff, not even his more intimidating bodyguards, like Basheer, but that changed in the spring of 2008, when Michael returned to Las Vegas and moved into another rented house, this one on Palomino Lane, six miles northeast of the previous year's property. This time, the address appeared in a local newspaper, and several of my friends and I went there on separate occasions, only to be harassed by a new security guard who I'd never seen before. I'll refer to this guard as Reginald, even though that wasn't his real name.

Reginald would wait until after dark to approach young women like me and make various threats against us, always out of earshot of the other guards. He made the atmosphere so unpleasant that I gave up trying to see Michael at his house, and instead met with him at the Palms resort, where he continued to go to the movie theatre and also to use the recording studio there. One time, Reginald was there too and I welcomed this as a positive, because although his behaviour had clearly been out of line, I had given him the benefit of the doubt and assumed that it had come from a sense of protectiveness, which no security guard could be faulted for. But even after seeing Michael respond lovingly to me, he continued to be as aggressive as ever, if not more so, perhaps frustrated that his intimidatory tactics had failed to scare me away.

At that point, I decided to tell Michael about Reginald. I had never before complained to him about anything, but I felt that he had a right to know how one of his employees was behaving behind his back. It was a few weeks later that I next saw Michael, thanks to a group of lovely fans from Spain who'd flown in to Las Vegas in time for Michael's fiftieth birthday, on 29 August. These fans were entirely unfazed by Reginald's threats, even when he went so far as to call the police on them (a waste of police time since they were committing no crime!), and their fearlessness gave me the courage to wait with them outside Michael's house. Equally bewildered by Reginald's behaviour, they helped me to get word to Michael about him via a carefully worded letter, and a few days later, just after 1 a.m. on the morning of 6 September, Michael called me, for the first time in my life.

What followed was the most intimate conversation I'd ever had with Michael, during which we laughed and cried and poured our hearts out to each other. He began by expressing his upset at what Reginald had been doing to my friends and me. He said, "I got your letter. I didn't know they were doing that. I am so sorry. I would never let anything happen to you. You're so precious to me. I have a problem with this security. I'm not happy with them. I have a problem with them. I didn't know they were doing any of those things, what they were doing to you. It didn't come from me. None of it was from me. I'm so sorry about it. I'm going to do something about it. Don't worry. I'm going to change things."

I asked him if he was in control of his security team, as it had upset me to hear him say that he had a problem with them. "Oh no, don't you worry, I'm in control," he said. "I'm in control of them. I tell them what to do. They don't tell me what to do. Things are going to change, you'll see. I can't fire people. I'm like my mom in that way. But I'm going to get rid of them. I'm in charge of them."

I knew that some of the security guards who had been around Michael since the trial were affiliated with the Nation of Islam, whom his brother Jermaine had introduced into his life at that very vulnerable time. Michael told me on the phone, "You know, they're so respectful around me and the children, always bowing and very respectful. I didn't know they were doing these things behind my back, were being so two-faced. I didn't know any of it. You know, during the trial, I had them all over Neverland, and I needed them then. I needed their protection. But now it's different and I'm going to change things. Oh God, I'm sorry, I'm sorry, I'm sorry…"

He kept apologising over and over, his voice heavy with tears, and I kept begging him to stop and telling him that it wasn't his fault. I did emphasise to him that it was only one guard who was causing all the problems, though I knew at least some of the others must have been aware of it and turning a blind eye. "Oh, I'm so sorry, from the bottom of my heart," he said. "Tell all the fans that. Tell them it didn't come from me. I'm so sorry. It's not me. It's the security. I'm not doing it."

Michael must have taken immediate action because when I went to his house the next day, Reginald was behaving entirely differently, asking us all if we had any gifts or letters we wanted him to pass along to Michael, and offering to buy us pizza. A week later, Michael brought up what I'd told him about Reginald during a conversation at his house with three other fans and me.

"How are my security treating you?" he asked. "Now tell the truth. Tell me."

I said, "Lately, they're fine," and my friend Ines from Germany agreed. "Yeah, lately they're fine," she said.

Michael wagged his finger at us, perhaps fearing we were just being polite. "Now tell me," he said, emphatically. "Tell the truth. Tell me. I want to know. How are they treating you?"

Edina, who was visiting from California, said, "They're okay now, but in May and June, they were kind of mean."

Michael said, "Well, thank you for telling me. Tell me names. Give me names. I want names."

"I don't know their names," said Edina, but I did, and I told him Reginald's full name and how he'd tried to get some of us arrested by falsely claiming we'd tried to go on the property.

Michael repeated the name and said, "You have to tell me when that happens. You are so precious to me. You are my world. I want them to treat you like that, as precious as you are." Then he turned to his personal assistant, Michael Amir, and said, "Aren't they so precious? They are so kind. Make sure they're treated right," and after confirming Reginald's full name with Amir, he repeated it again while making a face and shaking his head. A few weeks later, Reginald disappeared from the house, and I never saw or heard of him again.

*   *   *

It was always Michael's essence that I connected with, but my first experience of him in person was as a superstar, performing to packed stadiums, mesmerizing the audience with his crystal voice and electric dance moves. My next experience of him was as a man, expressing himself through words and gestures, in public and in private. And in 2008, I began to experience him as a father, something I'd only caught glimpses of in the past, for example in September 2003 at Neverland Valley, and in 2007, on the few occasions that we'd all spent time together.

During our phone call in early September 2008, I asked Michael how his children were and he said, "Oh they're great, they're great. Prince is becoming a young man. And Paris is becoming a young lady. They're growing up. I love them. They play all the time. We have so much fun." I told him what a privilege it was to observe the relationship between him and his children, and he responded, "Oh, you're so sweet, God bless you. You should hear the prayers that Blanket says. He's so sweet. You should hear what he says, Talitha. He tells me I'm such a great dad. And he thanks God that he has me for a dad. And he says that every night. And it's such a gift. It just melts my heart. I don't let the children listen to the media. I don't let them see the tabloids. I try to protect them from all of that. They don't really know. The governess, their nanny at the time, Grace, tried to tell them who I am but I don't want them to hear it from the tabloids. I want them to get it from you guys. So when I put the window down, I want them to feel that love. Because that's what it's really all about."

"You're right," I responded. "We are a reflection of what you've given to the world. We're a reflection of everything you've put out there and all the people whose lives you've touched. That's what we represent. It's right that they see you through our eyes because we see who you really are. You're such a wonderful father, Michael."

"Oh thank you, thank you," he said. "My father was very into discipline but he wasn't very nurturing. He wasn't very affectionate. So, I try to give that to my children. I take them out. I take them to the movies. I take them to games arcades. I want them to have fun. I want them to have the childhood I never had."

Over the following month and a half in Las Vegas, almost every time that I saw Michael, I also saw his children, and I began chatting with them as much as, and sometimes even more than, with him. I bonded with the older two especially, Prince, then eleven, and Paris, ten, over our shared love of our pets, in their case the dog and cat they'd told me about in December, Kenya and Kaity, and also a black cat called Thriller and a yellow-naped Amazon parrot called Skyberia, and in my case, a three-legged Maine Coon cat called Cookie.

The children and I would share anecdotes about our pets' antics and photos of them, and Paris would sometimes write me thank-you notes and give me sweet little gifts, including a snapper bracelet that she took off her wrist and put on mine, and a necklace with a gold snowflake that she and her dad picked out for me while out shopping together. This was my first time as an adult being around children, both Michael's and the local kids who would drop by after school, and it was through them that I learned that I have a natural affinity with children, and that they tend to relate to me less as an adult and more as one of them.

Michael's three children were a reflection of who he was as a father, as he'd raised them singlehandedly, with help only from their nanny, Grace. They were happy and balanced, privileged but not spoilt, confident but not cocky, spirited but not brash, and while they were each their own person – Prince, outgoing and funny; Paris, profound and gentle; Blanket, quiet and timid – they all shone with a quality of innocence and wonder that he had nurtured in them, by shielding them from the harshness of the outside world, both in relation to him and in general, and by giving them a childhood that was rich in play and imagination.

The children were home-tutored wherever they went, and they spent their free time engaging in activities that harnessed their intellect and creativity; Paris loved telling me about the latest book she was reading, or how many she'd read that week, and Prince about the new scale model he was working on. They were allowed online only on children's websites, while under supervision, and watched movies together as a family. In fact, they did everything possible as a family, they were a unit, and when Michael talked about the future, he always spoke in terms of "we," meaning him and his children, because they were a part of him; they were his world.

It was always a joy to witness the dynamic between Michael and his children, so playful and loving. Oftentimes, his SUV, now one of two identical dark blue Cadillac Escalades, would roll through the gate and the back windows would slide down, unleashing a wave of chatter and merriment. Michael would discipline his children gently when necessary, reminding the boys especially to say "thank you" when any of my friends and I paid them a compliment or gave them a gift (Paris rarely needed any such reminder.), and one time, one of them reprimanded him, with hilarious effect. It was in late September and, in thanks for another beautiful letter, I had given Michael a dozen cookies to share with his children. The next time I saw them all, I asked them if they'd enjoyed the cookies, and the children responded, "Cookies, what cookies?"

Michael looked at me sheepishly and said, "Oh, I didn't tell them about the cookies yet. I put them away and when they do something good, I'll give them a cookie."

"Oh," I said, "but did *you* eat some because you were supposed to eat three of them? At least. Big ones."

My friends and I were always encouraging him to eat more because we knew he often neglected to eat and sleep enough.

"Oh, I didn't know that," said Michael. "I ate the Spider-Man cookie. Did you give me the Spider-Man cookie?"

I had actually bought themed cookies for each of the children and explained this in a note on the box. "Yeah, that was supposed to be for Blanket because he loves Spider-Man," I said.

Blanket was on Michael's lap and at that, he swung around and began pounding him with his tiny fists, making us all erupt in laughter.

The press often ridiculed Michael for covering the faces of his children while in public, even though anyone who knew anything about his life could surely understand why. He wanted to shield them from the gaze of the world so that they could go out without him and not be recognised, as they often did in Las Vegas, sometimes spending an evening playing arcade games at the entertainment centre Chuck E. Cheese. He wanted to spare them from the media scrutiny that he had been subjected to since he was a little boy, performing with The Jackson 5, and that had led to humiliating comments being made about his appearance. These comments mainly revolved around the cosmetic surgery he'd had (just like so many others stars, who endured nowhere near the same level of criticism) and the disorder that afflicted him called vitiligo, which caused his skin to lighten and was evident up close from the light patches on his arms and hands. But most importantly of all, he wanted to protect them from harm, something he explained on camera to Martin Bashir, who omitted his explanation from his 2003 documentary, as it would have normalised a behaviour that Bashir wanted to portray as bizarre.

Michael came close to tears while explaining to Bashir that he was terrified that if his children were identifiable, someone might kidnap and murder them. This clip was included on Maury Povich's rebuttal video, along with an interview with Elizabeth Taylor, a former child star, in which she said that it had been her idea to have the children wear masks in public. In private, the children wore no such coverings, and in Vegas, apart from on Paris's birthday in April 2007, when she wore a veil over her face while she and her father walked through the Wynn together, I only ever saw them wearing baseball caps, which Michael made sure were pulled well over their faces as they walked from their SUV to a casino resort or other public building, in case any paparazzi were lurking nearby. One time, in late 2008, Michael told me that now that his children were getting older, he wouldn't be able to insist for much longer that they kept their faces hidden on such occasions, that he would have to leave it up to them, and that this scared him a little.

*　*　*

Another group of people who Michael spoke lovingly about during our phone call in September were my friends, both known and unknown, and me, for I consider every true fan to be a friend of sorts, part of my extended family. He said, "Tell the fans that I'm so grateful for all your love and gifts and the books and the cards and the letters and the drawings for the children. I'm too shy to say these things to you face to face. I'm too shy to stop sometimes. I'm sorry, I don't mean to do that. I don't mean to be rude. I know you guys wait for me and I feel so bad when I look down out of my hotel room and I see you all in the cold. And I would take the blankets off my bed and give them to you because I feel so bad. And I send out pizza because I feel so bad. But I'm so shy. I grew up on stage. So when I'm on stage, I'm at home, I'm powerful, I can move mountains. But off stage, I'm so shy. Oh Talitha, I'm so shy, I'm so shy, I'm so shy, I'm so shy, I'm so shy, I'm so shy, I don't know why but I'm so shy. And I don't mean it. When I don't stop, it's just because I'm shy. I want to see you guys. I would love to be able to stand in front of you and say all of these things but I can't do it."

As shy as Michael was, and he was, tenderly, painfully, beautifully shy, he always stopped to talk to us as he left and returned to his house in Las Vegas that fall. After the Spanish and other fans who'd come for Michael's birthday left, I was alone for a while, and then the half a dozen other followers who visited from Europe throughout that period began to trickle in, in ones and twos, and stay for about a week at a time. Most of them were from England and some, like Justin, aka Waldo, had first seen Michael as teenagers in the late 1980s and been following ever since. They all told me that this was the most accessible they'd ever seen him and their most amazing time within his world.

Michael talked about his love of us, of all of his fans, again during a conversation with Joanna and me on 19 October, the day before he left his Las Vegas home for the final time. We told him how his love had reached us from afar throughout our childhoods, opening our minds and hearts, and shaping who we had become. Michael urged his children to listen as we poured our hearts out to him, and then he said, "We're much more than we think we are...I'm clairvoyant. I feel that energy. It's all push and pull. You inspire me. I see your souls even when you don't say a word...I live for you. I live for your quintessential innocence and your love, the innocence of children. I tell them [meaning his children]. We talk about all of this. I tell them about innocence and love."

About a handful of local fans also dropped by the house now and again that fall, including a lady and her two adult children, who I'd first met on a prior trip to see Michael in Las Vegas and who he'd known as a family for years. And on weekdays, a bunch of kids who went to nearby schools would often come and hang out for an hour or so, and we would make cards for Michael using the supplies of sparkly paper, stickers, and stencils that I kept inside a box at the back of my car.

These preteens and young teenagers had not even been alive during the *Thriller* and *Bad* eras, when Michael had been at the height of his career, but they were well aware of his music and who he was, and they were drawn to him, as all children were. The impression I formed of Michael over the thirteen years I spent in his world was based not only on my interactions with him, but also those of others, including other fans, friends, family members, employees, and associates, that I observed, as well as anecdotes that they shared with me, and I had both seen and heard how children of all ages responded to him, how they clung to him and followed him around, because they knew what I knew, what I'd known intuitively since I was a child, that he was made of goodness and light.

*Heaven on earth: Me standing outside Michael's house on
Palomino Lane in Las Vegas, September 2008.*

One time, when the school kids and I were hanging out together,
making cards for Michael, a woman drove by his house shouting abuse
directed at him, which she'd done a few times before and which I'd
hoped and prayed he'd never heard. Well, on that afternoon, those

kids leapt to their feet and took off after her car, shouting threats and expletives, because just as they knew Michael represented love, they knew that woman represented a hatefulness and ignorance that was all too prevalent in the world, and that was all too often directed at him.

All of the other neighbours I encountered while waiting outside that house were warm and welcoming, including a couple who owned two horses, called Oreo and Nabisco. They would walk the horses up and down the road, and they told me once that Michael and the children were welcome to ride them any time. So, the next time I saw the Jackson clan, on their way out, I relayed this invitation to them, and as their SUV rolled away, lo and behold, the couple and the horses appeared. The SUV pulled up next to them and the guy extended the invitation again, as the children climbed over the back seat to pet the horses, and Michael thanked him profusely.

The most meaningful incident involving someone from the neighbourhood, however, occurred on the afternoon of 27 September, while five of us were gathered around the SUV, chatting with Michael. Midway through, a lady approached and said something to one of the security guards, who said to Michael, "She's a schoolteacher."

"Let her in," said Michael. "I want to meet the schoolteacher."

I stepped aside and the lady leaned in and she shook Michael's hand and said, "We're really happy to have you here in the neighbourhood. You're very welcome."

Michael thanked her and introduced her to Blanket, who was the only one of his children with him.

"Oh, and is he three or four years old?" asked the teacher, as Blanket was quite small for his age.

"No, he's six," said Michael proudly.

"Oh, he's six. He's a first-grader then," she replied, and beamed at them both.

Michael never talked to me about the pain of being falsely accused of child molestation, but I understood it to be as he described it to actress Anjelica Huston, who starred with him in his 1986 film *Captain EO*, when they ran into each other at his doctor's office in Los Angeles in 2009. She later shared a heartbreaking account of this, her final encounter with him, with the Italian newspaper *la Repubblica*.

She said Michael talked to her about his humiliation at being falsely accused and about his sorrow at the loss of Neverland. "I remember his words," she said, and quoted Michael: "'They ruined my dream. I had this dream, perhaps childish and foolish, a place designed to celebrate the innocence of that childhood that I never had, and they took it from me. I love children, I could never do them harm. I spent all my life loving them and trying to do good things for them. The libel of harming a child, that breaks my heart. It is an unbearable pain, those accusations are unjust and terrible...'As he said these things, he began to cry. I held him in my arms...He was so skinny and frail."

I knew that nothing could eradicate that unbearable pain, but I hoped that by extending the hand of friendship to Michael, that sweet schoolteacher at least provided a balm to soothe his wounded heart.

*   *   *

Prior to late 2008, Michael had talked to me several times about going on tour in the future, always saying the same thing, that instead of doing tours on the scale of those in the past, involving eighty-two concerts in thirty-five countries in the case of *HIStory*, for example, he wanted to do a few exclusive shows in major cities. In September, during the same encounter in which the schoolteacher featured, he told five of us – four followers visiting from Europe and me – that he was returning from "a meeting about the tour."

"Oooh, tour!" we all responded, and Maria, from England, said, "Well, we would love you to tour but the most important thing is that you take care of yourself and don't take on too much."

"Thank you, tell that to them," said Michael, pointing at Blanket, and presumably meaning his three children.

"Why?" I asked. "They want to see you on stage?"

"They want to *be* on stage," said Michael. "They can't wait to get out there. But I'm... Well, I don't know."

"Oh, you could have them up for 'Heal the World' or something like that," I suggested, as his performance of that song always featured children from a local choir, and Michael agreed.

"Yeah, that's what I'm thinking," he said.

Maria then reminded him of when he had invited her to be on stage with him during "Heal the World" at a *HIStory* concert in South Africa, in thanks for an interview she'd done defending him on TV.

It was clear that Michael prioritised his role as a father above any other; his children were his main focus and the centre of his world. But he was also a creative genius and a humanitarian, through and through, and he often talked about the projects he was working on and his commitment to healing the world. He told me during our phone call in early September, "I'm working really hard all the time, really hard. I go around the house and the kids get mad at me because I make so much noise. I'm always banging on things and making sounds."

He said about writing new music, "I promise you, you're going to hear it all real soon. I'm such a perfectionist, Talitha. I write so many songs. I write hundreds of songs, and it's so hard for me to choose the ones that are good enough for you to hear." And he said later, "I have pencils and pens and paper all over the house. And when I feel it, it just comes, and I write and write and write. It's non-stop. I can't turn it off." He told me that the main message that he wanted to convey through his next project was one of environmental awareness. "The thing that I care about the most, and I'm being completely honest here, is our planet. There's going to be so much on my album about the planet. I feel so strongly about what's happening to our world."

Most, if not all, of Michael's fans had connected to him in the first instance through his music, and he often asked us what our favourite songs were, an impossible question to answer because we all had far too many to mention. Asked this question during our phone call, I listed several, including "the classics, like 'Billie Jean' and 'Smooth Criminal,'" to which he responded, "You wouldn't believe how quickly I wrote those songs, Talitha. It was like I was picking up on something that was already there. God sent me those songs and I was an instrument of nature. They just came to me all of a sudden." A week later, on 12 September, he asked the same question of four of us outside his house, and we all began talking at once, calling out the names of songs we loved, but he became distracted by his children and held up a hand, signalling to us to hold on.

Then, once the children had settled down, he turned back to us and said, "So, tell me again, what are your favourite songs?"

"'Give In To Me,'" said Edina, to which Paris responded, "Oh, I love 'Give In To Me.'" "'Will You Be There,'" continued Edina. "'Speechless,' 'Someone Put Your Hand Out...'"

"'Someone Put Your Hand Out,'" repeated Michael. "Oh, thank you for saying that. Oh, bless you, I love that one. I wrote that years ago while in Florida."

"'The Lost Children,'" I said.

"Ah, 'Lost Children,'" said Michael, and clapped. "Oh, I'm so happy you said that. I always wanted to write a song like that, talking about the children of the world. There are so many children out there, wandering around, lost, millions of them. I have a mother and a father but I've always been alone on tour. So, I feel their pain. And they are all my children. I would take them all in my heart. If I could, I would."

As a humanitarian, Michael was completely devoted to the children of the world; he donated hundreds of millions of dollars to helping them throughout his life, often anonymously, and took time out of his schedule to visit orphanages and children's hospitals wherever he went.

*   *   *

My role in Michael's world was that of a fan, a follower, a supporter, and a friend, and this was one I felt I occupied not only on my own behalf but on behalf of all of the people who loved him and never got a chance to tell him so. I felt a responsibility to this mass of strangers, these friends of sort, to direct as much love and light and positivity towards him as I possibly could, to make him feel cocooned and shielded from the darkness that had targeted him for years.

Since the early days, when I had watched Michael from the front barrier of concerts and enjoyed brief exchanges with him in London and New York, my main method of communicating with him had been via the written word, often in the form of lengthy letters. And now that I was seeing him almost every day, I still found myself sitting under the shade of the tree that bordered his property, leaning over my notebook, pen in hand, reaching for the expression to contain what was uncontainable, channelling all of the love that had bloomed in my heart since childhood into literary form.

I also found myself writing to him on behalf of my thirteen-year-old self, because I was still her in a sense, alone in my own world with

Michael, except now what had been internalised was being externalised, expressed and reciprocated, as that inner part of me looked on in awe at the embodiment of what she had wished so fervently into existence. It was this feeling that inspired a poem I wrote called 'Loving an Angel,' which went as follows:

'Loving an Angel'

I remember being thirteen
Seeing an angel on the screen
His face was beauty, his eyes were love
I knew he came from up above

I longed with all my heart to meet
This giver of love, so pure and sweet
They called him Michael, a star, a king
He became my world, my everything

I wished and wished, and my wish came true
The universe carried my soul to you
And though I see you a thousand times
I'll never lose what's yours and mine

For deep inside, I'm still thirteen
Peering out at this wondrous dream
I can't believe it, I'm so amazed
My life's a wonder, I'm in a daze

Look and see the love that's mine
This love reflects the light you shine
For in the darkness, you were there
You gave me hope, you made me care

In your presence there is no fear
And earthly ties all disappear
My inner child sprouts wings and flies
My spirit soars across the skies

I love you with a love so pure
That through the ages will endure
My soul is yours eternally
You are my gift, my destiny

You are my angel, my sweetest song
You are to whom my heart belongs
You are my childhood dream come true
Thank you Michael for the wonder of you

I gave that poem to Michael shortly after he left Las Vegas, on Halloween night in Los Angeles, written inside a giant Snoopy card. A couple of days later, he called my friends and me while we were waiting outside the Hotel Bel-Air, where he was staying, and he told me that he loved the poem so much that he'd read it to his children.

My literary creation that evoked the greatest response of all from Michael that fall in Las Vegas, however, was an article for the teen magazine that I wrote for, about the work teenagers in various countries were doing to save the planet. Knowing that this was a topic close to Michael's heart, I gave the article to him on the evening of 18 October, as he and his children were leaving home to go to the Planet Hollywood restaurant at Caesars Palace, and when they returned, a couple of hours later, and the window slid down, Michael immediately reached for me and began showering me with love.

He told me that he'd read the article to his children over dinner and that it was so beautiful and that I was so beautiful and that I had a beautiful soul and that he wished that there were more people in the world like me. He kept caressing my hand and squeezing it tight, and then he reached out and wrapped his arms around me, almost pulling me through the car window in an embrace. I felt light-headed at his response, and the next day, I cried happy tears while listening to "Man in the Mirror" and reflecting on the impossibility that the man who'd recorded such beauty could ever love me so.

Michael also wrote letters to me that fall, to me alone and to my friends and me, and he also wrote a letter to friends but not me, including some who weren't even there! That latter one came on 22 September, as a result of a visit from Maria from England and the letters she'd brought from other followers, three from England and one from Spain. After delivering the letters to Michael, Maria left and I was at the house alone when a security guard came out and handed me a bag with a letter inside. He said, "Michael told me to give this to you," but, when I read the letter, I knew that it wasn't for me, and that Michael must have meant for me to give it to Maria, which I did when she returned.

The letter, written in black marker ink, read:

"I truly love and miss you all, you all are truly wonderful, I will always adore all of you, you hold a very special place in my heart always, every song I write, I write for you, every breath I take is for you, I exist for you! The best is to come, I promise. I love you forever, Michael Jackson."

Michael usually signed his letters to me "Michael Jackson & family," but one he wrote, to three of us that fall, in which he told us that he loved us "to the ends of the earth," he signed, "Michael, Prince, Paris, Blanket," giving it an extra special touch.

Equally eloquent and expressive are my letters from Paris from that period, each of which she signed with her full name, and a heart over the letter *i*. One she gave me on 12 October, along with the snowflake necklace, which she described as "an early Christmas gift" from them all. She also thanked me for the decorative shoebox I'd given her and her brothers, filled with cute stationary and small toys, referring to it as a "wonderful box of happiness."

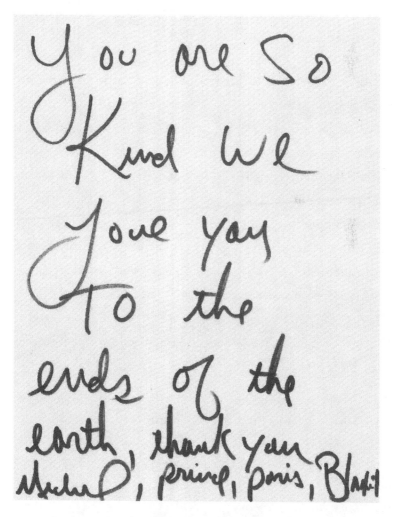

A message that Michael wrote to two followers visiting from Europe and me just after we'd met him at his home in Las Vegas, and that he had a security guard deliver to us, along with ice creams for us to enjoy, September 2008.

The following May, in Los Angeles, I put together a similar gift for the children, and this time I decorated the lid of the box with the words "Box of Happiness" in sparkly letters. The children later re-gifted that box to their personal chef, Kai Chase, with sweet notes to her inside, in a typically thoughtful gesture. And Paris used some of the stationary and stickers from it to write a letter to my friends and me, addressing it, "To the loving and kind fans," and signing it, "Lots of love, Paris & family."

In my heart, those final seven weeks in Las Vegas are contained in a box, or perhaps a bubble, of happiness, with all of my memories stored inside, of Michael and the children and the fans and the school kids and the horses and the bunnies that would pop up in the lawn in front of the elementary school across the road from Michael's house. I remember with crystal clarity how it felt to be immersed in those days of joy and sunshine, and those nights of starry magic, as I walked up and down the street with my earbuds in, listening to Michael's music, lost in the sound of his voice and the dream that I was living, for I knew even then, even before he left that house for the final time and that bubble of happiness popped and disappeared, that nothing would ever compare to the peace, tranquillity, and carefree nature of that time and place inside Michael's world.

EIGHT
In public, in private

It was a typical day in my life in the spring of 2009. While getting ready to drive to Michael's house, which was about five miles from my apartment, in the wealthy Los Angeles neighbourhood of Holmby Hills, I took the time to check my emails and clicked on one from a sender I didn't recognise. "I'm sick and tired of seeing you in every photograph of Michael," it said. "Stay away from my husband!"

I chuckled to myself, bemused but also slightly unnerved by this message from a stranger, who was no doubt referring to the dozens of paparazzi photographs of Michael and me that had appeared online over the previous months, of me in the background, smiling and looking on, or, probably more upsetting to the sender, talking to him, holding hands with him, being held by him. The email may have been amusing, and it certainly was to my friends when I shared its content with them, but it was also an unsettling reminder of how public my presence in Michael's life had become.

For most of my time in Michael's world, I had felt invisible to the fan community at large. Unlike some of the more high-profile followers, I'd never joined or frequented online fan forums, though I certainly understood and appreciated their value, and I'd never shared photos or stories of my experiences with Michael with anyone outside of my immediate circle, other than once during the trial to defend him to the press.

However, the anonymity I'd enjoyed for so long ended in early 2007, after paparazzi photographs of me with Michael at Los Angeles International Airport and, a few weeks later, the Wynn in Las Vegas appeared online. They became the subject of much scrutiny, with some fans speculating that I was everything from Michael's new nanny to his secret girlfriend, until fans who knew me intervened to set the record straight.

At first, curiosity drove me to the links that friends sent me to these discussions, where I was referred to in the early days as The Girl in the Red Coat, because of the red coat I'd been wearing at the airport, or, on Spanish forums, Little Red Riding Hood. But then I stopped reading them, because I didn't want the flattering things that were being said about me to go to my head, or the hurtful things, like that I was a stalker or that I must have been sleeping with Michael's bodyguards to get close to him, to upset me.

At the end of the day, I knew that most of the participants in these discussions had never met me and so were not talking about me personally but rather a projection of me, an image in a photograph, and forming opinions based on that. I did hear from friends about further discussions that arose, amid rumours that I was seeing Michael at his home in Las Vegas, for example, and following the two messages that he asked me to share with his fans, one during our encounter at the Green Valley Ranch in December 2007, and the other during our phone call in September 2008.

The first message, which I posted in a popular forum using Dani's login details, went as follows: "I was with Michael yesterday and he asked me to tell *all* his fans that he loves you all very much. He said, 'Tell all the fans that I love them very much…Tell them that I was very sorry that I had to postpone the event I was going to do with Al

Gore in London. We had to postpone it but we are hoping to do it next year instead.

"'I have so many exciting events planned for next year in Europe,'" it continued. "'I am going to release all the details real soon.' He says he is working on music and writing new songs all the time, and plans to release a series of singles, rather than an album, next year, 'because the music industry has changed so much and the day of going in a record store and buying an album is gone.' He and his children are looking forward to spending a magical family Christmas together."

And the second message, nine months later, read: "Michael asked me to give you all this message. He specifically asked me to put it on the Internet so that everyone hears it, so that's what I'm doing. He says, 'I love you all from the bottom of my heart. You're a quintessential part of everything I do, of everything I create. I feel your purity and innocence from all across the world. I feel your love and it inspires me to create music every day. I love you all so much.'"

Nothing, however, fuelled the online focus to the extent of the many paparazzi photographs of me with Michael that captured him out and about in Los Angeles after he moved there from Las Vegas in late October 2008. Shortly after he arrived and checked into the Hotel Bel-Air, his location was publicised and fans began to gather there, and at first, I worried that they would resent me for my apparent closeness to Michael, which I knew some people (like the sender of that irate email, one of several such messages that I received that spring and summer) did.

I had met only two of the LA-based fans once before, when they'd stopped by the house in Las Vegas one evening that fall and we'd bonded over a pizza that Michael's security team had delivered to us. And thankfully, the other fans turned out to be equally lovely. Over time, we became a unit of seven, consisting of Jill, who was originally from England and had seen Michael for the first time at his home in Encino, Los Angeles, in the 1980s, while on vacation with her family, Samantha, Talin, Arus, Yana, Angeli, and me. Jill had followed prolifically in the 1990s, and she, along with most of the other girls, had been to the courthouse to support Michael during the trial and seen him various other places over the years, but our paths had never before crossed, and I felt so grateful that they finally had.

Me looking on as Michael signed autographs outside the Hotel Bel-Air, October 2008. (Photo: National Photo Group)

After seeing Michael at the Hotel Bel-Air in October and November, I took time out to visit my family in Ireland and, after

Michael moved into his home on Carolwood Drive in Holmby Hills and it became clear that he was there to stay, to relocate to Los Angeles. It was mid-February before I became a daily presence in his world again, and over the following months, I was often joined by some or all of my new friends, as well as other American and European fans.

The other main fixtures around Michael during that time were the three employees who accompanied him wherever he went: his personal assistant and head of security, Michael Amir Williams, who he referred to as Brother Michael and who was always very poised and professional; his main bodyguard, Alberto Alvarez, who was firm but kind; and his driver, Faheem Muhammad, who had a more laid-back vibe.

Beyond us and them was another layer of people who had been absent for almost all of my time in Las Vegas, and they were the paparazzi, who we referred to as "paps," and the autograph hunters, who collected autographs from celebrities to sell. There were a couple of paps who were something of a hybrid of pap and fan. They would wait with us all day at Michael's house, and sometimes when he went out and there were no other paps around, they would put their cameras away, both because they didn't want to cut short our time with him, since the presence of cameras made him uncomfortable, and also so they could meet and talk to him as well.

Unfortunately, many of the other paparazzi, who began coming in their droves in later months, were vulgar and aggressive. They would often argue in front of Michael, and drive dangerously in pursuit of him, and one time one of them accidentally hit him on the head with his camera while he was leaving the doctor's office in Beverly Hills and getting into his SUV.

A couple of the autograph hunters were known to Michael, and he always responded to them positively. One of them was Bryan from

Canada, who I'd first seen at Los Angeles International Airport in March 2007. When Michael was planning Paris's eleventh birthday, which was on 3 April 2009 and which she insisted be a Michael Jackson-themed affair, despite his objection, he asked Bryan for vintage posters of him, similar to those that he had signed for him in the past, for use at her party, and Bryan happily obliged.

There was also an autograph hunter called Mike, who had followed Michael around New York on a bicycle as a teenager in the 1980s, and whenever Michael saw him, he would tell him that he remembered him from that time. Autograph hunters, like paparazzi, were typically demonised by fans, who accused them of using Michael as a commodity, but he didn't seem to mind signing whatever they gave him, perhaps because he knew that most of the items would likely end up in the possession of fans.

One time, I was talking to Michael through the open window of his SUV outside his house when about twenty-five autograph hunters, who had followed him back from the doctor's office, crowded around me and began passing him things to sign. "Be careful of her," he shouted at them, fearing I would get crushed, but really I was used to it and didn't mind at all. He then sat and signed an entire stack of albums, adding messages and drawings to some, while we chatted.

This became so commonplace and held him up so many times – often to the benefit of my friends and me! – that his security team eventually imposed a new policy: from then on, autograph hunters would no longer be allowed to hand items directly to Michael; they would have to hand them to Amir/Alberto/Faheem, and Michael would sign only four items per person and either keep the rest or return them unsigned. Both Bryan and Mike said that they welcomed this decision because they never asked for more than a few autographs at a time and this would dissuade those who did, and sure enough, the number of autograph hunters did seem to decline after that.

* * *

In the week after Michael arrived in LA and checked into the Hotel Bel-Air, there was a flurry of activity. He went out every day for the last five days in October, including to a Halloween store with his children, shopping on Rodeo Drive in Beverly Hills and at a Borders bookstore in Westwood, to a Kentucky Fried Chicken drive-through restaurant, and to the home of his dear friend Elizabeth Taylor.

Dani, who was visiting from Germany, and I saw him everywhere he went, and one of the photos of Michael and me, holding hands outside the Hotel Bel-Air, appeared on the homepage of the tabloid news website TMZ the next day. After that, Michael retreated, more or less until early March, and during that period, he was spotted out and about on only a few occasions, including at his doctor's office in Beverly Hills several times and at a bookstore in Santa Monica on New Year's Eve.

We did hear but not see Michael on a few occasions at the Hotel Bel-Air in November, including when we talked to him on the phone, and when he talked to us from inside his room and then sent Prince and Paris out with gifts for us all: beautiful letters from him, several red roses, and food from the Indian restaurant Chakra in Beverly Hills, where he would attend his parents' sixtieth wedding anniversary the following May. On one magical evening, he also came out himself, wearing pyjama bottoms, slippers, and dark shades, and sat inside the gate at the side entrance (an entrance that's no longer there) to talk to us all for almost an hour.

Following a trip to London in early March to announce a series of concerts, however, Michael became much more active, and I soon began seeing him almost daily, including outside his house, where he would stop and roll down his window to talk, just as he had in Las Vegas, though normally only for a minute or two, possibly because it was located near a busy street corner and so felt less private and/or because he had a much busier schedule now; outside the various studios where he was rehearsing for the concerts; at his doctor's office in Beverly Hills; out shopping on the city's Westside; and in the hotel lobby of the Wynn in Las Vegas, where he stayed for two nights in April.

I TRuly Jove all
of you I AM Recording
Tonight, for all of you, you
re My True inspiration FoReuer.
I Am living for you, and the children,
Be alive, Be free, feel Consciousness
Sub conscious, being GoD.
I love you   Michael and family

One of the letters that Michael wrote to my friends and me and that his two eldest children delivered to us at the Hotel Bel-Air in November 2008. Whenever he wrote a letter to two or more of us, we would draw lots, and the winner would keep the original and then make copies for the other recipient(s). I won this letter and kept it inside a sealed plastic bag, and when I opened that bag for the first time, more than a decade later, I was overwhelmed by the scent of Michael's cologne, which he would spray on every letter and which it had retained even after all those years.

Michael and me holding hands on his return to the Hotel Bel-Air, October 2008.
(Photo: National Photo Group)

Michael and me chatting outside the Hotel Bel-Air, October 2008.
(Photo: National Photo Group)

Once again, as well as recording every detail of every encounter, I made daily notations on my wall calendar, and it's clear from a glance that April and May were the most amazing months for me. "The seven hugs month!" I wrote on the April page, meaning he'd hugged me on seven occasions during that thirty-day period, and both months are littered with asterisks, which I reserved for days that were particularly magical.

*   *   *

One of the places where my friends and I got to meet Michael the most was at the office of his doctor, a dermatologist named Arnold Klein, on Roxbury Drive in Beverly Hills, where he went over twenty times in 2009, often staying for several hours. We later discovered that he had been going there to undergo a painful procedure to address the lasting damage caused by an accident that had occurred while he was filming a Pepsi commercial in 1984, and that had resulted in second- and third-degree burns to his scalp.

Throughout March and much of April, whenever Michael went to the doctor's office, I waited at the railing beside the back door to the building, and talked to him on his way out, and again through the open window of his SUV, where he often sat for several minutes, signing items for autograph hunters. It never occurred to me to wait inside the building, as I considered this out of bounds, but that changed on 22 April, while I was waiting there to see him with two of my friends, Yana and Angeli.

At the front of the building was a café and, after waiting for several hours, Angeli and I went there to get something to eat. Her food was ready before mine and she offered to wait, but I insisted she leave and return outside, as I didn't want to be responsible for her missing

Michael. Well, as she was walking through the building to the back door, Michael's driver, Faheem, emerged from the stairwell and whispered to her, "Wait here, he's coming. Don't tell the paps!" referring to the dozens of paparazzi who were waiting outside, with their cameras trained on the doorway.

Me chatting to Michael as he left Dr. Klein's office in Beverly Hills, March 2009.
(Photo: National Photo Group)

Angeli asked Faheem if she could tell me, and he said yes, and just at that moment, I came around the corner and he disappeared back up the stairs. We were about to call Yana when she appeared, and then the three of us waited together, giddy with excitement. A few minutes later, the door to the stairwell opened and Michael stepped out, wearing jeans and a black jacket, and exclaimed in joy at seeing us. He hugged each one of us, and then we gathered around him to chat.

Yana, who was originally from Russia and had met Michael for the first time at the Hotel Bel-Air the previous fall, showed him her tattoo, the MJ logo, as it appears on the cover of the *HIStory* album, on her hip.

"Oh, that's great!" said Michael. "Take a photo of that, Faheem." Faheem pulled out his iPhone and took a photo of it and showed it to Michael, who said, "No, get a wider shot, with her hands," so he took it again.

Then, realising that I hadn't shown Michael my tattoo in almost six years, since I'd spent a day with him at Neverland in 2003, I turned around to show it to him again.

"Oh wow, that's beautiful," he said, and then he began lowering the straps on my shoulder, which my friends took great pleasure in teasing me about later.

"It's a picture of you with an autograph underneath," I said, feeling flushed at his touch. "It's not an autograph you signed [meaning for me personally, as it was copied from a book] because I got it before I ever met you. I just wanted you to be a part of me forever. And now you are."

"Oh, that's sooo sweet, I love it," said Michael, and he had Faheem take a photograph of it too.

"Michael," said Angeli. "I wanted to ask you if you're coming to the US."

Michael just stared at her for a moment, so I intervened: "On tour, she means on tour!" and we all laughed about that afterwards, because of course we knew what she meant but it made no sense to him.

"Yeah," he said, enthusiastically. "They want me to do giant stadiums. I'm going to do a giant stadium in New York City."

Then Yana gave him a golden coin, which had a picture of him and said on one side, "The greatest entertainer in the world," and on the other, "The brightest star," and which he absolutely loved.

Our interaction ended in the usual way, with him and us expressing our love to each other. It was sweet and gentle and affectionate, typical of so many that I experienced that year, involving some or all of my six new LA friends. After that day, Michael's entourage allowed us to wait inside the building to see him, a trend that continued until late May, when too many people, including autograph hunters, began to congregate there, and they had to put a stop to it.

Another one of my more memorable encounters with Michael at the doctor's office occurred three days later, on 25 April, and while it began with the usual sweetness, it ended with us both feeling rather upset, through no fault of our own. While waiting outside Michael's house that afternoon, I sat in the back of my car attaching photographs of my friends and me to decorative sheets of paper, and writing messages to Michael to accompany them.

The photos were from an exhibition in Beverly Hills of more than 1,400 items from Neverland Valley, including the golden gates I had wept while walking through for the first time, the paintings I had searched for hidden images, on Michael's urging, the animatronic displays from the movie theatre, furnishings, clothing, awards, and so much more. It was organised by a prominent auction house called

Julien's Auctions and a man claiming to be Michael's manager called Tohme Tohme. They said they'd agreed with Michael to cancel plans to auction the items but to go ahead with the exhibition for the enjoyment of his fans.

I was still working on the card when, at around 5.30 p.m., I glanced up and saw that the gates of Michael's estate were open and one of his two Cadillac Escalades was pulling out. I leapt out of my car and the window of the SUV rolled down, and Michael leaned out, calling me to him. But the SUV kept rolling, towards Sunset Boulevard, so I ran back to my car, and as I glanced behind, I saw that there was only one fan car still parked there, whereas earlier there had been several. Inside the car sat Maria from England, who told me later that she too had been making a card for Michael so hadn't noticed the SUV emerge or my response to it. "Maria!" I shouted, before jumping back into my car to follow the SUV, which drove about two miles southeast, to the doctor's office in Beverly Hills.

I kept up as best I could, but Michael's people had him out of the SUV and inside the building before I arrived. I was certain that I was too late to see him but then I realised, to my amazement, that he was standing in the doorway waiting for me. He had waited for me!!! "I wanted to say hi to you," he said, and he reached for me and we held each other, my heart fluttering with joy. He was wearing a pair of colourful red and orange pants, and I started playing with the tassels on the waist and telling him how cute they were, making him laugh. Maria arrived then and he hugged her and told her, when she expressed surprise that he remembered her, "Of course I remember you!" Then he remarked on my Hello Kitty shoes and we talked about the love Paris and I shared of the brand.

There was a rumour that Michael was going to attend the

Neverland exhibition, and indeed some of my friends were there now, hoping that he'd make an appearance on this, the final evening. So, I asked him, "Michael, are you going to the exhibition?"

"What exhibition?" he asked.

"The Neverland exhibition," I clarified.

"Oh no, that's not happening anymore. I'm keeping all my things. That was never supposed to happen."

Maria said, "We're really happy that you're keeping everything. Michael, I went there this morning and saw my tapestry, the one I gave you three days before Prince's birthday. You had it in the children's nursery, do you remember?"

Michael looked confused. "You went to see it?"

"Yeah," said Maria, "at the exhibition."

"But the auction is called off," said Michael. "It was a big mistake. I don't even want to talk about it. It makes me so angry."

It was only then that we realised that Michael knew nothing about the exhibition, even though the entire world knew about it, even though it was happening less than two miles from his house.

"Oh," said Maria, and echoed my thoughts by saying, "I'm sorry we brought it up."

"That's okay," said Michael. "I love you guys."

I'd seen Michael upset before, but this was the first time I felt like I'd caused the upset, by bringing up the exhibition, and Maria felt likewise, though of course he had every right to know about it, and the people who were truly to blame were the ones who'd organised it, and seemingly the cancelled auction as well, without his consent. "That was never supposed to happen," he'd said. He'd been utterly betrayed, and we, his fans, had been betrayed too, as we'd been led to believe that Michael had sanctioned the exhibition, that he'd approved of it, and that he'd wanted us to go and see it. Had we known his true feelings about it, we would have boycotted it entirely.

After Michael went inside, I called my friends and told them what had happened, and when we saw Michael later, leaving the building, I handed him a note explaining that we'd assumed he'd known about the exhibition all along (which I'm sure he realised) and apologising for upsetting him, but more so for the betrayal that he had endured. I never did give him the card I had been making that day, with photos from the exhibition, and so it remains, half-finished, in my possession to this day.

*   *   *

On several occasions, Michael left the doctor's office and went shopping, and we all followed him in a convoy of cars. Sometimes, the SUVs, with the one Michael was in at the front, and the other, peopled by security guards, directly behind it, would circle Beverly Hills or West Hollywood, trailed by a long line of cars, occupied by fans, paps, and autograph hunters, driving bumper to bumper through the busy streets in a snake-like formation. We would wrap around blocks, with those at the back sometimes breaking red lights to keep up, until the two SUVs pulled up somewhere and everyone spilled out.

Michael always encouraged us to follow him; he would tell Faheem to drive slowly so that we could keep up, and sometimes tell us where he was going, so we could drive ahead of him and greet him there. Wherever he went, my six friends and I would all contact each other, in case any of us got left behind, or in case any of us weren't there but could make it to the destination on time to see him, and over time, we developed our own linguistic shorthand: "121" referred to the SUV Michael typically travelled in, as its licence plate began with those digits, while the security SUV was "122," and "randoms" referred to entourage members other than the three main guys, Amir, Alberto, and Faheem.

The shopping expedition that afforded the best opportunity to see Michael was one I missed out on almost entirely, and yet it turned out to be an experience like no other. I had given up a long time ago trying to rank my encounters, but this one occupies a singular place in my heart, not so much for its content but for its context, as described to me by two people who watched it unfold from a close vantage point.

Left to right: Alberto, Michael, and me, taken just after Michael left an antique store in Beverly Hills, April 2009. (Photo: National Photo Group)

It was 27 April and, shortly before noon, Michael had gone to the doctor's office in Beverly Hills and stayed there for about four hours. As he was leaving, he stopped to talk to six of us, including Talin, Arus, Yana, and me, inside the building. He had his children with him and he sent the older two to hug me, telling them, "Go hug Talitha," and then we all chatted for a while. He was wearing a green jacket and I admired it, and he told me that it was a gift from Dr. Klein.

"Name your top three songs," he said.

"'Speechless,' 'Will You Be There,' 'Lost Children,'" I said.

"'Speechless,'" said Talin.

"'Whatever Happens,'" said Arus.

"Am, am, am, 'Earth Song,'" I said.

Michael said, "'Speechless' is top of the list, huh?"

And we all said, "Yeaaah!"

He had handed a letter Arus had given him to Blanket, and he dropped it then and Michael bent over and picked it up, telling his youngest son, "Oh, you dropped the letter, you have to be more careful." And he walked out holding Arus's letter, which had a beautiful photograph of her on the front that the paparazzi captured, making it quite the talking point among the fan community.

After Michael left, we all scattered to our cars to follow, except Talin, who sadly had to return to work. He went to an antique store on Melrose Avenue that coincidentally shared the name of his 1979 album, *Off The Wall*, and Arus and I waited by the door to greet him as he left. Then we got back in our cars and followed him to the designer clothing store Ed Hardy, a line owned by the French fashion designer Christian Audigier, who was a friend of Michael's.

It took me a while to find a parking spot on the busy Melrose Avenue, and when I got to the store, the other fans told me that Michael had called them all to go inside with him, but only three of them had made it, including Yana. Arus and I tried signalling to Michael's entourage to ask if the rest of us could come inside too, but they ignored us, so we phoned Yana to see if she could help us, and she promised she'd try.

Michael was in the store for about thirty minutes. At first we could see him through the large storefront window, but then he went to an area at the back, out of sight. My phone rang; it was Yana. She told me to go to a big window near the back of the store, that Michael was in the restroom and that when he came out, she would tell him that we were there. Arus and I went there and waved when we saw Michael, but we didn't think he saw us, as he didn't respond.

Nobody came to get us, and when we saw the entourage escorting the children out to the SUV, we knew Michael would leave at any moment. I was disappointed, of course, and kicking myself for not getting to the store on time, but I was also happy for the fans who'd made it inside, especially Yana, and appreciated that I had been incredibly spoilt up until then and that it was okay to miss out on one opportunity to meet Michael; it wasn't the end of the world, even if it felt like it at the time!

Arus and I were walking to the front door, which was crowded with paparazzi and onlookers, so we could at least see Michael leaving, when Faheem came running out calling my name: "Talitha, Talitha, Talitha, come here!" I grabbed Arus's hand, and Faheem escorted us through the store's front door as several of the onlookers grumbled, "How come they get to go in? It isn't fair!" and one of the paps responded, "They follow him everywhere. You go girls!" Faheem led us to Michael, who was engaging in conversation with Yana, telling her, "Oh, I wrote a story just like that one time," which she later told me was in reference to a short film she'd made at film school.

"We need to go, you have one minute," Amir whispered in my ear as I approached, and then Michael came and wrapped his arms around me, making me melt. The encounter had the same heavenly quality as so many I'd experienced, and ended with Michael telling me that he was going to sing "The Lost Children" for me on stage in London, as he knew it was one of my favourite songs. I withdrew when I heard Amir calling my name, and for a moment it didn't look like Arus would get to say hi to Michael because another fan was blocking her way, so I said, pushing her forward, "Michael, this is Arus. This is my friend Arus. Say hi to Arus." And he wrapped his arms around her, and then said, "Hi, Arus, bye, Arus," making her laugh.

My interaction with Michael was as glorious as ever, but it was hearing accounts from Yana and the autograph hunter Bryan, who were both inside the store with him, that earned it an extra special place in my heart. When we got back to the house, we all gathered around Yana to hear the details of her encounter with Michael. She told us that when she first went into the store, she felt too shy to talk to him, and that he was on the phone for a lot of the time.

After we called her, she told Michael Amir that we were outside and asked him if we could come in, and he said, "Oh, that's not for me to decide." So, she asked him if she could ask Michael, and he said, "Oh, come on, don't do that. They see him a lot. They'll have plenty of other chances. Just enjoy your time here." I don't think Amir had anything against us, but he just couldn't be bothered helping us, and wanted to get Michael in and out of the store as quickly as possible and keep him on schedule.

As time went on, Yana became braver and began talking to Michael, and he told her several things about the tour, including that he planned to perform the song "Human Nature" and that the show would be three hours long. When he came out of the restroom, she thought he would see Arus and me, waving to him through the window, where she'd told us to stand, but he was speaking with the store manager and so didn't notice us there. When he was alone again, she approached and said, "Look at the window, Michael. The girls are over there. Talitha is there." Michael said, "Who?" Yana said, "Talitha," and Michael responded, "Talitha is there?"

Then she said he went to one side, so that he could look out and see us but we couldn't see him. And then he began saying, "I want Talitha. Talitha's there. I want Talitha. I want Talitha. I want Talitha." She said he kept saying it, over and over again, and Amir responded, "Sir, we have to go now. The children are waiting." And Michael said, "No, I want Talitha. Where's Talitha?" Amir said, "Oh, you want Talitha? Sorry, I didn't hear you say that." He said he'd get me, and then Faheem said he'd get me, but while Faheem was gone, Amir again tried to get Michael to leave, but Michael would take a few steps and then stop and say, "Where's Talitha? I want Talitha. I'm waiting for Talitha." Yana said to me, "He was like a child in a candy store: 'I'm not leaving until I get my lollipop!'"

As she was telling this story, standing on the sidewalk outside Michael's house, I was squealing in delight and disbelief, and the other girls laughed at my reaction, telling me, "Well, you know he totally loves you." And I did know it, but I could never quite believe it, the way you know dinosaurs existed but it's difficult to wrap your head around the fact that our planet was once inhabited by these giant beasts. The confirmation of that love was always surprising to me, no matter how many times it happened or in how many different ways. It was the reason why Talin had nicknamed me Dory, after the amnesiac fish in the film *Finding Nemo*, because I'd met Michael more times than anyone she knew but reacted with so much joy every time that it was like I'd forgotten every past encounter and thought I was meeting him for the first time.

The next day, Michael went to the doctor's office again, and while I was waiting for him, I went to the café to get something to eat. Bryan came in and told me about his time in the store with Michael. He said he couldn't believe how much Michael had wanted to see me, how insistent he'd been, and that he had never seen him like that before, so firm with Amir. He said the impression he'd got was that Michael had felt that I belonged in the store with him, not standing outside. He said, "Everyone always says, 'Michael really loves Talitha,' but this was the first time I got to see it for myself."

In the years that followed, in the blackness of my grief, such was the enormity of my loss that I tried to repress all of my memories of Michael and downplay his feelings for me. I would tell myself that he behaved the way he did towards me not because he loved me and wanted me around, but because he knew that I loved him and wanted to make me happy. But then this encounter would come back to me, cutting through that denial. When Yana had pointed me out to him, he could have just waved and pointed at me, which would in itself have evoked a Dory-like response of excitement, but he had wanted to see me, so much so that he'd refused to leave the store until his entourage had come and got me and brought me to him.

This, and other accounts from other people, let me know that Michael loved me even when I wasn't there, and acted that way even when it wasn't for my benefit, through expressions that were out of my sight and earshot. A few years after his passing, the bodyguard Bill, who had worked for him in Las Vegas and been with him at the Green

Valley Ranch resort in December 2007, reached out to me via email. He told me that Michael had always referred to me as his friend and that whenever he'd seen me out and about, he would tell his security team, "Let her in. She's okay. She's with me."

Also, a week after Michael's passing, his nephew Taj Jackson returned a letter I'd given to Michael, with photographs of a friend and me, that he'd found in the bedroom of his LA home. And months later, a family friend called me from the last house where Michael had lived in Las Vegas, on Palomino Lane. He told me that he was there with Michael's father, Joseph, that he was helping him to clear it out, and that he'd just found a photo of me on Michael's bedside dresser. It was a photo I'd given him of Joanna and me, taken outside his house, and on the back I'd written a cheeky message, referring to us as his girls, which of course we all were.

He loved me when I wasn't there, and he loved my friends too, and always kept us close. He told us repeatedly and emphatically how much we all meant to him, and his make-up artist, Karen Faye, told us LA girls that he'd had a photo of the seven of us in the dressing room of the last studio where he rehearsed, the Staples Center in Downtown LA. His love for us, for all of his fans, was as real as our love for him, the bond equally heartfelt and absolute.

*　　*　　*

Michael went out on ten days in March, twenty-two in April, and nineteen in May, and he stopped to talk to us everywhere he went, often two, three, four times a day. It was an amazing time to be around him, and we LA-based fans were all very lucky. As well as availing of these opportunities to see him in public, I also had four encounters with him in private that I owe entirely to my friendship with Robert*

*Not his real name

from England, who I'd met for the first time in Tokyo in early 2007 and who'd visited the house in Las Vegas in late 2008 several times. As well as being an avid fan of Michael's, Robert was also a lifelong collector of memorabilia related to him, and when he gifted him with rare and collectible items in Las Vegas, Michael responded with so much enthusiasm that he decided to bring him more – a lot more.

Having secured a private meeting with Michael at the Hotel Bel-Air to present him with boxfuls of memorabilia in October, Robert came to Los Angeles again in late November, and this time he invited me to come and see Michael with him, a gift that I will never be able to repay. On 28 November 2008, the day after Thanksgiving, Michael Amir escorted Robert and me into a suite at the Hotel Bel-Air to wait for Michael. Normally, whenever I met Michael, it was in a sense unexpected, as I never knew when he might emerge, but while waiting in that room, I knew that I was going to see him at any moment, for a prolonged time, in an intimate setting. My heart was racing with excitement, but as soon as he appeared, with his three children, his presence filled the room and a sense of tranquillity washed over me.

After Amir left, Michael greeted us both, shaking Robert's hand and enfolding me in a warm embrace, and we said hi to the children, who sat down on the sofa with their dad. It had been over two weeks since I'd seen Michael, which felt like a long time then, a testament to how spoilt I'd become, and all of my senses drank him in: how he looked, how he moved, how he sounded, how he smelled. He was wearing a long black dress coat and dark shades, looking every bit the superstar.

It is strange, and obviously offensive, to me when people make fun of Michael's appearance, which they often do based on distorted photographs of him published in tabloids, because in person, he was beautiful, and it wasn't only fans like me who thought so. While waiting to see him at the Palace hotel in New York in the early 2000s, one of the employees there, a middle-aged man, had come out to talk to my friends and me, and he had said, "I don't care what people say about him. When you see him, you know that he's beautiful. He has a beautiful aura. He's actually beautiful inside and out."

Once Michael and the children had settled down, I asked them how they were enjoying their stay at the hotel, and Michael said, "Hmm, I like it except for the spiders. We call it 'The Spider Hotel.' There are spiders everywhere!" This initiated a funny conversation about arachnids, during which the children tried to scare me with their descriptions of the apparently enormous spiders that occupied the hotel grounds. I reminded Michael of the spider bite on his leg that he'd shown my friends and me at Neverland five years earlier, and he said he liked tarantulas, like the ones at his zoo, but "not the little ones. You can't see them coming!"

We continued chatting as Robert unloaded the boxes of memorabilia and presented it to Michael, and some of the items triggered memories from my childhood, like the range of soft toys that came out in the late 1980s, called Michael's Pets. I told Michael that I had had the pet Bubbles, fashioned after his pet chimpanzee of that name, as a little girl and that I'd slept with it every night. And when Robert gave Michael merchandise related to the 1978 film *The Wiz*, I shared with him my first memory of him, seeing him as the Scarecrow and not knowing who he was. "And you didn't know it was me?" he said, intrigued. "But you loved the Scarecrow." He seemed to consider that, perhaps appreciating its significance, that I loved him even before I knew who he was.

Michael had never revealed to his children who he was to

the world, the magnitude of his fame, but now that they were getting older, they were beginning to grasp it and were curious to see all of the memorabilia related to him, Paris in particular.

As Robert presented it, Michael remarked, "I don't show them all this stuff."

"Why?" I asked. "You should."

And Paris responded, "Yeah, we want to see it, Daddy!"

He then told us he was working on some new merchandise, including a pair of branded trainers by Nike.

After being cooped up in the hotel for weeks, the children were bursting with energy. They kept climbing over the furniture, and Michael kept reprimanding them and apologising to us. I chatted with them as much as I did with Michael, and at one point, I asked Paris what she was getting from Santa.

"Oh, I don't believe in Santa," she said.

"Oh, really?" I responded, surprised, and Michael exclaimed, "I can't believe you said that!"

"But *you* believe in Santa, don't you?" I said to her younger brother, Blanket.

"No, I don't," said Blanket, proudly.

"I can't believe you guys," said Michael, shaking his head.

"I believe in Michael," said Blanket, and giggled.

"Oh, so do I," I said. "He's better than Santa."

"But Daddy's not as much fun as Santa," said Blanket, and Michael laughed hard as I argued to the contrary.

Michael repeatedly thanked Robert for the merchandise, telling him he was "the Man," and he kept telling me that he loved me. "You're always so good to us," he said. "I love you. We all do." Just before we left, we posed for a photograph together, my first posed photograph alone with him, and he hugged me tightly and then turned me around to face the camera, and I leaned my head against his chest and listened, for the first and last time, to the sound of his heart beating, a heart that radiated all the light and love in the universe, that sustained the life of a man who was almost too good, too pure, too beautiful to behold.

*   *   *

Although my encounters with Michael were the central element of my time in his world, the thing I spent most of my time doing was waiting – waiting for Michael. I waited entire days outside his hotels and houses without seeing him, sometimes in the latter case all alone, and would pass the time by hanging out with my friends when they were there, working on writing assignments, making cards and letters for Michael and his children, and daydreaming about all that had been and might yet be. It wasn't always easy and, of course, I felt terribly bored and restless at times, but even when the part of me that is in need of constant distraction wanted to leave, the deeper part of me wanted to stay.

I had the opportunity to go to Michael every day for months at a time in 2007, 2008, and 2009, and yet I never lost sight of the fact that this was the exception rather than the norm, that just to be in proximity of him, to co-exist with the possibility of seeing him at any moment, was a rare and precious gift. While waiting to see him, to no avail, outside his house on the corner of Carolwood Drive and Sunset Boulevard in Holmby Hills for over a week in February 2009, I often thought of a line from his book *Dancing the Dream*: "[T]he steps of his house seemed softer than any pillow." To this day, I would rather be sitting on the steps of Michael's home, waiting to see him, than lying on a bed of rose petals, endowed with all the riches of the world.

Me delivering a gift from my friends and me for Blanket on his seventh birthday, at the gates of Michael's home in Holmby Hills, February 2009.

My wait to see Michael ended around 9 p.m. on 23 February, when Robert had his next meeting with him, this time inside the Holmby Hills house, which he and his children had moved into shortly before Christmas. The front gates, which were still hung with Christmas wreaths, a mark of Michael's love for the festive season, swung open, and I drove inside. Two security guards directed me to park on the right, next to a fountain, and then helped us to unload the suitcases and boxes of memorabilia from my car and carry them to the house.

A man in a floppy white chef's hat opened the door to greet us, and we stepped into a large foyer that led off to a grand staircase and several rooms, including one at the far end with a piano, and two living rooms, one on each side. The man, who introduced himself as the head chef, led us into the living room on the left and offered us a drink, which we politely declined. At the other end of the room was a glowing fireplace, hung with a lavish Christmas wreath, and between two sofas was a coffee table topped with books about art, and a globe I recognised from the library at Neverland, with a plaque dedicated to the *Thriller* album mounted at the base.

Michael, accompanied by Prince, descended the staircase, wearing his signature fedora, a black jacket, and a pair of eyeglasses, and once again, I felt the soothing effect of his presence as it swept into the room. In that blissful period of my life, people often told me that I was naïve, and in retrospect, I do believe that the light of Michael's energy blinded me to the darkness of the world. But even those who were far more hardened and cynical than I would ever become often spoke about Michael's aura as an almost tangible thing. It was so powerful that even if I'd lost all of my senses, I still would have known when he was close by, because I would have felt his presence, deep in my soul.

As Michael greeted us, with a hug for me and a handshake for Robert, he made a point of telling us that Paris and Blanket were on their way, and sure enough, they entered the room a few moments later, wearing matching red promotional t-shirts from the musical *Annie*, which they said they'd all seen and enjoyed very much. We chatted about Christmas and the recent birthdays of the two boys, as Prince had turned twelve on 13 February, and Blanket seven on 21 February, and the Oscars, which had been on the previous night and which Michael said they'd all watched together. "Daddy guessed right for every nomination winner," said Paris, proudly. "He knew who was going to win in every category!"

Then Robert began presenting the memorabilia, while Michael sat in the armchair at one end of the coffee table, with Prince perched beside him, we sat on one of the sofas, and Paris and Blanket sat on the other, across from us. "I know you find it hard to believe," said Michael, after Robert had presented him with a rare Jackson 5 game, "but I don't get all this stuff. I'm too busy doing other things so I don't get time to collect it." Robert asked him what he was going to do with it and he said he wanted to open a museum and display it all there. He and the children responded enthusiastically to many of the items, and Michael said about Paris, "She wants a Michael Jackson theme for her birthday party. I said *no*, but that's what she wants."

I looked across at Paris, who was reading a passage from the *Moonwalker* colouring book to Blanket. She was a few years younger than I had been when I'd begun collecting Michael Jackson memorabilia, and so I could relate to her fascination with it all. When Robert handed her a cushion adorned with an image of her father's face, she held it to her, with an expression of serenity that seemed far beyond her years, and I understood in that moment the depth of her love for him, which was all the love I held in my heart layered upon that of a dear and devoted daughter. It was a scene that would come to haunt me, when I considered in later months the unfathomable nature of her loss.

When we'd last seen them all, at the Hotel Bel-Air in November, Paris had told me, with obvious regret, that she'd never seen *The Wiz*, and when I'd asked her why, she'd said, "Daddy won't let me watch it." But this time, when Robert presented memorabilia related to the film, Michael told me, "They've seen that now."

"Oh my goodness," I said. "You finally let them watch *The Wiz*!"

"Yeah," said Michael. "Paris tricked me. She pulled a fast one."

"Why, what did she do?" I asked to a chorus of laughter.

"Oh, she got around me," said Michael, and the children began chattering about how much they loved the film and what their favourite scenes were.

"I love the part with the flying monkeys," said Paris.

"And I love it when The Wiz keeps changing his collar," said Prince.

Michael and me, inside the foyer of his home in Holmby Hills, February 2009.

Later, *The Wiz* came up again and, my curiosity piqued, I asked Paris, "How did you do it?" She giggled and, shaking his head with laughter, Michael told me, "I told her she could pick any video she wanted. It was her night to pick. And she said, 'Really? Anything? Anything for children?' And I said, 'Perfect. If it's for children, that's perfect.' And she said she wanted to see *The Wiz*. She tricked me!"

Michael was the biggest superstar on the planet, with millions of fans, but he was himself a fan of many artists, especially those associated with the Golden Age of Hollywood. Knowing his affection for the 1930s' child star Shirley Temple, Robert gave him a book and several magazines about her, to which he responded enthusiastically. He said he'd met her once, in San Francisco, and I asked him what that was like.

He paused for a moment and then said, "She was embarrassed. She was shy."

"Oooh, because of who you are?" I said, assuming it was because she'd felt intimidated by the level of his fame.

"She asked me if I felt ashamed of her," he said.

"Ashamed?" I responded, perplexed. "But why? Why would you feel ashamed of her?"

"She thought I'd gone there expecting to meet the little girl."

"Aw, so you knew how she felt then," I said, as I remembered him describing in his autobiography *Moonwalk* how he'd felt when his brothers had brought fans to meet him and they'd been disappointed that he was no longer the cute little boy they'd expected, but a gangly teenager suffering from acne.

"Yes, I did," said Michael. "But I hadn't gone there to meet the little girl. I'd gone there to meet the woman."

Robert gave Michael a stack of magazines with him on the cover, including the *Hello* magazine published in 2000 with a photograph of him and Elizabeth Taylor on the front, accompanied by the words, "Elizabeth and Michael – A very special love." "Look, look," he said, showing it to his children, to whom she was godmother to the eldest two. Michael often talked about Elizabeth, who, although he never said as much, I believe was his soul mate, owing in part to the affinity they shared as former child stars. In November, when he'd come out to talk to us all for an hour at the Hotel Bel-Air, he'd told us that he was planning to build a house next to hers, in the city of Bel Air, so that he could take care of her.

Prompted by the sight of the *Hello* magazine, which he passed to me to see, I asked him now, "How is Elizabeth, Michael?" He said nothing for a while, just stared into the distance, and I was afraid that I'd upset him by asking, but then he said, "She's in and out of the hospital. She sneaks in and out without anyone knowing. I shouldn't really be telling you that." "That's okay, I won't tell anyone," I promised, feeling sad at the potential loss of his dearest friend, who was in her late seventies and said to be in failing health, though as it turned out, she would outlive him by almost two years.

Our time with Michael and the children might have gone on all night had it not been for a phone call from Michael Amir. A security guard came and handed the phone to Michael, saying, "Michael Amir wants you to know you have a telephone conference," and Michael, after listening for a few moments, said into the phone, "Here's [Robert]," and handed it to him.

As Robert later told me, Amir said, "Michael has an important phone conference. I need you to help me. You help me, I'll help you. Wrap this thing up."

"Okay, should I give the phone back to Michael?" Robert asked.

"No, no, no. Hand it to security."

Normally, it was Michael who initiated the conclusion of our time together, gently explaining to us that he had to go, but when Robert relayed Amir's message to Michael, he seemed entirely disinterested, leading to a bizarre scenario in which we had to try to end our visit, despite his apparent reluctance to do so.

When it came to these private visits, Amir was the middleman between Michael and us, and so we knew it was important to appease him, even if this meant acting contrary to our natural inclination, which was to spend as much time as possible with Michael. Taking the signal from Robert, I began emptying the remaining items from the suitcases, which lay open in front of the fireplace, and moving them into the foyer, as Robert sat down in front of Michael and explained, "Michael, that was Michael Amir. You have an important phone conference. I don't want to keep you from your business." "Oh, okay," said Michael, and just went on looking at the memorabilia and chatting with us. Finally, after repeated urgings from Robert, he got up and excused himself to use the restroom, promising us he'd be right back.

I wheeled the empty suitcases out to the car but when I tried to go back inside, a security guard stood blocking my way. It was clear that he was in cahoots with Amir in trying to end our visit and keep Michael on schedule, but when Michael came back and saw me there, he reprimanded the guard, saying, "What is she doing outside in the freezing cold?" I stepped back into the foyer and our visit concluded in the usual way, with more hugs and chatter and posed photographs, including one that Prince took of Michael, Robert, and me together, all beaming into the camera.

Robert's next visit with Michael was at a studio in Burbank, called CenterStaging, in April, and the final one was once again inside the house, on the evening of 16 May 2009, and though shorter than the first, it progressed in much the same manner. This time, the house was filled with the sound of music, and we heard Michael before we saw him, telling someone upstairs, "I love that song. That's one of my favourite songs. I love it. Turn it up, turn it up!" Moments later, he glided into the room, wearing a studded jacket and shades, bopping to a song by The Temptations. Throughout our visit, my focus shifted back and forth between the children, who wanted to show me the Lego scale models they'd been working on, and Michael, who was standing in front of the fireplace with Robert, as he unloaded the memorabilia and showed it to him.

Michael and me, inside the living room of his home in Holmby Hills, May 2009.

I played with the three children, admiring Prince's yellow digger and Paris's pirate ship, both intricate models with lots of moving parts, and bounced the ball that Prince had made from rubber bands and that they told me they were using as "a basement detector." And then I drifted over to Michael, who offered me candy and asked to see my tattoo again after catching sight of it. He talked to us about his plans for London and told us he was buying a house in Las Vegas and wanted to have us over for dinner there.

As the visit wound down, we once again posed with him for a series of photographs, including a group shot captured by Paris, and then Michael held me for a long time and I told him in an outpouring of emotion how much I loved him and how proud of him I was. As Robert and I left, he and the children lined up at the door, waving and blowing us kisses, and, with all of us blissfully unaware of the nightmare that would play out there only weeks later, Prince said confidently, "See you next time!"

*   *   *

My memories of that final stretch of time, from when Michael moved to Los Angeles in late October 2008 until his life ended there in late June 2009, have a very different quality to all others related to him. Every other series of recollections, whether associated with the *HIStory* tour or Neverland Valley or my first year in Las Vegas, is contained inside its own bubble of time, that began and ended with my heart whole and intact, but that final period is attached to the end, and, in my mind, it is weighed down by it.

Nonetheless, these memories of Michael are precious to me, as are the mementoes relating to them: the many photographs that captured us together, in public and in private, and the many letters and messages that he wrote to my friends and me during that time. If I had to point to a favourite image from our final weeks together, it would perhaps be one taken on 21 April, when Michael left the doctor's office and went shopping once again, and Robert and I caught up with him in an alleyway in Beverly Hills, as he walked from one store to another. Flanked by his entourage and preceded by a cluster of paparazzi who were capturing his every move, he stopped suddenly, curled an arm around me, and drew me to him.

Under an umbrella: Michael holding me in an alleyway in Beverly Hills, April 2009. (Photo: National Photo Group)

He was wearing a surgical mask that he'd most likely got at the doctor's office, a veil, and a fedora, and was holding an open umbrella over his head to shield himself from the gaze of the cameras and the glare of the sun, which was potentially deadly to him, because people with vitiligo are highly susceptible to skin cancer. But in the image, his eyes are visible and they're directed at me as I lean in to him, with a huge smile on my face. My posed photos with Michael are lovely, but so are the paparazzi photos, because they capture us in a moment of spontaneity, and this one, in my mind, represents above all Michael's shyness, a quality so sweet and tender that it made my heart ache. It suggests that while he tried to keep the world – the prying, scrutinising, scathing world – out, he let me in, a privilege that I will never feel worthy of but be eternally grateful for.

As well as writing letters to my friends and me while at the Hotel Bel-Air, Michael would sometimes return letters or photos I'd given him with messages written across them, and he wrote me a beautiful message for my thirty-second birthday, on 25 February 2009. Among my most treasured messages are a set he wrote to Yana, Angeli, and me on 6 May, after we'd met him at his house, the studio, and then the doctor's office. We'd overtaken him on his way back to the studio and when he arrived, his SUV stopped and Alberto held something out of the window.

At first, none of us responded, as we assumed it was for the autograph hunters who had been around earlier, but then Alberto said, "It's for you guys!" and so I approached and took it. When I saw what it was, a series of messages written by Michael on sheets of lined paper torn from a notebook and pages ripped from magazines – telling us he simply adored us and that he loved us "sooo much" – I began squealing in delight, and then the girls saw what it was and joined in. And I always imagine how that must have felt to Michael, to be the cause of such excitement as he drove into the studio, where he was preparing to transform into the superstar who could drive an audience into a state of hysteria with a single gesture or move.

A photo of Michael and me, taken inside a hotel suite at the Hotel Bel-Air, that I gave to him in the spring of 2009, with a message on the back, and that he later returned to me, signed from him with love.

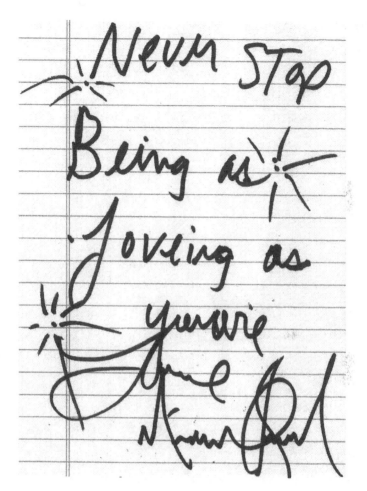

One of my many beautiful messages from Michael that I will cherish forever.

*   *   *

Taken in isolation, without the context of what was to come, and omitting the deep concern and sense of foreboding that came to define my final days around Michael, my only negative experience during that period in Los Angeles began on 16 May, when I became the target of intense jealousy. That jealousy had been bubbling under the surface for a long time, but it was that final visit inside the house, to which no other fan gained access throughout the time that Michael lived there (that is to say, nobody there in the capacity of a fan, as certainly, many of the employees and associates who entered would have categorised themselves as such!), that unleashed it.

When Robert and I had first entered the house, on 23 February, only two of our friends, who we trusted implicitly, had been outside the gates when we'd driven through them. But in May, we walked through the gates, escorted by Faheem, under the gaze of several fans. This led to ramifications that Robert and I had gone to great lengths to avoid, by keeping secret our February visit, and by downplaying our time with Michael at the Hotel Bel-Air in November and CenterStaging studios in April. These measures weren't for the benefit of our friends, who were always supportive and happy for us, but for those few who had been demonstrably resentful towards us, and me in particular. Following the visit, they expressed anger and frustration at us but also at Michael, for what they perceived as ongoing favouritism.

I can't say that any of this came as a surprise to me, as I'd seen it many times before. I had seen certain fans lie to their so-called best friends to exclude them from an opportunity to see Michael, out of a sense of one-upmanship, and fans turn on those who they perceived to be getting "too close" to him. Absolutely, Michael loved all of his fans, but absolutely, he connected with some more than others, and this was only natural because he was human, and anyone would connect with some more than others from any given group.

I accept that it wasn't fair that some fans had more opportunities to see him than others (though if you met him even once, you were luckier than most people on the planet) or that he responded to some more favourably than others, and it was natural to feel an emotion similar to envy but without the underlying resentment, to wish that you had the same opportunity or evoked the same response.

I had felt envious in that sense in Munich in 1999, of fans who had met Michael when this was for me an as of yet unfulfilled dream, and when people told me that they were envious of me a decade later, I understood what they meant and respected their honesty; I feel envious of that past version of me now. I wish I could be her again, if only for a moment, to experience the joy I once knew.

Envy in this sense was natural within that world, but some fans couldn't stop that envy mutating into something bordering on hatred, which they directed at the cause of it, in this case, Robert and me, and, to a lesser extent, Michael. They seemed to be fixated on our relationship with him, rather than their own, and to have lost all sense of the wonder of being around him, which they surely must have wished for with the same fervour as I had as a young girl living in the Irish countryside, gazing up at the stars.

The fan world was highly emotive, and it brought out the worst in people, but it also brought out the best in people, and in those final weeks, I saw displays of tremendous strength of character, at times when it would have been all too easy to become infected with the jealousy that pervaded. When Robert and I emerged from Michael's estate on the evening of 16 May, some of the fans came straight over to congratulate us, including a French couple who later texted us to say: "Lucky, lucky, lucky. We envy you two but we are so happy for you." And the next day, Talin called me to say that she knew some fans were unhappy about our visit but that she definitely wasn't one of them, which of course we already knew.

Another tendency I had observed over the years was for fans to express their jealousy by relaying the experiences of others in a way that lessened their content in terms of quantity and quality, but if anything, my friends, so devoid of jealousy were they, went to the opposite extreme. One evening in June, I was waiting for Michael outside a venue in Inglewood called The Forum with Talin and Angeli when they began recalling an encounter I'd had with him at the doctor's office a few weeks earlier.

After Michael had emerged from the staircase and stopped to sign some items for autograph hunters, I had walked with him around the corner into a wall of cameras, which were filling the doorway, from floor to ceiling. "I'm really embarrassed, Talitha," Michael had said, and then he'd repeated it several times. "I'm embarrassed. I'm embarrassed. I'm so embarrassed." And, with my heart aching, not quite knowing how to comfort him, I'd responded, "Oh Michael, don't be embarrassed. It's okay, they're all here for you. I'm here for you too."

When recalling this exchange outside The Forum, the girls kept calling me Michael's "girlfriend," and I guffawed and said, "Girls, come on! If I'm his girlfriend, what am I doing out here in the cold?" And they said, "Well, we know it's not like that but there is something special between you and Michael. You're like his comfort zone, his security blanket. He feels so comfortable with you." It was one of the sweetest assessments anyone had ever made of my relationship with Michael, one that defied categorisation, as I believe did his relationship with all of his fans, which was based on a soul-to-soul connection, and, in my case, in my mind, had a fairy-tale-esque quality.

Had I been surrounded by fans of a different nature in LA, my time there might have been tainted by the jealousy and tension that emerged towards the end, but those girls created an atmosphere around Michael that was harmonious and loving during what would prove to be his final months on earth, and I will forever love them for that.

As an aside, I do realise that we were all women, and not girls, but I refer to us as such because everyone did, including Michael, and for my own part, I feel like I was more girl and less woman in that context, because, even at the age of thirty-two, I maintained an innocence that would soon be shattered, as the world I'd known since childhood collapsed and I was plunged into a different reality, one in which evil lurked in the shadows and, in the space of a heartbeat, I was forced to grow up in the cruellest of ways.

NINE

This Is It

n 3 March 2009, shortly after 7 a.m. Pacific Standard Time, my phone rang. It was Michael. He had left Los Angeles the previous night on a flight to London, amid rumours that he was planning to announce a series of concerts there. "I just landed," he said, and I laughed and said, "And I just woke up." I asked him how his flight was and how the children, who I could hear chattering in the background, were, and then I said, "Michael, are you *really* doing thirty shows in London?" "Oh well," he teased, "I'm going to announce something... You'll see!" Two days later, I watched live on television as he took to the stage at London's O2 Centre for a press conference to confirm that, for once, the rumours about him were well-founded, though initially only ten concerts were planned.

When Michael returned to LA, on 8 March, four of the LA girls and I waited to greet him at a private terminal located at Los Angeles International Airport, called Landmark Aviation. We watched his plane land and, almost an hour later, his two SUVs emerge, but unfortunately he was being escorted by two squad cars, and so for once he didn't stop to say hi to us. We jumped in our cars to drive back to his house and, after the squad cars had departed, the two SUVs split up and I ended up behind the one Michael normally travelled in, aka 121, driving east on Wilshire Boulevard.

As we approached a major intersection, the traffic light turned red, and after a moment's hesitation, I did something I hadn't done since

I'd followed Michael around LA with my friends in the early 2000s: I unbuckled my seat belt, jumped out of my car, and approached the back window of the SUV, and to my absolute joy, the window slid down, revealing Michael inside with his three children.

I gushed with delight at seeing them all again and told Michael how proud I'd felt of him while watching the press conference. It had been the first time in years he'd participated in a live televised appearance, and all the hype surrounding it had served as a reminder of the magnitude of his fame. "I got up early to watch the press conference and I was thinking, 'That's my Michael!' I couldn't believe it," I said, making him laugh. I relayed some messages from my friends in England, and the children showed me miniature airplanes they'd made during their flight home.

"Oh, be careful of the traffic," said Michael, as the motorists in the next lane moved forward to turn left, and I can only imagine what they must have been thinking, seeing a car abandoned on the road behind an SUV with a girlish figure leaning in its back window. When Michael returned to the house, the security guards waved us inside the gates and, as we stood chatting to him through the open windows of his SUV, he asked us repeatedly, referring to his announcement about the tour, "Was it a surprise?" and we all assured him that yes, it most definitely was.

Over the following months, Michael went to several different studios in Los Angeles to prepare for the concerts, which soon ballooned in number from ten to fifty, and were to be part of a tour titled *This Is It*. On two days in late March, he went to a dance studio in Van Nuys, and on 28 March, he went to a studio in Burbank called CenterStaging, where he went on a total of twenty-two days between then and the end of May, and where he often stayed for six, seven, or eight hours at a time. On two evenings in May, he also went to a nearby sound design studio, on Magnolia Boulevard.

Left to right: Angeli, Talin, me, and Arus waiting to greet Michael on his return from London, with gifts of balloons, sunflowers, and handmade cards, at Los Angeles International Airport, March 2009.

On 15 April, he went to the Nokia Theatre (now the Microsoft Theatre) in Downtown LA to audition about sixty male and sixty female dancers for his upcoming tour. And on four days in early June, he went to Culver Studios, a movie studio in Culver City, to work on a video production to be included in the concerts. It was during this same period that he began rehearsing at a venue in Inglewood called The Forum, where he went on eleven days in June, before relocating to the Staples Center in

Downtown LA, where he rehearsed on the last two nights of his life.

*   *   *

I met Michael outside every one of the studios where he rehearsed for the This Is It tour in 2009, and inside one of them, but by far, the one where my friends and I met him the most was CenterStaging. The first time he went there, on 28 March, I waited for him with two other fans, Talin and Yana, and the autograph hunter Mike. When Michael emerged, he rolled down the window of his SUV to say hi to us, and then he reached out and wove his fingers through mine and said, "Thank you, Talitha, for everything you've done for us. I love you so much." This initiated a particularly gushy exchange, and all the while, he continued to entangle my fingers and caress my hand with his thumb.

After expressing my love in various ways, I said, "Michael, I can't stop listening to your music now and imagining you on stage."

"Really?" he said. "Which songs are you listening to?"

"I'm listening to the Brunei concert. Oh Michael, there's this thing you do at the end of 'Earth Song.' Do you remember?"

"No, what did I do?"

"Oh, you do this a capella thing. Oh my God, it's amazing. I'm obsessed with it. You have to do it in London at the end of 'Earth Song.' You have to. It's so powerful."

I promised to give him a copy of the audio, which was from the royal concert he did in Brunei in 1996, and when Talin told him he also had to include the song "Speechless" in the set list, he sang us a line from it, making us all squeal.

Afterwards, I felt bad because I knew I had dominated our time with Michael, something I always tried to avoid doing, ever cognisant of all the time I'd already had with him, but when he had enfolded my hand in his, I had got carried away and forgotten for a moment that anyone else was there. I tried apologising to the two girls, but they wouldn't hear of it, and Talin told me, "That was awesome. You have to do that every time. None of us can talk to him like that. You made him stay for ages. We're just happy to be there with him longer and hear his voice."

I was so happy and relieved by their response, and from then on, whenever Michael went to the studio, he would stop to say hi to us on his way in, and then we would wait outside, usually for several hours, leaving only to get food or use the restroom. When anyone saw Michael's SUV approaching the gates, they would shout, "This is it!" and we would all gather at the open windows to chat with him, and if there was a lull in the conversation, one of the girls would inevitably elbow me or whisper in my ear, "Say something else, keep him talking!"

Obviously, we talked a lot about the tour, such as in the following exchange, from 24 April, when there was a cluster of us fans on one side of the SUV, and a cluster of autograph hunters on the other. One of the girls held up a sign she'd made that said, "Fans this side," and when Michael saw it, he turned and gave us all of his attention.

"How is everything going with the show?" Maria asked him.

"Oh great, I'm working really hard," he said.

After a momentary distraction from the other side, he caught sight of Talin and asked her, "What song did you want me to sing?" and she said "'Speechless.'"

"'Speechless,'" Michael repeated. "I'm going to do it but I'm going to alternate it with 'Stranger in Moscow.'"

"Oh," I said, "you're going to have different set lists."

He nodded. "I'm going to switch back and forth between them."

Talin said, "We're so happy you're going to sing that song."

And I asked, "Are you going to do 'Earth Song?'"

"Well, you know, I *always* do 'Earth Song,'" he replied.

"And what about 'Man in the Mirror?'" asked Talin.

"I always do that one too," said Michael, even though this wasn't strictly true, as he hadn't performed it on the *HIStory* tour.

Following a brief silence, Arus whispered to me to say something else, so I told him that a story had appeared in a newspaper in Ireland saying that he was going to perform there, and asked him if this were true.

"Oh, I love Ireland," he said. "I have such an affinity with the country…"

"Yeah, but are you going to play there?" I asked again.

"I don't know yet," he said. "We haven't committed to anything. I'm getting a lot of requests. The Giants Stadium in New York City wants me to play there. China are asking me."

"*China?*" I repeated.

"Yeah."

"Are you going to do Japan?" I have a particular love for that country and longed for a reason to return there.

"Japan," said Michael, nodding. "India is interested…"

Finally, it was Faheem who brought our time together to a conclusion, telling us, "Okay guys, we really have to go now," and we all thanked him and told Michael that we loved him and waved him goodnight.

We then hopped back in our cars to drive back to the house, and on these semi-daily expeditions, there was often no security SUV and I would sometimes end up right behind Michael in LA's slow-moving traffic. I would catch glimpses of his silhouette through the back window of his SUV, and the movie he was watching on the screens installed inside, and I would blast his music while basking in the wonder that I was immersed in, one that I could hardly have conceived of when I'd travelled to Prague for the opening concert of the *HIStory* tour and begun my journey through his world. Now, thirteen years on, I was watching his next tour evolve from close quarters, while savouring the anticipation of seeing him return to the stage, from where he would no doubt dazzle and enthral a new generation of fans.

* * *

My most amazing encounter with Michael at CenterStaging was inside the studio with Robert, on 16 April. After driving through the gates, Amir escorted us into a dance studio, where several people were milling about, including Michael's choreographer, Travis Payne, who I recognised from the *HIStory* tour, and his former manager Frank DiLeo, who had managed him during the *Bad* era, in the late 1980s, and been a prominent figure at that time.

Amir led us into a room on the left that had a one-way-mirrored window, so you couldn't see into it from the outside, but you could see out from the inside, and watch what was happening on the studio's hardwood floors and mirrored walls. Inside the room, amid a stack of toys and a scattering of fan letters, were Michael, wearing a black jacket, white t-shirt, and eyeglasses, and his youngest son, Blanket.

At first, Michael was standing in the corner and seemed rather shy, a trait he would typically express by hiding his face and avoiding eye contact, but as we talked, he seemed to lose his shyness, and he came forward to hug us, telling me, "Sorry I'm a bit sweaty from dancing," to which I responded by assuring him that he smelt great, and he really did. He always wore cologne, reportedly Tom Ford's Black Orchid, and would apply it before meeting "his girls," and even spray it on the letters he gave us. Robert asked him if he was tired and he said, "Yeah, I've been working so hard. Right now, I'm still at the conceptual stage. I'm still putting the show together. I couldn't get an ending. I need a strong ending and I couldn't think of one. But today, I got it. I got it."

Michael's favourite photo of us together, locked in a tight embrace inside a studio at CenterStaging in Burbank, April 2009.

I asked him if he'd had a chance to listen to the copy of "Earth Song" that I'd given to him, and he said that he hadn't but that he knew now what I meant, that it was a version he'd also sung at the World Music Awards in 1996. "Where it gets really loud at the end," he said. And I said, "Yeah, yeah, yeah, and you're doing this ad lib of 'what about us?' and clicking your fingers." And then he started singing it to me, and I felt like I'd died and gone to heaven. It was one of my favourite live performances, one I hadn't been able to stop listening to in recent weeks, and here was Michael, inside a private room at the studio where he was rehearsing for his next tour, singing it to me!

I gave him a photo of my friend Dani and told him that she was going to be in London for the tour, as so many of my friends were. It is a tragic twist of fate that the vast majority of the fans I'd befriended over the years never came to Los Angeles in 2009, which provided countless opportunities to see Michael during his final months, because they were saving all of their vacation time and money to attend a series of concerts in London that would never come to pass.

I also gave Michael a photo of Jill, whose artistic photography he and his daughter, Paris, adored, something that they would express in a recorded message to her a few weeks later, and that Michael reiterated several times. Before leaving, we posed for a series of photos, including one of Michael and me holding each other that he told me later was his favourite of us together. As I hugged Michael goodbye, I told him again how much I loved him and how proud of him I was, and Robert said, "You sold out fifty concerts and broke three world records. You're the only one who could do that."

*   *   *

It was one thing to hear about the upcoming tour from Michael, but another to hear the rehearsals for it, something we got to do for the first time at CenterStaging, where we were waiting on the evening of

22 April when the pulsating rhythm of "Smooth Criminal" filled the air, triggering an eruption of cheers. This was the song at the centre of my favourite segment in *Moonwalker*, and I savoured the prospect of seeing it performed live again, of watching Michael hitting every dance move and leaning across the stage at a gravity-defying forty-five-degree angle. Next came "Thriller" and then "Jam," and the following night, we heard all of these songs again in addition to "Billie Jean," the performance that held a special significance for me from my *HIStory* tour days.

Our most extensive audible exposure to the tour, however, came during Michael's first rehearsal at The Forum, on the evening of 4 June. After he arrived and went inside, we all climbed the steps to the row of doors that encircled the arena, some of which we were able to prise open a few inches to better hear the audio from inside. And there we stood, with our ears pressed against the blue, metal doors, listening to Michael's songs interspersed with his live vocals and requests like, "I want more lift when they're climbing the fences," during "The Way You Make Me Feel," as well as stage directions from other people, such as, "Michael, turn around, look up at the chandelier," or, during "Thriller," "This is where Michael transforms," presumably into a werewolf, as this was a standard part of his live performance of that song.

While resisting the urge to squeal in excitement, I listened with my friends to the following songs in this order: "I Just Can't Stop Loving You," "Dirty Diana," "Beat It," and, after a short interval, "Wanna Be Startin' Something," "They Don't Care About Us," similar to the version he'd performed on the *HIStory* tour, intermingled with the "HIStory" song, then "Jam," a few verses of "Stranger in Moscow," and, following another interval, "Smooth Criminal," the beginning of "Thriller," with a new sound and a slower tempo, "The Way You Make

Me Feel," and a medley of Jackson 5 songs, which he ended by singing "I'll Be There" live.

My friends and me listening to Michael rehearse for the This Is It tour at The Forum in Inglewood, June 2009.

The following evening, when we arrived at the venue, there were barriers around it, and we only got to stay on site for about an hour before security guards came and told us that we couldn't be there anymore, that it was private property and that we would have to wait at the exit instead. Before being driven out, however, we did get to listen to "Workin' Day and Night," "We Are The World," and "Heal The World" over and over, and I wondered if he'd alternate the latter two songs, as they were both powerful anthems with similar messages of peace and love.

*   *   *

We experienced an arguably even greater audible treat emitting not from a rehearsal studio but from a building at the back of Michael's Holmby Hills estate. On several occasions, we sat in our cars by the side of the house at night, listening with widened eyes to new music accompanied by new lyrics, carried through the air by Michael's crystal clear voice. On the evening of 22 May, several of us listened for hours as he worked on a song with a powerful bass and a rising crescendo, trying to make out the lyrics, as they were slightly too muffled to decipher. Now and again, we would hear him clapping or yelling excitedly, and when we heard the door open and the sound of footsteps, we all called out his name: "Michael! Michael! Michael!"

After we'd assured him that there were no paparazzi present, he came over to the concrete baluster railing above to chat with us, something he did a total of five times that evening, sometimes accompanied by his children.

"Oh my God, we can hear the music. It's so amazing. It sounds amazing, Michael," we told him the first time.

"You can hear the music?" he said, ducking down in embarrassment.

"Yes, and it sounds incredible, we love it!"

We asked him what the lyrics were, but he said he was still working on them, and we asked him the song's title but he said he hadn't decided on a title.

"That's something we come up with later," he explained.

After our final exchange, which ended with him saying, in response to us, "Good night. God bless you. I love you more. I love you most," we heard the children howling at the moon, and we responded in kind, bursting with excitement at having heard the raw version of what could become Michael's next number one single and part of the soundtrack to our lives, feeding into our ears through headphones, blasting from the stereos in our cars and homes, and perhaps even, one day, filling a venue during a live performance.

*   *   *

As testament to the vast gulf between media reports about Michael, which often depicted him as a has-been, and the reality of his appeal, the more than one million tickets to his fifty This Is It concerts at the O2 Arena in London sold out in a matter of hours when they went on sale in March. And on 9 April, I witnessed first-hand the level of frenzy he could still cause by his presence alone, without any of the embellishments of his superstardom. Normally, when he went out anywhere in LA, he sneaked in and out of buildings unbeknownst to passersby, but on that afternoon, when he went to the antique store Lladró on Rodeo Drive in Beverly Hills, word spread among the nearby shoppers and tourists, and a crowd quickly formed.

By the time he left, hundreds of people were pressed up against the window at the front, trying to catch glimpses of him shopping inside, while hundreds more were around the back by the garage, standing on the roofs of their cars and on concrete flower pots, waiting for him to emerge. As his SUV drove out, he rolled down his window to wave, and people took off after him, cheering and calling his name. It was so chaotic that two squad cars had to escort him away, and yet I knew it was nothing compared to the pandemonium that would ensue in London, where he would be based between early July 2009 and early March 2010, though he had told Robert and me that he was considering returning to the US during a three-month break in his schedule at the end of the year.

During those final months in LA, I tried to prepare myself psychologically for my time in London, where I knew I would likely be the focus of more attention, in person rather than just online, than I was accustomed to or comfortable with. Robert had told me that he'd seen discussions about me on fan forums in which people had expressed their intention to befriend me when I came to England for the tour, so that they could get close to Michael, and one night, outside the gates of Michael's Holmby Hills estate, Justin had brought over a sweet Japanese girl to meet me, telling me she'd asked him to introduce her to "the famous girl."

I knew that I might have to navigate some tricky fan politics in the months ahead but I was determined to stay grounded and true to myself. And at the same time, I expected that it might be a very humbling experience for me, as I'd been so spoilt for so long, in having ongoing access to Michael for months at a time, sometimes alone and more often in the company of only a few other fans, but in London, I would doubtless once again be one among the masses, vying for even momentary exchanges with him.

Michael had promised Robert and me that he would continue to invite us to visit him and his children, at their London home, and that he would give us tour passes so we could attend all fifty concerts, and he'd told me that he wanted to have me on stage with him, I assumed during "You Are Not Alone" or an equivalent song, during which a female fan was plucked from the crowd at every concert to join him for part of his performance. But during the final weeks in LA, I knew that he was under a lot of pressure to no longer show favouritism, and I'd known all along that the future was a great unknown, and that there was no guarantee of anything except what I'd already experienced.

Regardless of what access I would have, I was excited about the next phase of my adventure, certain that as long as he was safe and happy, I could cope with whatever came my way, both within his world and without.

TEN
The final days

y initial concerns regarding the *This Is It* tour arose in March 2009, about a week after Michael had announced it to the world at a press conference in London, when the number of concerts skyrocketed, from an initial ten to an eventual fifty. This was no longer in keeping with what Michael had been saying for years, that he no longer wanted to do large-scale tours, but rather a series of exclusive concerts in major cities. I worried that he was being pressured into taking on more than he'd intended, owing to the feverish demand for tickets. However, when I talked to him the day after the final twenty concerts were announced, bringing the total to fifty, he seemed excited about them, and this was the impression that he continued to give throughout the following months.

The first indication that I received that he was unhappy about the logistics of the tour came on 29 May, less than a month before the end. At about 2 p.m., Michael's Cadillac Escalade emerged from his estate and we all gathered around it to chat with him. He was wearing a silver, sparkly jacket that we all admired, and when I handed him the latest card I'd made, from a large sheet of shiny cardboard, with sparkly lettering and a photo of us on the front and lots of messages and poems to him written inside, he pointed at me repeatedly and said, "Thank you for these cards, they're inspirational!" He also thanked another fan, from Holland, for the baby photos she'd been giving him, which he clearly adored.

It had become more difficult in recent days for us to talk to Michael, especially at the doctor's office, where his entourage had stopped allowing us to wait inside the building, because of the increasing number of people who had begun to congregate there, and where swarms of paparazzi arrived every time, likely tipped off by a local worker. They would occupy the entirety of the railing by the back door, and descend on the SUV when Michael emerged, making it impossible for us to talk to him through the window, as we normally had. Determined to find a way to convey our love to him, even through the chaos, Talin had made signs for us to hold: four large green sheets of cardboard that spelled out "We" "Love" "You" "Michael."

Left to right: Samantha, Jill, Talin, and me holding "We" "Love" "You" "Michael" signs outside CenterStaging in Burbank, May 2009.

After Michael left his house on 29 May, we followed him partway to Burbank, assuming he was heading to CenterStaging studios, where he had gone on the previous three days. Talin, Jill, Samantha, and I then drove ahead of him on the freeway, got off at his usual exit, and waited for him there, on the side of the road, holding up the four signs for him to see. Our plan worked, and after Michael had driven past us, we overtook him again so that we could hold up the signs as he arrived at the studio. His SUV stopped outside the gate, and we and the other fans gathered around it. He told us, laughing, how much he loved the signs and how sweet they were, and we all admired his jacket again, as well as his curly hair, which made him look like the Michael of past eras, when he'd always worn it that way. "You look like a superstar," I told him, and he responded, "Aww, thank you!" and Talin said, "He *is* a superstar," making me laugh; she was quite right.

Ever since the first tickets for the fifty *This Is It* concerts at London's O2 Arena had gone on sale, in a two-day pre-sale that had begun on 11 March and during which the 750,000 available tickets had sold out in four hours, there had been concerns about them expressed by fans. For one thing, buyers were limited to purchasing a maximum of four tickets to the entire tour, whereas most fans wanted to go to far more than four concerts, some to all fifty if possible. Some fans had found ways around this, by using a second credit card with a different address, for example, but not everyone had access to such resources. Another problem was that most tickets, especially to the coveted front rows of the venue, which was to be entirely seated, didn't go on sale directly to the public but via a ticket resale agency called Viagogo, which was charging several hundred pounds in some cases for tickets with a face value of £75.

As a result, the front of the arena would likely not be occupied by mega-fans, as the front of Michael's previous concert venues had been, but by wealthy people who could afford the steep purchase prices. And, in fact, many of Michael's biggest fans would not be in attendance at most of the concerts, because of the limitation on ticket purchases. This wasn't just a problem for fans, but would also likely be objectionable to Michael, who often talked about the exchange of energy between him and his audience, and who liked to engage with fans he recognised during every performance. In the previous weeks, several fans from Europe had written to Michael about these concerns, and after he went into the studio on the afternoon of 29 May, Alberto came out to take one of them to see him, because he wanted to discuss them with her.

About fifteen minutes later, this fan came out, and Alberto told the remaining nine of us that we could go in now. At first, he told us that we could each go to see Michael alone, or in groups of two or three, but when we entered the studio, which was on the opposite side of the road to the one that Robert and I had visited in April, Amir came out of a room and said that we were all to go in together and stand in a line across from Michael. We filed into a large room, with dim lighting and scant furnishings, and stood in a line, as instructed, across from Michael, who looked like a billion dollars in his jewelled jacket and with his perfectly curled hair, and whose eyes were blissfully uncovered by shades.

"I love you, I love you, I love you," he said. "I wanted to tell you that I didn't know that the concerts were seated. I didn't know about that and I'm going to do something about it. They did that without my consent. They just did it for obvious reasons."

Several of us spoke up in response, saying, "To make money, we know. We know it's not your fault," and Jill said, "We know how complex this is and how many people are involved."

"They did the schedule wrong too," said Michael. "It was

supposed to be day, show off, day, show off, day, show off." He'd obviously meant to say, "Show, day off, show, day off, show, day off," but of course we understood his meaning.

Jill replied, "We are worried we won't be able to keep up with you," making him laugh.

"I put everything I have into the shows," said Michael. "I work so hard. But I'm only one man. There is only so much I can do." His voice quivered with emotion as he said this, making my heart ache.

"Michael," I said, "please don't push yourself too hard. Please look after your health. You are more important than anything. You don't have to do all fifty shows. If it's too much, just cancel them. Don't let anyone pressure you into doing anything you don't want to do. Only do what you want to do. It's *you* who we love."

"Oh, thank you," replied Michael, "you're so sweet, thank you. Bless you. I also wanted to say that I'm sorry that we don't put the window down sometimes but it's for security reasons. I know you wait for me and I love you so much."

Of course, he didn't need to apologise for this, or for anything; he owed us nothing and yet, he gave us everything, and in fact the only time he didn't roll down his window was when his SUV was being swarmed by paps.

"Don't worry," we all told him. "We understand, Michael. We love you. We love you more."

"Thank you for your love and thank you for your loyalty," he said.

Then he clasped his hands and closed his eyes and bowed his head, and he remained like this, in perfect stillness, for about half a minute, and I don't think I took a single breath in that time. The force of his energy grew so powerful that it drove all of the breath out of me, replacing it with the purifying light that was the essence of his soul.

When Michael looked up, his expression was one of loving serenity. For a while, nobody spoke, and then Amir asked if anyone had any gifts to give him, and a girl from the east coast called Sandy, who I'd first met in 2001 and was probably the most prolific American follower, crossed the room to give him a jacket that she'd made for him. He hugged her and told her emphatically how much he loved it, and he must have really meant it, because when he left the studio that evening, he was wearing it in place of the silvery jacket that we'd all admired.

Back outside, my friends and I went over everything Michael had said to us. One of the fans from Europe asked me why I hadn't told him that the O2 arena was entirely seated, but I'd assumed that he'd known that the arena was seated, just like I'd assumed that he'd known about the Neverland exhibition, and I was shocked to discover that, once again, he'd been kept in the dark. He'd told us that he was "going to do something about it," and sure enough, on 10 June, a man called Cooper, who had worked as part of the production team on every one of Michael's tours since *Victory*, which Michael had done with his brothers, as The Jacksons, in the US and Canada in 1984, came out to talk to my friends and me at The Forum.

Cooper told us that he had heard that Michael was planning to install a front pit in the O2 Arena, a standing area at the front, just like the one on the second leg of the *HIStory* tour, to which those fans who'd queued up the longest would gain entry, and that he'd been told not to put too many lights near the front of the stage for this reason. He also told us that Michael would continue to rehearse at The Forum until 19 June, and then move to the Staples Center in Downtown LA, which turned out to be true, and that he would rehearse there until 2 July, before leaving for London.

What preoccupied me the most following our encounter on 29 May was not Michael's lack of knowledge regarding the arena so much as his expressed dissatisfaction with the tour schedule and the pressure he was obviously feeling. "I am only one man," he'd said. Why *hadn't* he known that the arena was seated? Why *was* the schedule not to his liking? This was his tour, not the concert promoters AEG Live's, not the president and chief executive Randy Phillips's, not the tour director Kenny Ortega's; it was his. He was the star, he was the reason more than a million tickets had sold out in a matter of hours, he was who people were willing to pay hundreds or even thousands of pounds to see. Everyone else was expendable, but as history would so tragically prove, he was the single essential component, so why wasn't he the one calling the shots, why wasn't he in charge?

This was the nature of the conversation between my friends and me outside CenterStaging that afternoon, and all of us resolved to check in with Michael whenever possible over the coming weeks, to point out all of this to him, to remind him that he was the boss, and to tell him that we were there for him and would support him no matter what, and that he didn't need to do the tour for us, as he so often said he was, telling us, "I'm doing this for you, I'm doing this for all of you." We didn't want him to do anything for us except take care of himself. I'd told him, "It's *you* who we love," and I've always felt grateful that I did, because it was one of the few opportunities I had to express this sentiment to him in person in what would prove to be his final weeks on earth, though I repeated it in several letters thereafter: "Please don't push yourself too hard. Please look after your health. You are more important than anything…"

When Michael left CenterStaging that evening, we all chatted to him through the windows of his SUV as usual, and jumped in our cars to drive back to his house. Normally, he turned right out of the studio to head towards the freeway, but this time he turned left, and we all guessed that this meant that he was going to the same sound design studio on Magnolia Boulevard that he'd gone to ten days earlier. We greeted him on his arrival there, and he hugged me before disappearing into the building, where he stayed for about an hour. When he came out, one of the fans asked for a photo with him, and then everyone took a turn, approaching him and posing for a picture.

At first, people stood with Michael at the open door to his SUV, but by the time I reached him, he was sitting on the back seat, so I climbed inside and sat down beside him. "Hi, Michael," I said, as I got in, and he lit up with a smile and said, "Hi, Talitha," drawing out the last syllable, making it sound like "Talithaaa." My heart soared at the sound, for it was so rare a thing for Michael to learn the name of a fan and address them by it, a privilege I'd seen extended to no more than a handful throughout my time in his world, a gift sought by many but extended to so few.

And here he was, saying it again, floating the three syllables into the air, turning them into a song, uttering the sound in a voice that had reached across the world and touched the hearts of millions, saying my name, a name so uncommon that I'd been asked all my life about its origins: "Is it Irish? What does it mean?" "It's Aramaic," I'd reply, referring to the ancient Semitic language, spoken in Biblical times. "It means 'little girl.'" And so every time Michael said it, he was saying, in the language of Jesus, "little girl." "Hi, Little Girl." And as I sat down beside him, I wondered how he saw me, this little girl turned woman, with a slender body, fair skin, brown eyes, and long, dark hair. Did he see only that or did he also see the little girl inside who was, as I'd written in my poem 'Loving an Angel,' "gazing out at this wondrous dream?" I think he did, he must have, because he looked at me with such tenderness, such sweet affection.

Michael wrapped his arms around me and held me to him, then turned me around to face the camera, and Alberto took a photo of us. And then we fell into each other again, and we held one another, bodies pressed together, embraced, enfolded, enwrapped, his arms around my back, pulling me closer, closer, closer, until I lost all awareness of the edges that separated us. We were one in that moment of perfect love that required nothing of each other, that had no worldly desire or context, that needed only to exist.

My hands wandered across his back, his shoulders; his hand cupped the back of my head, stroked my hair, caressed my face. We sat cheek to cheek, skin against skin, his lips on my face, kissing me softly, my lips on his, sprinkling him with kisses, light touches of warmth on his snow-white skin; his voice in my ear, my voice in his, channelling our love, speaking across each other, a stream of expression. My beautiful, my sweet, my angel, how is it that you exist, I wondered, that the world can contain such a miracle, human in form, divine in nature, held in place by this fleshly vessel, which I cherish as I do the soul contained within.

I knew only this moment, this dream, this reality; I was with him, as one with him as I would ever be again. For it is the great tragedy of my story that for every first, there is a last, the last time we held each other, which was on that blessed evening, the last time I heard him say my name, which was a few days later, the last time I talked to him, which was hours before the end. I heard Alberto's voice in the distance: "Talitha, come on now. There are other people waiting. Talitha, Talitha, Talitha." The other people, my friends, I had forgotten that they were there, that anyone else existed, but they were waiting their turn; I had to go. I tried to pull away but he was holding me tight, he wouldn't let me go, and so I leaned in to him one last time.

Held for the final time: Michael and me inside his SUV, outside a sound design studio in Burbank, May 2009.

*   *   *

That evening, I floated to heaven, but the next day, back on solid ground, something terrible happened, something that hadn't happened during my entire time in Michael's world, or ever as far as I know: the words that Michael had said to us in the studio were reported by a British tabloid, a British tabloid of all things, the bane of his existence, the lowest of the low. I do not know how this happened, though I've heard that it was unintentional, that someone told someone who told someone who sold the story to the press. Whatever the source, it felt like another betrayal, of him first and foremost, but also of us and of what he'd shared with us in private, behind closed doors.

The newspaper article, which also stated, accurately I might add, that Michael had said on another occasion that he'd gone to bed thinking he was doing ten concerts and woken up to discover he was doing fifty, is likely the main reason why, in the following weeks, we enjoyed far less access to Michael than we had in previous months. Granted, there were other contributing factors: our numbers swelled and included at times fans who behaved in a frenzied way when they saw Michael, by running at his car and hanging on to it as he tried to leave. The number of paparazzi and autograph hunters also rose, all eager to get what they could before he departed for London, as did the number of security guards. One day in mid-June, a few of us ran into Alberto at The Forum and he apologised to us for the restricted access, explaining that Michael was "in London mode now."

These additional factors aside, several people who worked closely with Michael on *This Is It* told us after his passing that his entourage had been under strict instruction to keep us away from Michael following our meeting with him at the studio. They said that the powers that be hadn't wanted any more media reports claiming that he was unhappy about the tour, because it made them look bad and, heaven forbid, might affect sales of those remaining high-priced tickets. They also hadn't wanted anyone telling him to cancel the shows if he didn't want to do them. Their priority was profit, not Michael, and so it was in their best interest to keep him isolated and controlled, not strengthened and empowered.

I did get to see Michael every day that he went out in June, which numbered sixteen in total, and included four visits to the doctor's office, four to Culver Studios, eleven to The Forum, two to the Staples Center, and an outing on 7 June to the El Capitan Theatre in Hollywood, where he and his children watched a screening of the movie *Up*. One time, his entourage had us all line up outside The Forum and then approach his SUV one by one to talk to him, and another time, two of my friends, Yana and a lovely guy called Ariel, and I waited at a traffic light by the venue, and when the SUV came, it pulled up and Michael rolled down the window to talk to us. I used every such opportunity to ask him how he was and to urge him to take care of himself. But overall, most of my exchanges with him in this final month were too brief to allow for any real conversation.

*　　*　　*

It was 16 June 2009, nine days before the end, that represented a turning point for me, when my concerns for Michael deepened and took on a sense of urgency. By then, I had developed suspicions that, as well as being a source of stress – as Michael had made clear to us in the studio – the tour was also having a negative impact on his physical well-being, something Michael Amir confirmed that afternoon by telling Robert that Michael was stressed out and not sleeping properly.

It wasn't unusual, particularly in recent weeks, for Michael to leave the doctor's office in Beverly Hills in a groggy state, and we assumed, correctly as it turned out, that he was undergoing a procedure that required sedation, the effects of which hadn't always worn off by the time he left. I didn't like seeing him this way but I at least understood the cause of it, and it never seemed to last very long; I would often meet him again, ten to fifteen minutes later, on arrival at his next destination, by which time he would have returned to his usual, alert and engaging, self.

On 16 June, Michael went to the doctor's office in the afternoon, after which he went to The Forum, where he rehearsed for several hours. He returned home about midnight and I spoke with him briefly through the window of his SUV outside the entrance to his estate. He seemed confused and incoherent; he couldn't understand what I was saying and repeated my words to him several times. This was such a jarring departure from the Michael I knew that after he left, I turned to my friends and my first words to them were, "What's wrong with Michael?" I now understand that the confusion and incoherence I witnessed were caused by severe insomnia and what's referred to as "lupus fog," brought on by the stress of the tour.

I'd known for quite some time that Michael suffered from the autoimmune disease lupus, and indeed, it's common for people with vitiligo to also suffer from an autoimmune disease of some kind. In lupus patients, stress can trigger a flare-up, which can, in turn, cause something known as "lupus fog," a set of cognitive impairments that can include concentration and memory problems, confusion, and difficulty expressing oneself. When, several months later, I watched video clips of people displaying symptoms of lupus fog, they were eerily reminiscent of the condition I'd seen Michael in that night, and on a few occasions thereafter.

At the time, however, I knew none of this; all I knew was that something was wrong with Michael, an assertion that was further confirmed over the following days, each of which ended with my friends and me huddled together outside his house, with worried expressions and speaking in hushed tones. What was wrong and what could we do about it? We knew he wasn't happy about the tour, that he was stressed out, that he wasn't sleeping well, that he was skinnier than he should have been, given the physical demands of touring, and now that he was visibly incoherent for reasons we couldn't fathom.

Our access by this stage had become limited to a few seconds here and there, an occasional hand squeeze or momentary exchange, and while we continued to communicate our thoughts and feelings to him in writing, it didn't feel like enough. We needed to do more but we didn't know what or how, or even if it was our place to intervene, because what if there were factors involved that were beyond our knowledge or understanding?

We remained in this state of limbo, crippled with uncertainty, until 21 June, when we received an email from a French fan called Marika, who had visited Michael at Culver Studios with another fan earlier that month to present him with a jacket they'd made. She wrote that when Michael had taken off his jacket to try on theirs, they had been shocked by how skinny he was, beyond "scary skinny," she said, "a skeleton."

On return to France, Marika had written to Michael's longtime makeup artist and friend, Karen Faye, who was working on the *This Is It* tour. Karen had replied, saying that she was aware of Michael's condition and was "doing everything humanly possible" to help him. She asked Marika to keep her observations to herself, no doubt out of concern for Michael's privacy, but Marika decided to share them with us, and though it didn't prevent the horror that would unfold four days later, I'll always feel grateful that she did.

In her email, which she sent to about thirty followers, Marika pointed out that the only other people (his children aside, obviously) around Michael on a daily basis were employees. "No family, no friends, no one," she said. "On the set, I watched people around Michael. Everyone was avoiding Michael, looking somewhere else. They were all working on their video. Too [much] money involved. You don't want to be fired because you told Michael Jackson to eat. You all know Michael's employees will never take the risk to lose their job. They don't love Michael this much." She then urged us all to help him. "So please, let's all discuss it together, to find a way to save him. And I don't think 'save' is too exaggerated," she said.

Marika's email unleashed a sense of panic among my friends and me. We'd known that Michael was skinny but hadn't known that he was "a skeleton." As Marika had written, "I feel that I witnessed reality. For once, he didn't have a coat on, a big shirt, big trousers. For once, I saw the reality of his situation." Just over an hour after receiving Marika's email, I responded, to all of the people on the email list. I began by thanking Marika for bringing everything out into the open and then I wrote the following:

I know some people won't want to hear this but Marika is right. My friends and I here in LA have just begun to realise how serious things are, how dangerous it will be to Michael's health to continue with the shows. We've been waiting for months for him to bulk up and gain weight/muscle, as he's done before every other show. But he remains extremely skinny. Of course, he puts on a brave face and tells us everything is fine, but Karen Faye's response to Marika confirms our fears and assures us that we're not being paranoid fans making up stories in our heads.

We have all been urging Michael to take care of his health, not to push himself too hard...I told him a few weeks ago not to feel pressured into doing anything he doesn't want to do, and to cancel the shows if they are too much. That was the last time I got to speak to him properly. Since then, security have been limiting our access to Michael, so we only get a few seconds to see him every day, no time for any real conversation...And after all, what impact is one voice going to make?

*Even combined, we the LA fans represent fewer than ten voices...What we need is a chorus of voices, one hundred, one thousand...as many as possible, all telling him to **stop the shows because we don't want him to die**. We really need Michael to understand that we care about **him** (his health, his happiness, his **life**) far more than we do about seeing "Michael Jackson" back on stage* *performing. We need him to know that by cancelling the shows, he will not be "letting down the fans" (as he no doubt believes) but that by going ahead and ending up in hospital, or worse (the unimaginable), he is hurting everyone who truly loves him – his children, his family, his friends, and all of us.*

We can still give our letters to Michael; at this stage, that's the only contact we can rely on. So please, everyone who believes this email and wants to do something, sit down and write a letter today and email it to me (or someone else you know in LA/coming to LA) and I will give it into Michael's hand. Include a photo and which country you're from. Michael is not good with names but he will recognise your face as someone who cares. And I think the message is a million times stronger if it comes from people all over the world, all saying the same thing, not just a bunch of girls in LA. Write what you like, of course, but please don't hold back. The time to be direct is now.

And by the way, Marika is right about another thing too: Michael is all alone. As you may know, I've been around him on and off for two years, and he doesn't have any friends around him. He has his children, he has security, now he has industry people as well. But when it comes to people who love him truly, see what's going on now, and are in a position to do something about it, we're pretty much all he's got.

That same day, I began receiving letters from fans around the world. My friends and I printed them out and put them together with our own letters, and each day, the stack grew. Michael didn't go out on 21 or 22 June, so the next time we saw him was at around 6 p.m. on 23 June, when he went to the Staples Center in Downtown LA for the first time. When he left his home, there were more people waiting outside than ever before: clusters of fans, paparazzi, and autograph hunters, but also groups of onlookers, which represented a new element. The hype of the tour had piqued their interest, and they longed to catch a glimpse of him before he returned to the stage and reclaimed his musical throne.

Everyone descended on Michael's SUV, but somehow I managed to slip through and have a few moments with him at the window. He reached out a trembling hand and, as I held it in mine, he kept saying something to me, but I couldn't hear him over the surrounding chaos and the rumble of the engine. It was beyond frustrating, after months of frivolous chatter, to be unable to speak with him now, when it mattered the most. My friends and I followed him to the Staples Center, but he didn't stop on the way in or on the way out, and we got to see him only briefly as he drove back through the gates of his estate that night.

"Michael's hand was trembling," I told my friends that evening, fuelling the sense of urgency that we all felt to initiate the three-step plan we had come up with. Step one involved handing over the letters, while explaining to Michael that they were from fans from all over the world and that they were extremely important. Step two involved reading him a short statement expressing our concerns. If, at that stage, he told us that he was fine, really fine, we would do no more. But if he told us that he needed our help, we would move on to the third and final stage of the plan, which was to be initiated only with Michael's blessing or as an absolute last resort.

That final step involved circulating an open letter to everyone involved in Michael's life who we could reach: family members and friends, like Elizabeth Taylor, who lived locally, entourage members, security personnel, and other employees, and everyone involved in the *This Is It* tour. The letter, which was similar in content to the statement we'd prepared, read as follows:

A message about Michael Jackson's current health
To all concerned: You are receiving this letter because you are

someone who works with Michael Jackson, or who knows him on a personal basis. This is a letter written on behalf of many of Michael's fans, including the group living in and visiting Los Angeles who have had contact with Michael over the past half a year.

To get straight to the point, we are gravely concerned about Michael's physical condition and how it appears to have worsened over recent months. With him about to undertake a gruelling fifty-date concert tour, we felt we could no longer be silent and that it was time to express our worries – to him and to everyone in his close circle of friends, family, staff, and colleagues.

What we have witnessed is a shockingly underweight man who appears to be in trouble, physically and emotionally, and who is single-handedly carrying a huge burden on his shoulders, a burden he has spoken out about. We are not privy to information about his personal health or medical conditions, and we understand we may be misinformed or unaware of certain details. We respect Michael's right to privacy and we do not wish to invade it.

But the fact is that we believe Michael's health is at risk and that he may need some help, possibly professional help from a doctor. Whether the weight loss is the problem or whether it is a symptom of another condition, we strongly feel that it must be confronted and treated, without delay. If you, for even a moment, have had a concern about Michael's current condition, then we beg you to do whatever you can to help him, support him, encourage him, reassure him. If you are in a position to act and you see what is going on, then you can't in good conscience ignore what you see. You are involved.

Even as fans, we have struggled with this, talked ourselves out of this, been in denial of it, but we've now seen too much and can no longer stand back and stay silent. We may be crossing a line, but we are willing to do so because Michael's health and happiness matters to us more than anything else. Remember, we are in a position where financial and professional gain is not a factor. Our motivation is simply love. We are strongly dedicated and *loyal to Michael and our support for him is unwavering, but we cannot support a tour that will damage his health, possibly worse...*

We are turning to you now because you may be our best hope, our only hope. We feel frustrated to see this situation unfolding, we feel helpless because we are on the "outside," and we feel terrified of the outcome if nobody steps up to help. Please don't turn your back. We are willing to risk our reputations and our good standing with the man who matters most to us. We pray you are willing to take a risk for him also. He said it to us himself a few weeks ago, he is "only one man," and he probably could use some support and assistance right now.

If you agree there's an issue with Michael's health, please ask yourself what is the right thing to do, and do it. We are relying on you, for Michael's sake.

In retrospect, I wish we had distributed this letter as soon as we'd written it, but out of respect for Michael, we'd wanted to approach him first, to bring our concerns directly to him before we brought them to anyone else. We'd also thought that time was on our side, that Michael would be in LA for almost two more weeks, based on what Cooper had told us at The Forum and the date of his first concert in London, which was 13 July. I also wish that we could have shared our concerns with the fan community at large and invited everyone to write a letter, because every fan deserved to know what we knew and to have their voice heard, but we already had suspicions that we were being shut out because of our influence over Michael, and feared that if word of our plan got out, we would find ourselves shut out even more and unable to enact it.

*   *   *

On 24 June, the last day before the end, the scene at the house was just as chaotic as it had been on the previous day, and we knew that we wouldn't get a chance to speak with Michael there, so we came up with a plan. Jill and I had been elected to hand over the letters to Michael and read him the statement, though I did get cold feet at one point and ask Jill to do it alone. Like we wrote in our open letter, I was worried that we were crossing a line, and I was afraid of losing favour with Michael by being the one to hand over the letters, but then I realised that such a concern was selfish; it had been my idea for everyone to write him the letters after all, I couldn't possibly renege on my promise to deliver them to him.

The risk of putting myself on the line, of reaching out and being poorly received, of suffering some personal loss, great as it might have seemed to me, did not compare to the risk of doing nothing, of failing to stand by the commitment I'd made and watching his health further deteriorate, to the point where he collapsed from a lack of sleep and nutrition, or worse, the unimaginable, the unthinkable, the unspeakable. I had been privileged beyond measure and, just like with great power, with great privilege comes great responsibility. As fans who were put in the position we were in, who were given direct access to Michael, I felt that we had a duty of care towards him, an obligation to put him first, no matter what.

The plan we came up with on 24 June was not to try to give the letters to Michael at the house, where we knew it would be impossible to speak with him properly, but at the Staples Center, where we thought it might be possible if Jill and I were the only two people waiting at the entrance when he arrived. We knew that when there were a lot of people, Michael's entourage sometimes didn't stop, telling him that it was a security risk or perhaps that paparazzi were present, but if there were only two of us, no such excuse could be given, so it would be entirely up to Michael whether to stop or not, and we felt certain that he would, because he always did.

We shared our plan with the other fans waiting at the house, and every one of them gave us their blessing. They all agreed that when he arrived at the Staples Center, assuming he was going there that evening – an assumption that our plan hinged on – they would not approach the entrance, in order to give Jill and me the best chance of success. I can not overestimate the selflessness of this act, because every one of us treasured every opportunity to see Michael, no matter how fleeting, and it would be an act made all the more selfless, infinitely so, by the significance that evening would soon take on.

Jill and I went ahead to the Staples Center, and when we approached the entrance, an opening to an underground garage on Chick Hearn Court into which Michael's SUVs had disappeared the previous evening, we saw two security guards standing there. At first, I wanted to avoid them, because I was afraid that they'd ask us to leave, but then Jill went over and told them that we were there to see Michael and would approach only if he called us over, and they agreed to allow us to wait by them. After that, we could relax a little, though my tummy was still aflutter; so many people were relying on us to deliver their words of love and concern to Michael, we couldn't let them down.

Shortly after 6 p.m., our friends called us: Michael had just left home and was heading our way. They kept calling us to update us on his location: he was still on route to Downtown LA, he was nearing the exit now, he would arrive at any moment. At 6.50 p.m., his dark blue Cadillac Escalade turned onto Chick Hearn Court and began heading our way. Michael leaned forward between the two front seats. The sunlight was streaming into the car and it shone directly on him, lighting up his features, making him glow. We waved and I held up the letters, to show that we had something for him, what would become our final collective offering, our final gift, our final expression of love.

The SUV rolled to a stop in front of us, the driver's window slid down, and Faheem called us over. I leaned in to see Michael and then saw, to my surprise, that Michael Amir was sitting next to him. I was taken aback. I had never before seen anyone other than Michael's children, not a family member, not a friend, and certainly not an employee, in the back of the SUV with Michael. Why was he there, on this of all nights? I will never know. I tried to hand the letters, which numbered about thirty and were inside a clear plastic bag, to Michael, but Faheem reached for them before he could, so I withdrew them, and then I tried again. The same thing happened. The letters went in a few inches, Faheem put out his hand to take them, and so I withdrew them a second time. It was on the third attempt that I was successful, and the letters passed directly from my hands into Michael's.

As I spoke, telling Michael that the letters were from fans from all over the world and that it was really important that he read them, he began turning them over in his hands. On one side was a letter from Maria from England, and on the other side was my letter, which was written on colourful sheets of cardboard. On the front was a photo of Michael and me holding hands, a large, pink, glittery heart and, written in colourful, glittery letters, the words "Because we love you." My letter, my last letter to Michael, read as follows:

Dearest Michael,

The fans have been talking among themselves for weeks about their concerns for you. We are talking to each other now. The time to be silent is over. We love you too much for that. That is why today, we are reaching out as one.

We have reason to believe that you are not healthy enough to perform fifty concerts and feel pressured into going ahead with the tour even though your heart is not in it. You suggested this to us when you talked to us inside the studio in Burbank, but the weight of your words is just beginning to sink in now. We've all been in denial for too long. I know I have been, imagining you are superhuman, forgetting that under that brave exterior lies a fragile, sensitive human being with the weight of the world on his shoulders and nobody to help him carry it.

Won't you let us help you shoulder that burden now, like we have so many times in the past? Won't you listen to our concerns and finally understand that we love you Michael, and not merely the artist, the performer. We love your soul, your light, your heart, and we would die if you left us. I know I would. I would die inside.

It's not easy to do this, to be so direct, to risk you shutting us out, but that's how much we love you, enough to risk losing the love you have for us. And if we don't speak up, who will? Your children are too young to understand what's happening, your employees are too scared to lose their jobs, your industry colleagues are too blinded by their own self-interest, your family and friends are not around you every day to see what we see – the strain you're under, your undernourished body...

I am sure you believe that by postponing or cancelling shows, you will be letting down the fans. Michael, you're wrong. By pushing yourself to the point of exhaustion and collapse, by risking your health, maybe even your life, you are hurting everyone who truly cares about you – your children, your family and friends, and all of us, Michael. And most of all, you are hurting yourself, the most precious soul on this planet.

If we are right and you don't want with all of your heart to begin a fifty-date tour in under three weeks, then please Michael, I beg you, don't go ahead with the tour. Don't do it for the fans because no true fan wants this. Don't do this for your children because they need their daddy, healthy and strong. Don't do this for AEG because all they care about is money. Only do this tour if and when your heart is in it, only after you have rested and recovered, feel fit and healthy and strong. Only under these circumstances should you go ahead.

If we are right to be this concerned, then please Michael, postpone the shows, cancel the tour, get help to be healthy, shut out AEG, pack up and escape to South Africa or the Middle East or China, do whatever you need to do to get out of this forced commitment, and let the lawyers clean up the mess, let the spokespeople deal with the media backlash. None of that matters compared to your health and well-being. You don't need the money and you certainly don't need to prove yourself to anyone. You are Michael Jackson. There is none other.

If we are totally wrong and you are healthy enough to go ahead with the tour, if you want with all of your heart to do fifty shows, then please just see all this as misguided concern. Know that no matter what you decide to do, we will be there for you, just as we have always been there, to support you and love you, to stand by you, proud as always to call ourselves your fans. We are yours. Without you, there is nothing.

You are not alone Michael, remember that, never alone.

I love you with all my heart,

Your Talitha

I had written hundreds of letters to Michael during my thirteen years in his world, all in recent years signed "Your Talitha," but this was the first letter I'd ever written to him in which I'd expressed my fear of losing him, passed from my hands to his, hours before the end. It was also, as far as I know, the first time that a group of his fans had rallied together to try to save him from what they perceived to be a threat to his life, namely the stress caused by the upcoming tour. We were right and we were wrong: the stress of the tour is what killed Michael, but not as a direct result of the impact it was having on his physical and psychological well-being, which was the basis of our concern.

Michael didn't die from exhaustion or starvation or lupus or vitiligo or the back injury he'd endured when the cherry picker he was on collapsed at the MJ & Friends concert in Munich in 1999 and that he still suffered from, or any of the other ailments that afflicted him. He died because the stress of the tour caused him to suffer from severe insomnia, which necessitated the presence of a doctor, namely Conrad Murray, who killed Michael by committing a deadly act, an act that would have killed him regardless of his condition, that would have killed him even at his strongest and most resilient, that would have killed anyone. We could not, in a million years, have predicted that. Conrad Murray was the wild card that none of us saw coming.

In the days after we lost Michael, several of my friends from outside his world, friends I'd confided in for years, told me, "You knew." They did so based on how drastically the tone of my conversation regarding Michael had changed in the days just prior to the end. Instead of gushing to them about the excitement of seeing him, I had been talking about my fears of losing him, and I did have a sense of impending doom, of a shadow that foreshadowed the darkness that was to come. Many fans I know have reported similar feelings of dread, some as early as March, when he did the press conference in London, announcing the tour.

Whether it was simply based on what we observed with our five senses, what we saw and what we heard, or on some deeper intuition, hardly matters; the point is that we did know to be afraid, we did know that the stress of the tour was posing a threat to Michael's health and even his life, and we did act on those fears to the best of our ability. What we did not know was that Conrad Murray was going to kill Michael. If we'd known that, Michael would still be here, because we would have moved heaven and earth to stop him.

As Michael turned the letters over in his hands, I kept repeating the same thing, that they were from fans from all over the world and that it was imperative that he read them, and he nodded and acknowledged that he understood, and promised that he would. Although our time together was brief, he appeared to me to be his usual self that evening. I saw none of the symptoms that had alarmed me so in recent days, no confusion, no incoherence, no trembling hands. He was sharp and alert and engaging. He was the Michael I'd known and loved since I was a little girl.

I asked him if we could have thirty seconds to read him a statement, which was the part of the task that Jill was to carry out, and he said yes but then Michael Amir said no, that we could do it on the phone instead. Amir held up a phone, as if to call me right away, and told Michael that he had my number. We thanked Michael, told him we loved him, and stepped away, and then, remembering that she had a photo to give him – one of the photos she'd taken, one of the photos he loved so much that he'd asked her for bigger prints, for enlargements of what to him were beautiful works of art – Jill ran to the SUV again as it rolled away and handed her photograph, her last gift for Michael, to Faheem.

The SUV descended into the garage. Jill and I turned to leave, and immediately, my phone rang. It was a call from a blocked number. It was Michael. I picked it up but all I could hear was static. "Michael, can you hear me?" I asked. The call dropped, and then my phone rang again as we made our way to a nearby set of steps, where the other fans, who had been watching our encounter with Michael from across the road, came to join us. "What's going on?" they asked, and Jill told them that we'd given the letters to Michael and that he was trying to call now, to hear the statement, but that he'd gone down into an underground garage, and the reception was obviously bad.

The second call dropped, nothing happened for a while, and then my phone rang again from a blocked number, but this time, I heard only silence. I received another such phone call later that night, and my friends and I took this as a good sign, that Michael was persistently trying to call, that he was eager to hear the statement, and that he would surely call again as soon as he had better phone reception.

Jill and I felt a tremendous weight lifted off our shoulders, because along with our fears, we also had a sense of hope. We were confident that by working together, we could help Michael, and that by handing him those letters, we'd taken the first step. All of this, we told each other, would soon be resolved. We spent the evening, as usual, hanging out with our friends, and Talin gave me a lovely gift, a Hello Kitty shirt and a card that now serves as a memento of that final night, when we unknowingly stood on the precipice between then and now, with our hopes, and our hearts, still intact. In it, she wrote:

Dear Dory,

This is just to thank you for everything in the past couple of months. If it wasn't for you and Yana, I would've never managed to have coffee with Michael a few times a week. We've definitely had some memories that we'll remember forever. Let's hope the best is yet to come!

You are truly one of the sweetest people I've ever met and you deserve all the great things that come your way.

Love, Talin

Dory was Talin's nickname for me. She said, "If it wasn't for you and Yana," because out of our little group of seven, we were there the most and would call everyone as soon as Michael went anywhere, and "coffee with Michael" was her sweet term for seeing Michael. For weeks, I'd been preparing not only to say goodbye to the intimacy of my time with Michael in the US, but also to my LA friends, who were some of the sweetest people I'd ever met. Only a few of them were planning to come to London for a few of the concerts, none for the entire tour, and I knew I'd miss them all terribly

I can only tell my own story, because only my story is mine to tell, but I had seen all of these beautiful people experience what would become part of their own stories, in some cases their first meeting, their first hug, their first photo with Michael, which was really just a continuation of what had begun for all of us in childhood, when we'd awoken to his presence in the world. And on that final evening, we were all still full of hope that regardless of what happened with the tour, we would soon see Michael happy and healthy again, and enjoy many more adventures together with him over the long years ahead.

*   *   *

The sun set on the last day of Michael's life. Jill, Samantha, and I went for a stroll around the Staples Center, and we came to a narrow window that looked onto a stage, and on that stage was Michael, performing to the opening beats of his song "Dangerous." I gasped and froze, and we clustered together to watch him perform the song in its entirety, hardly daring to make a sound, fearful of attracting the attention of the security guards we'd seen circulating the building, who'd no doubt send us away if they found us there.

Michael was wearing a t-shirt that one of our friends, a girl called Irina, who was originally from Romania but lived in New York and who'd met him for the first time that year, had given to him. It was black with white lettering that said, "Curls for my girls," referring to his new hairstyle, which had made us all squeal the first time we'd seen it. He seemed to be walking through the performance rather than giving it his all, but it was still incredible to see. At the end, an angel ascended and wrapped a pair of golden wings around him, and, to the outro of the Jacksons's 1980 song "This Place Hotel," they descended together through the floor of the stage. And that was the first and last time any of us saw any of *This Is It* performed live, a performance during his last hours on earth that ended with him disappearing from view in the arms of an angel.

Not only that but the stage that he was on was the same stage that his children would stand on two weeks later, at his memorial service on 7 July, unveiled for all the world to see, grieving their father. In front of the stage he would lay, frozen in time, inside a golden casket, and beyond him we would sit, near the front of the packed venue, pouring our grief onto the floor, forming puddles of tears at our feet. If only the future had cast a more perceptible shadow, if only we'd looked through that window and seen the scene that would soon replace the one before us, the image that would be projected onto the backdrop of the stage, of Michael's name bookended with the years that contained his life, we would have bent time and space to annihilate it from all existence. But on that final night, when fate hung in the balance and every possible future still lay ahead, we remained innocent of what was to come.

*   *   *

Because Michael had not stopped while leaving the Staples Center on the previous night, the three of us had made a plan. Instead of waiting by the underground garage, we would wait at the traffic light at the end of Chick Hearn Court, in the hope that when Michael reached it, the traffic light would be red, in which case he would almost certainly roll down his window to talk to us, as he always did, in which case we would hand him Jill's phone, with a call placed to my phone, so the two phones would be connected. Then, as he drove away, Jill would read him the statement on the phone and we would talk to him about our concerns.

This had been our original plan, but because Michael had repeatedly tried to call me – or so we thought – we abandoned it, confident that he would call again once he left the Staples Center. Instead, we waited with the other fans by the underground garage, and when Michael left, at around 12.30 a.m. on 25 June, he rolled down his window all the way, leaned out, with a huge smile on his face, and waved to us. When his SUV came to the traffic light, it was red, and it stayed red for over a minute, and I felt a twinge of regret for not going through with our original plan, but we reassured ourselves that it was okay, that Michael would soon call again.

It was only later, weeks after his passing, that I learned that we had been misled, and purposefully so, by the only "fan" I knew who didn't put Michael first when it mattered the most. I will refer to this fan as Gollum, after the creature in *The Lord of the Rings*, because some European fans had referred to them as such, owing to their attitude towards Michael, their jealousy and possessiveness of him.

As one example of Gollum's behaviour, one time an Australian girl, who'd been travelling through the US, came by the house to see Michael. Gollum told her repeatedly that he didn't live there, and when she didn't believe them, that he had put them in charge of who was and wasn't allowed to wait outside, and that she'd have to leave. Fortunately, the girl then approached us, and we welcomed and encouraged her, and were with her outside Culver Studios on 8 June when Michael, hesitantly, after asking her repeatedly, "Are you sure?" signed her wrist so that she could have it tattooed. It had been that girl's one and only chance to meet Michael, weeks before the end, and Gollum had tried to rob her of it, and on that final night, they robbed us of our final possibility of speaking to Michael and of changing his fate.

Gollum had not come to the Staples Center on that final night, but waited at Michael's house. However, they had kept in contact with one of the fans who was at the Staples Center, a visiting fan who was innocent of their nature. As soon as Gollum heard that Michael was trying to call me, they began calling me from a blocked number, so I'd think it was him. Another fan at the house told me that Gollum had muted their phone and then held it up, laughing, as I said, on the other end, "Michael, Michael, Michael, can you hear me? I can't hear you..." We were trying to reach out to Michael, to help him, to save him, and Gollum was trying to intercept the calls and laughing about it. The other call I received later that night was also from Gollum, and not Michael as I'd thought, and so Gollum was the reason we abandoned our original plan and gave up what would be our final chance to speak with him.

In all of the testimonies at all of the trials relating to Michael's passing and in all of the interviews that people who had been around him during those final days did, not one person, not one, as far as I know, ever said that they'd done what we were trying to do that night, what we'd done in our letters, letters that we'll never know if he read or not, letters that went into his hands and then disappeared out of all knowledge (though there were claims that they were seen in Michael's dressing room and in his car that night, and that he asked for them to be brought into his house on his arrival home), and what we were planning to do on the phone – to confront him directly with our concerns and urge him to put his health first.

Gollum had been openly hostile to me since we'd first met, outside the Hotel Bel-Air in the fall of 2008, and yet I'd told them about the letters and invited them to write one too, because I'd believed that even if they hated me, they loved Michael and deserved to be included. Gollum knew what we were trying to do and purposefully sabotaged our efforts, and because of them, I will never know if our original plan would have worked or not, and if it would have changed nothing or if it would have changed everything, because what if Michael had listened to us, read our letters, heard our concerns, and decided to cancel or at least postpone the tour until he was ready, until he was in a better place, physically and psychologically? What if he'd felt a weight lifted off his shoulders, knowing that he had the blessing of his fans to put his health first, and what if he'd gone home and told Conrad Murray to leave, that he wanted to try to sleep naturally? What if? I'll never know, and so only the question, the torment of not knowing, the regret of abandoning that original plan, remains.

Regardless of what anyone else did or didn't do, I'm responsible only for what I did or didn't do, and I carry the burden of that, because ultimately the things that I did, the actions that I took, the plan that I made, for everyone to write letters to Michael and for me to deliver them into his hands, failed. I failed. And I live with that failure and the terrible guilt that it evokes. I let him down and I let everyone down, and that's on me, and I'm so sorry. I would give my life to change the outcome and return him to those who grieve him as I do.

Around 1 a.m. on 25 June, Michael arrived home. While we were waiting for him, a silver car drove through the gate and we heard one of the security guards saying that it was "the doctor." I'd noticed that silver car on several occasions but learned the identity of its occupant only on that final night. In the open letter we'd prepared, we'd written, "We believe Michael's health is at risk and that he may need some help, possibly professional help from a doctor," and so, on overhearing the guard, we remarked to each other, "Oh, a doctor, that's good." We assumed that the doctor was there to help Michael wind down after his rehearsal, never imagining the monstrous act that he would commit only hours later.

As Michael approached the gate, he cracked his window open a few inches and stuck out his hand, and I pressed a note, reminding him to call me, into his fingers, squeezing them in mine, one last time. His fingers curled around the note, and he withdrew his hand, and as his SUV passed inside, we all shouted our final words to him: "We love you, Michael. Goodnight, Michael. Sweet dreams. See you tomorrow!"

About an hour later, members of Michael's entourage emerged. One of them handed Talin an autographed photograph that Michael had signed to her on his arrival home that night. It was the first autograph she'd ever asked him for, by slipping the photo into his SUV with a note attached to it on an earlier occasion, and after a lifetime of signing autographs, after signing hundreds of autographs that year alone, it was the last autograph Michael would ever sign, and I'm glad it went to someone who loved him with all of her heart.

As Michael Amir was leaving, I asked him what had happened with the phone call, and he apologised, explaining, as we'd assumed, that the reception at the Staples Center was really bad. And then he said, "Michael asked me to remind him to call you tomorrow," meaning later that day, of course, meaning 25 June, the day all possibility, all promise, all hope would be lost.

*　　*　　*

If Michael left this earth before I did, something I'd always hoped would never happen – given that I was almost twenty years younger than him, however, I'd known it was a possibility, though I'd hoped his familial longevity (his grandfather Samuel Jackson had lived to be one hundred, his father lived to the age of eighty-nine, and his mother, at the time of writing, is still going strong at ninety) would compensate somewhat for the age gap – but if it did happen, I thought I would know it instantly, that no matter where I was or what I was doing, I'd feel it and I'd know. However, I woke up on 25 June with not the slightest inkling that this was the day that would carve me in two, between then and now, before and after, whole and broken.

I do not know what time Michael died because nobody but his killer, Conrad Murray, a man who lacks all credibility in my mind, knows, but it was almost certainly during the morning hours of 25 June, when I was likely still sleeping. I had stayed awake until well after 2 a.m., and my sleep had been briefly interrupted several times, but I didn't wake up for the final time until shortly before midday. If I'd sensed Michael's departure, if I'd shuddered or cried out in my sleep, I had no sense or recollection of it on waking.

At 12.04 p.m., Yana called me. "Has Michael called you yet?" she asked. "Not yet," I told her, and promised to let her know as soon as he had. A few minutes later, I called Jill, and we agreed to get ready and meet at the house, because I still wanted her to be the one to read the statement to Michael, as planned. At 12.28 p.m., I received a phone call from a friend who was waiting at the house. "An ambulance just went into Carolwood," he told me.

My heart tightened. This is exactly what we'd been afraid of, that Michael would collapse and have to be taken to hospital, but we didn't know anything yet; perhaps the ambulance wasn't even there for him, perhaps one of his employees had had an accident and needed help. I took a deep breath; there was no need to panic. My friend promised to keep me updated, and I got ready to leave my apartment and go to wherever Michael was.

Shortly after 1 p.m., my friend called again. The ambulance had just arrived at UCLA Medical Center and unloaded Michael on a stretcher. I fought down the first wave of panic. It's okay, I told myself. I had known this could happen. We all had. He was going to be fine. I typed the address for UCLA Medical Center into my GPS, and at about 1.30 p.m., I pulled into the courtyard outside a ten-storey L-shaped building and handed my car keys to the valet, who drove it down into an underground garage.

Michael's two Cadillac Escalades were parked outside the building, and I was the only person waiting there until Jill arrived, a few minutes later. We would often tell each other in the years to come that we were the first to arrive at this particular part of the hospital, which would soon become the focus of the world's media, the first to arrive and the last to know, because what most people would accept so easily, we never would.

Jill and I went for a walk around the building, while fielding calls and texts from friends who were on their way. We tried to reassure each other, and ourselves, that Michael would be fine. We knew that he'd been rehearsing at his house that week with his choreographer, Travis Payne, and we told each other he must have collapsed from exhaustion, which is precisely what we'd feared would happen. Maybe it was even for the best, we ventured, because now he would get to rest and recover. AEG would be forced to back off, he would have to postpone or cancel the tour, and nobody would dare to hold it against him, at least not anyone who loved him, and never mind about anyone else.

We turned our focus to the practicalities of relocating from Michael's house as our main base to UCLA. We recalled Michael's hospitalization in late 1995, when he had collapsed due to severe dehydration and hypotension while rehearsing for a HBO concert with mime artist Marcel Marceau, and spent a week at the Beth Israel Hospital North in New York. I had watched scenes on television, of supporters gathered outside the hospital, wishing I was among them, and now it would be our turn to keep vigil. We located a coffee shop that would suffice as a food source, and learned of alternative parking that would save us having to pay for the pricey valet service.

By the time we returned to the main entrance, a few more of our friends had arrived, a crowd of onlookers was gathering, and news trucks were pulling up outside. It was becoming more real by the minute. News stories began to reach us, a muddle of contradictions that veered back and forth. We tried not to give them much credence. After a lifetime of being lied to by the media, we had learned to question and doubt everything relating to him. One outlet was saying that he'd had a heart attack. Another was saying that he was in a coma. In the midst of this chaos of rumour and speculation, Yana sank to the ground with her phone pressed to her ear. We cried out, "What is it? What's wrong?" "It's TMZ," she said. "They're saying he's dead."

A chorus of pained and desperate no's followed this statement, and then our rejection of it. "TMZ? That's a tabloid. Since when do we believe the tabloids?" We helped Yana to her feet. She was crying. We were all crying now. Hearing those forbidden words, even though we paid them little credence, had sent shock waves through us, but we insisted they weren't true. I recalled a tabloid headline I'd seen that had said the same thing. It had been from the 1980s. They'd been trying to kill him off for years.

Despite my reassurances, I was crumbling inside. What had begun as worry and developed into fear was now full-blown terror. I needed someone to unsay those awful words, to un-associate Michael with "heart attack," "coma," and, above all, "dead," to tell me that he was fine, or at least alive. We realised that we were being filmed. Media cameras were trained on us, capturing the fallout of that shocking headline. Feeling violated, we headed into the adjacent building, the short section of the L. Inside, five of us squeezed into an alcove, away from prying eyes.

My family called me from Ireland. They'd heard the news, the very worst news. I told them that it wasn't true. "I'm right here," I said, "and I haven't heard anything," meaning that I hadn't heard anything official, from someone I trusted. It was a statement that I would repeat dozens of times that afternoon, to friends from all over the world. Unbeknownst to myself, I'd suddenly become a less reliable source than the tabloids that had hounded Michael for decades and tainted his name with lies.

Michael's former manager Frank DiLeo rushed into the building: finally, someone who could tell us what was going on. We called out to him. He glanced at us but didn't hesitate. He opened the door to a meeting room, inside which several suited men were sitting at a table. The door shut behind him. And there we were, shut out again, left to speculate about what his presence here meant.

A security guard approached us. When we told him why we were there, he asked us to leave the building. The hospital was on lockdown, he explained, for obvious reasons. We pleaded with him for information. He gave us none; in all likelihood, he had none to give. And so we were forced back into the glare of the sunlight and the media spotlight. We opened the door to the strains of "Heal the World." The crowd around the hospital had turned into a throng. We exchanged bewildered looks. Who were all of these people? Where had they come from? Why were they here, intruding on our private world?

It was weeks later, when a friend from Japan told me that she had watched live footage of me weeping outside UCLA on giant screens in Shibuya, Tokyo's equivalent of Time Square, that I began to process the public nature of what to me had been a private experience, that I realised that the information I had acquired gradually, torturously, at the end of a shadowy afternoon of hopeful denial, had been received instantaneously by most people, in the same way that I receive the news of other celebrity deaths.

After leaving the shelter of the hospital, my friends and I filed across the street and gathered around a picnic table, behind a cluster of trees. More friends arrived and we collapsed into each other, sobbing and shuddering. All we had to hold on to was hope, and each other. And we still had an abundance of hope, that the worst news stories were the result of sensationalism, and the more positive stories were true to life. Life. That's all I was wishing for now, was Michael's life.

Another friend arrived. Falling into his arms, I pleaded with him, "What they're saying... It's not true, is it? It can't be true." He shook his head. "I don't know." I didn't like what I saw in his expression. It scared me. Media cameras descended again, summoned by another outburst. Another guy I knew emerged from the crowd and steered us away. Almost since the moment I'd arrived at UCLA, my phone had been ringing with texts and phone calls. It had become the background noise to the most torturous afternoon of my life. I retrieved it and responded to some of the texts, telling everyone what I had told my family, that I was right here and that I hadn't heard anything, that it couldn't possibly be true. No way.

I scanned the crowd for the faces of the men who'd been by Michael's side all year: Amir, Alberto, Faheem. For months, they had watched us light up in his presence and melt in his arms. They must have known that we were out here, hearing these headlines, tormented by uncertainty. Why hadn't they come out to talk to us, to tell us that he was okay? The number of onlookers continued to multiply, mostly young people, students I guessed from the nearby UCLA campus. Among them, I saw no tears, only smiles. They couldn't possibly believe that anything terrible had happened to Michael. If they did, they would be wailing. I shared this thought with my friends. It strengthened our hope.

Before we knew: clinging on to hope, and each other. Left to right: Arus, Jill,
and me, outside UCLA Medical Center in Los Angeles, on the afternoon of
25 June 2009. (Photo: AP Photo/Reed Saxon)

We drifted across to a mound of grass opposite the building where Michael was. I pictured him behind all of that glass and steel and concrete, lying on a bed attached to... what? An IV to rehydrate his body? A machine to keep him alive? I had never been so desperate to know. Every moment felt surreal, the stuff of nightmares. Maybe it was a nightmare. Any moment now, I'd wake up and return to reality and reflect on this subconscious manifestation of the worry I'd been feeling, the dread that had been hanging over me for more than a week. I waited to wake up. The nightmare continued.

Four of us huddled together to avoid the cameras that were once again trained on us, and we unintentionally provided the media with a poignant image. The photograph, taken from behind and widely published thereafter, depicts four young women standing side by side, facing UCLA Medical Center, with their arms across each other and their heads bowed. It became a symbol of the world's grief for Michael and had an air of reverence that was fitting, but when that photograph was taken, I had not yet begun to grieve Michael because my heart had still been full of hope. That hope would soon diminish.

Another friend arrived. He'd heard from one of Michael's aunts that it was true. "No, it can't be," I argued. "It's just a rumour, a mistake." And then a news story emerged that claimed that Michael was in a coma. Normally, we would have received such news with horror. Not today. "Coma's not dead," we told each other. "Coma's not dead." If there were even a breath of life left in Michael, we would revive him, we would draw him back to us with love. I thought about the man I had seen at the Staples Center only hours before. There was no way that could be gone. No way. I scrambled to hold on to that final shred of hope. If I let go now, I'd fall forever.

Yana returned. She'd just bumped into Alberto. He'd told her it was true, that he was sorry. And still, I didn't believe it. I wouldn't believe it. I couldn't. Streams of tears were stemmed by impossible hope. We were all lying on the grass, a heap of limbs and tears, when a helicopter descended, its blades of steel chopping the air, and settled on a landing pad on the roof of the hospital. My friend Dani was on the phone from Germany. She told me that the helicopter was there to collect Michael's body. I cried out in denial and disbelief. "The 'corona' has confirmed it," she said in her German accent, between heavy sobs. I repeated the word aloud in confusion. "Corona? What's a corona?" Jill turned to me with a look of horror. "Coroner," she said. I dropped the phone.

Just then, another friend appeared and crouched down before us. "I'm so sorry, guys," he said, shaking his head, his eyes heavy with sympathy. "It's true." And that was it. That was the last moment before I let go, before I lost Michael forever. The truth crashed through the last of my defences and spread through me like poison. That final thread of hope tethering me to the earth snapped and I was sucked into a void. And then I was falling, falling through blackness, plummeting through outer space, cut off from everything and everyone, utterly alone.

It was all over. It was over. Michael, the man I'd loved since childhood, the man who was the centre of my world, the man who held all of my heart, was gone. Michael was gone.

EPILOGUE

Love, loss, lies

n the aftermath of Michael's passing, there are three facets that dictate my experience of him: the love, the loss, and the lies. The love and the loss are internal, and on 25 June 2009, the former gave rise to the latter, and the two became intertwined. The lies, however, exist outside of me, where they represent an ongoing assault on the truth I hold most sacred, the truth of who he was, the purity of his soul and all that he gifted to the world.

In the 1980s, the colour of Michael's skin became visibly lighter, and few people could explain why, giving rise to a rumour, a lie, that he was bleaching his skin. In 1993, during his televised interview with Oprah Winfrey at Neverland Valley, Michael revealed for the first time that he had a skin disorder that destroyed the pigmentation of the skin.

Michael's affliction with the skin condition, called vitiligo, has been confirmed by his dermatologist, Dr. Arnold Klein, his make-up artist, Karen Faye, and numerous other doctors, associates, and friends, and it is even listed on his autopsy report. I, myself, observed the light patches that are symptomatic of the condition, and yet, in the face of all of that factual evidence, of all of that truth, that initial lie still persists.

Similarly, the biggest and most evil lie about Michael, that he was a child molester, persists, despite an abundance of evidence to the contrary, despite the 1992 allegations resulting from a failed extortion attempt, despite him standing trial in 2005 and being cleared of all charges, despite the FBI releasing more than 300 pages of documents in December 2009, six months after his passing, revealing that they'd investigated him several times between 1993 and 2005 and found no evidence of any wrongdoing. None.

Michael's friend Elizabeth Taylor once said of him, in a 1993 interview with *Newsweek* magazine, "He'd rather cut his own wrist than harm a child," and the people who spent far more time with him than his opportunistic accusers, people like Macaulay Culkin and Frank Cascio, who were close to him throughout their childhood and up until his passing; Grace Rwaramba, who worked for him, first as his secretary and later as the nanny to his three children, for almost two decades; and countless others have said publicly that they never saw or experienced anything to suggest that Michael was capable of these horrific deeds.

And yet the lie persists, now perpetuated by a sordid documentary featuring two men who had earlier said the same thing under oath: that Michael had never done anything wrong. Nothing. Ever. One of these men, Wade Robson, had testified to this twice, as a child in 1993 and as an adult in 2005, when I sat in the courtroom in Santa Maria and watched as he emphatically denied any wrongdoing on Michael's part. Following a barrage of questions from the prosecutor Ron Zonen, who repeatedly tried to twist the truth about his friendship with Michael, Robson, clearly frustrated, said, "I'm telling you that nothing ever happened!"

It was several years after Michael passed, after Robson and his cohort Jimmy Safechuck had been deprived of the many benefits of Michael's friendship, after Robson had tried and failed to secure a role in a tribute show to his alleged abuser, that they changed their story and tried to sue his estate, reportedly for up to $1.5 billion, and then participated in a documentary called *Leaving Neverland* that I have heard enough about to know I'll never watch.

Just because somebody says something happened doesn't make it true. And just because somebody can prove that they spent time with Michael, a privilege enjoyed by many, myself included, does not mean that whatever they say happened actually happened, especially when it contradicts what they have said in the past and what other people who were there say happened, and especially when there's a financial motive attached to the claim.

Words alone are not evidence. They are just words. And now, because you can't defame the dead, people can say anything they want about Michael without fear of being sued, and then they can try to profit from their lies by suing his estate or participating in a sordid documentary or selling their story to the media, and there's no legal process to stop them. There is also no legal process to hold their lies up to the light and reveal them for what they are, which is what happened at the 2005 trial, at which Michael was exonerated on all charges.

*   *   *

There is another lie about Michael that I feel compelled to address, in part because – unlike the most evil lie against him, which, thankfully, has been widely contested many times and in many formats – it remains largely unchallenged, and that is the perception that Michael was a drug addict who brought about his own demise. The fact, proven beyond a reasonable doubt in a court of law, is that Conrad Murray killed Michael by administering a short-acting intravenous anaesthetic drug called Propofol without the use of the necessary life-saving equipment – a crime for which he was convicted of involuntary manslaughter in late 2011 and served less than two years in prison. What he did was lethal, and it ended Michael's life.

And yet, when people write or speak of Michael's death, they almost never say that he was killed or that he was a victim of homicide. No, they say that he died of an overdose, suggesting that he was a drug addict who took too many drugs by accident, or was suicidal and took too many on purpose. Just because somebody kills you by administering a lethal dose of a drug doesn't make you a drug addict, unless, of course, you're Michael Jackson, a man who has never been given the benefit of the doubt by the world at large, whose every word and action, and now even manner of death, has been misconstrued, misinterpreted, and misrepresented to present him in the worst possible light.

According to testimony at the criminal trial against Conrad Murray for involuntary manslaughter, when Murray realised that Michael had stopped breathing on 25 June, he didn't call 911; he called for Michael's twelve-year-old son, Prince, before calling Michael Amir on the phone. When the security guard Alberto Alvarez arrived on the scene, shortly after noon, he saw Murray apparently trying to give CPR to Michael with one hand on a soft bed, instead of with two hands on a hard surface, which is the proper method. Murray then enlisted Alberto's help in gathering up the vials that were the evidence of his crime – while Michael lay alone, not breathing.

When the paramedics arrived, around 12.30 p.m., following Alberto's phone call to 911, Murray told them, according to testimony by Los Angeles County Paramedic Richard Senneff, "It just happened right when I called you," and that he'd administered only a sedative called Lorazepam, a lie that he would repeat at the hospital.

Murray made no mention of Propofol to any of the professionals who were trying to save Michael's life that day, though there seems to be no doubt that Michael was dead long before they reached him, possibly for hours. Senneff also told the court, "When I first moved the patient, his skin was very cool to the touch, his eyes were open, they were dry and his pupils were dilated. When I hooked up the EKG machine, it was flatlined."

It was two days later, during his first police interview, that Conrad Murray admitted to administering Propofol to Michael, which he claimed he'd been doing every night for six weeks, and this story stuck, even though it came from the mouth of a proven liar and even though it makes no sense. It goes against all logic and it goes against the truth of who Michael was, and I refute it absolutely.

It's true that in 1993, Michael publicly admitted to having become dependent on painkillers, a dependence that developed as a result of a painful surgical procedure, and that was exacerbated by the horrendous stress he was under at the time, due to the false allegations against him. He immediately sought treatment, completed a programme at a clinic in London, and left, clean and healthy. Yet, the dark cloud from that admission followed him for the rest of his life and, mainly due to the circumstances of that final, fatal crime against him, even into death.

At a hearing in a wrongful death lawsuit brought by Katherine Jackson against AEG in 2013, several doctors who had treated Michael at various times in his life testified. They painted a picture of a man who had suffered from chronic pain due to a range of ailments, most notably the second-degree burn to his scalp that had occurred in 1984 and necessitated a lifetime of procedures, the back injury in 1999, and the cracked ankle he'd endured two years later.

The evidence showed that Michael went to great lengths to avoid any medication that might trigger a dependency. He often sought out alternative treatments and even had an opioid inhibitor surgically implanted in his abdomen to block the feelings of euphoria that some painkillers can cause. This is hardly the behaviour of an addict desperate for a fix.

The prescriptions and medications that police found at Michael's Holmby Hills home after his passing – among which there were no opioids or other drugs that people with addictions seek out – showed that he was actually non-compliant with the medications that he was prescribed. And the postmortem examination found no sign of the organ damage that would have resulted from drug abuse. Michael's struggle wasn't to cope with addiction but to cope with chronic pain and various health problems while taking the least, and least addictive, medication possible.

I accept that Michael had used Propofol while on tour in the past as a sleep aid, and that it should not be used as such. But anyone who has suffered from severe insomnia knows the torment of lying awake night after night, waiting for a release that never comes, and that's when you don't have to get up the next day and perform to a stadium full of people.

At a 2013 hearing in the lawsuit against AEG, a nurse who specialised in holistic health care and who had treated Michael in the final year of his life, Cherilyn Lee, testified that Michael had asked her on the last day that she'd seen him, 19 April 2009, to find an anaesthesiologist who could put him to sleep using Propofol. She said that Michael had said to her, "I'll be okay. I only need someone to monitor me with equipment while I sleep," and that he'd "kept telling me, 'You don't understand, doctors are telling me it's safe just as long as I am being monitored.'"

"I only need someone to monitor me with equipment." This is the condition in which Michael felt safe being given Propofol, because this is the condition in which it is safe; Propofol is administered to hundreds of thousands of patients every year and rarely proves fatal. It's possible, though it's never been proven, that Michael asked Murray to order Propofol with a view to administering it later in London, once the proper equipment had been acquired. But in my mind, there is no way that he asked Murray to give it to him in his bedroom in LA, where none of the necessary life-saving equipment was present. No way.

Michael was a highly intelligent man, a genius, and he understood the risks of using Propofol without the necessary equipment. He would never *ever* have done anything to risk his life, to risk leaving his children behind, and the insinuation that he would have is an insult to his name.

Murray told police that he'd been administering Propofol to Michael through an intravenous drip every night for six weeks. If that's the case, where were the IV bags from the previous nights? Where was the tubing? Where were the open Propofol bottles? Michael's room was littered with Murray's medical equipment, but not one piece of evidence that he'd administered Propofol even once before.

Murray also claimed that Michael begged him for Propofol. Okay then, where is the consent form? If a doctor is going to do something that risky – as in administer Propofol without the necessary, life-saving equipment – on the behest of his client, he's at least going to cover himself in the event of a fatality. And if he thought he was doing nothing wrong, why did he act like a guilty man after Michael stopped breathing, first by trying to hide vials at the scene and lying to the paramedics, and later by disappearing from the hospital and abandoning his car, which was still parked outside the Holmby Hills home, the scene of his crime?

An Irish doctor called Patrick Treacy treated Michael throughout his stay in Ireland in 2006 and became close to him during that time. In his 2015 book, *Behind the Mask: The Extraordinary Story of the Irishman Who Became Michael Jackson's Doctor*, he said, "[I]n my experience, Michael was not a drug addict," and this is coming from a doctor who treated him, not people who saw and misinterpreted a state of incoherence and confusion, such as that which I witnessed in Michael's final days, as a symptom of drug use and not severe insomnia and/or lupus fog. His doctor said he was not a drug addict, because he wasn't one.

Dr Treacy also referred to an incident during which Michael elected to have a painful procedure carried out without sedation because he refused to allow the doctor to administer a sedative called Midazolam without an anaesthetist present. He said that, after hearing Conrad Murray's claims, "I couldn't understand why someone who would not even use Midazolam without an anaesthetist present would use a drug as powerful as Propofol in his own home." He couldn't understand why Michael would have allowed Murray to administer Propofol in those circumstances, and other than the word of his killer, there is no evidence that he ever did.

But what proves beyond doubt in my mind the absurdity of Murray's claim is that his method of administration was lethal. In his 2010 book, *Getting Over Going Under: 5 Things You Must Know Before Anesthesia*, Dr Barry L. Friedberg, MD and author, stated, "The only thing more reckless Murray could have done was taking Jackson up in an airplane and pushing him out without a parachute." In other words, Murray couldn't have done what he did on 25 June and *not* kill Michael. If he'd administered Propofol to Michael in this manner for the first time six weeks earlier, Michael would have died six weeks earlier. Murray might as well have told police that he had held a fully-loaded gun to Michael's head every night for six weeks and pulled the trigger, but only blew his brains out the final time. That's how ludicrous his claim is, and yet it continues to gain credence, even among fans, and that, I believe, would have broken Michael's heart.

I firmly believe that the first time Murray administered Propofol to Michael was while he was sleeping and without his consent, and that it was the last time, that it was the only time. I do not believe that Murray intended to kill Michael. I believe that Murray wanted Michael to sleep because he knew that if he didn't sleep, he would possibly cancel the tour and Murray would be out of a job, a job he so desperately needed. According to prosecutors at his 2011 criminal trial, Murray had a history of financial trouble and was over $1 million in debt at the time of his crime.

In 2013, at a hearing in the lawsuit against AEG, concert tour director Marty Hom testified that when Murray originally got the job as Michael's personal physician, he asked AEG for $5 million a year, eventually accepting $150,000 a month instead, and attorney Kathy Jorrie testified that during Michael's final days, Murray inquired whether AEG would still pay him if the tour was cancelled. And in Murray's statement to the police on 27 June 2009, he said that he had given Michael an additional dose of the sedative Lorazepam that morning, after Michael threatened to cancel that day's rehearsal.

Just imagine that Michael went home on his final night, exhausted from another rehearsal, and said that if he couldn't sleep, he'd have to cancel the tour. In my opinion, Murray was a desperate man, desperate for the tour to continue so that he could cling on to the money and prestige that the job would afford him, desperate enough to use sedatives like Lorazepam to sedate Michael temporarily and then administer Propofol without his consent, to ensure that he slept soundly and the tour went ahead as planned.

In my opinion, the reason Murray behaved like a guilty man after he discovered that Michael had stopped breathing is because he knew what the world has yet to fully realise: that he was entirely to blame for Michael's death and that Michael was entirely blameless, the innocent victim of a terrible crime, one that would not only end his life but also further defame him, by attaching yet another lie to his name.

* * *

In my last letter to Michael, I wrote, "Won't you let us help you shoulder that burden now, like we have so many times in the past?" At the time of writing, I had no concept or expectation of the burden of loss I would soon carry, but for years, my friends and I had tried to help Michael carry the burden of lies against him, and now we shoulder that burden for him, as do all those who love him.

Many of the beautiful people who I met through Michael have spoken out publicly against the most evil of lies, including an American called Jenny who participated in a 2019 documentary called *Square One: Michael Jackson*, in which she talks about the time she spent at Neverland Valley when both Michael and Gavin Arvizo, the accuser in the 2005 trial, were present, and Caroline from Sweden, who talks about her visit with three other girls and me in February 2003, while Gavin was also there and while, his mother would later claim, he was being held against his will – a ludicrous lie that without the trial would have gone legally uncontested, as so many other ludicrous and defamatory lies about Michael have and likely always will.

This memoir is my own stance against the tsunami of lies that tormented Michael in life, the worst of which, as he told Angelica Houston in 2009, were a source of "unbearable pain," and that continue to torment those who love him, by tarnishing his reputation and all that he gave to the world. I hope that by telling my story, by sharing my truth, I can point to the truth of who he was, because while I was just a fan meeting her hero, I was also a human being having a human experience of another human being.

If you want to know the truth about Michael, then go directly to the source. That's what I did as a teenage girl, when I discovered him through his artistic creations and his own words, sung, spoken, and written, and nothing I observed or experienced later ran counter to my initial perception of him. If you already know the truth, if you see the purity of his soul, then trust in that, because you didn't need to know him in person to know him, to understand him, to connect with him, on a soul-to-soul level. In the deepest sense, I did not know Michael better at the end than I did at the beginning, and I did not love him more, because in that first moment of discovery, when I watched *Moonwalker* for the first time, I loved him absolutely, and I always will.

My story goes on, as do I, and, this great burden aside, I have a wonderful life and a million and one things to be grateful for, but as has been the case since the age of thirteen, part of me is always waiting to go to Michael, and one day I believe I will. When I close my eyes to this world, I will open them to the next, and there he will be, in his most magical iteration. I will see his black loafers and sequinned socks, as he steps out of the shadows, and my gaze will travel upwards, along a pair of black pants with white stripes running down the outer edges, to a silver sequinned glove on one hand, held out towards me, to a black sequinned jacket, and then, under a fedora, framed by curls, his face, his perfect face, smiling at me. He will say my name once more as I melt into his arms, and that, because every fairy tale deserves one, will be my happy ending.

"Never stop wishing or dreaming, for this is where the magic begins."

- Michael Jackson

Acknowledgements

In the Irish language, "go raibh míle maith agat" means "thank you" or, roughly translated in a literal sense, "may you have a thousand goodnesses," and so I say this to all of my family members and friends in Ireland, the US, and around the world for your love and support, with special thanks and a thousand additional goodnesses to all those referenced or mentioned in this memoir for allowing me to share aspects of their story in telling my own.

Special thanks too to the following... To Mum and Dad, for allowing me to take my first steps towards Michael. To Prince, Paris, and Blanket, for the memories that you are a part of and that I will cherish forever. To David, for all you've done to help make my dreams a reality, both then and now. To Talin, Shay, and Camilla, my companion on that magical night in Tokyo Disneyland, for gently prodding me every so often over the years, urging me to tell my story, reminding me that I had a story to tell; without your encouragement, it may never have been written. To Rhonda, whose wisdom, empathy, and intuition helped to release the fear and conflict that had been holding me back for years; because of you, my story finally found a pathway through the grief and onto the page.

To Clair and Moonstreet, for being there for me throughout the writing process, for your constant guidance and support, and to Moonstreet, Talin, and Arus, for being the first to read my story; your feedback was invaluable in fine-tuning the finished fairy tale. To Ariel, for the beautiful illustrations, and to Arus, for the stunning design; your vision, talent, and purity of heart shine through in every detail. It is your love, as well as my own, the love of all those who contributed in any way to my story, whose story it touches upon, whose story it represents, that is contained within these pages, and I thank you all, friends and fans, known and unknown, from the bottom of my heart.

Notes

Friedberg, Dr Barry, "The Michael Jackson Death – A Predictable, Avoidable Tragedy," *Getting Over Going Under: 5 Things You Must Know Before Anesthesia*, Goldilocks Press, 2010, p. 42.

Huston, Angelica, "Il ricordo di Anjelica Huston 'Un bambino sincero e fragile,'" Interview by Silvia Bizio, *la Repubblica*, 7 July 2009. www.repubblica.it/2009/07/sezioni/persone/michael-jackson-2/jackson-anjelica-huston/jackson-anjelica-huston.html

Jackson, Michael, "The Boy and the Pillow," *Dancing the Dream* (1st ed.), Doubleday, United States, 1992, p. 29.

Living with Michael Jackson. ITV (UK), ABC (US), 3 and 10 February 2003.

Michael Jackson Talks to... Oprah Live. Harpo Productions, 10 February 1993.

Powers, Margaret Fishback, "Footprints in the Sand," 1964.

"Tabloid Truth: The Michael Jackson Story," *Frontline*, season 1994, episode 10, PBS, 15 February 1994.

The Michael Jackson Interview: The Footage You Were Never Meant to See, Fox, 23 February 2003.

Treacy, Dr Patrick, "The Death of the King of Pop," *Behind the Mask: The Extraordinary Story of the Irishman Who Became Michael Jackson's Doctor*, Liberties Press, 2015, p. 324.

Made in United States
Orlando, FL
24 December 2021

12401096R00174